The Theatre of Les Waters

The Theatre of Les Waters: More Like the Weather combines original writings from Les Waters with short essays by a wide range of his collaborators, creating a personal and multi-faceted portrait of an influential director, revered mentor, and inspirational theatre artist.

The book begins with a critical introduction of Waters's work, followed by essays written by a wide range of Waters's collaborators over the past four decades. These essays are framed by shorter pieces of writing by Waters himself: reflections, inspirations, observations, and personal anecdotes. At the heart of this book lies the notion that the director's central position in theatrical production is defined by collaboration and that a study of directing should take into account how a director works with playwrights, designers, actors, stage managers, and dramaturgs to turn artistic vision into concrete reality on stage.

An insightful resource for early career or student directors in theatre programs, *The Theatre of Les Waters* sheds light on the art of theatre directing by exploring the work of a major theatre artist whose accomplished career sits at the heart of American theatre in the 21st century. Drawing on aspects of memoir, case study, interview, miscellany, biography, and criticism, this is also an enlightening read for anyone with an interest in how theatre artists bring their creative vision to life.

Scott T. Cummings has directed plays and taught courses in playwriting and dramatic literature in the Theatre Department of Boston College since 1994. He is the author of *Remaking American Theater: Charles Mee, Anne Bogart and the SITI Company* (Cambridge University Press, 2006), and *Maria Irene Fornes* (Routledge, 2013), as well as co-editor with Erica Stevens Abbitt of *The Theatre of Naomi Wallace: Embodied Dialogues* (Palgrave MacMillan, 2014).

The Theatre of Les Waters

More Like the Weather

Edited by Scott T. Cummings

Routledge
Taylor & Francis Group

NEW YORK AND LONDON

Cover credit: © Bill Brymer

First published 2022
by Routledge
605 Third Avenue, New York, NY 10158

and by Routledge
4 Park Square, Milton Park, Abingdon, Oxon, OX14 4RN

Routledge is an imprint of the Taylor & Francis Group, an informa business

Library of Congress Cataloging-in-Publication Data
Names: Cummings, Scott T., 1953- editor. | Waters, Les, 1952- Works. Selections.
Title: The theatre of Les Waters : more like the weather / edited by Scott T. Cummings.
Description: New York, NY: Routledge, 2022. | Includes index.
Identifiers: LCCN 2021039556 (print) | LCCN 2021039557 (ebook) | ISBN 9780367773250 (hardback) | ISBN 9780367773229 (paperback) | ISBN 9781003170808 (ebook)
Subjects: LCSH: Waters, Les, 1952—Criticism and interpretation. | Waters, Les, 1952–Influence. | Theatrical producers and directors—Great Britain—Biography. | Theater—Production and direction.
Classification: LCC PN2598.W246 T48 2022 (print) | LCC PN2598.W246 (ebook) | DDC 792.02/33092 [B]—dc23
LC record available at https://lccn.loc.gov/2021039556
LC ebook record available at https://lccn.loc.gov/2021039557

ISBN: 978-0-367-77325-0 (hbk)
ISBN: 978-0-367-77322-9 (pbk)
ISBN: 978-1-003-17080-8 (ebk)

DOI: 10.4324/9781003170808

Typeset in Goudy
by KnowledgeWorks Global Ltd.

To all the directors I have met on this long walk. Thank you for your advice and support and challenges. Special thanks to Martha Lavey, who I miss.

To my parents, Phyllis and Les. I hope they would have liked this book as much as, I know, they'd have found it puzzling.

To Annie and Jacob and Nancy and Madeleine for being my family and for being their remarkable selves.

Les Waters

For Barbara Boyk Rust. Who took interest. With love.

Scott T. Cummings

Contents

Illustrations

All productions featured in these photographs were directed by Les Waters.

Acknowledgements

First and foremost, it must be said that *The Theatre of Les Waters: More Like the Weather* is the result of a year-long collaboration between me and Les Waters. The book is as much *by* him as it is *about* him. The intimate nature of the look it offers into how one theatre artist engages with the world and the work required his active participation on various levels every step of the way. It is a joint effort.

Central to the book's strategy are the essays contributed by a wide range of Waters's collaborators over the years. Virtually everyone who was invited to write something said yes with enthusiasm and then exhibited great patience with me in the inevitable editorial back-and-forth necessary to bring each essay to fruition. I know that Les joins me in thanking them all for their words and their insights.

Given the special attention that Waters pays to the visual composition of his work onstage, the book would not be complete without photographic evidence of his productions. A large number of photographers were generous in taking the time to go through files and hard drives to make available for consideration many more images than we could use in the end and to allow their photographs to be used for little or no fee. This includes Mark Barton, Kevin Berne, Oana Botez, Andrew Boyce, Michael Brosilow, Bill Brymer, Julieta Cervantes, Antje Ellermann, Ken Friedman, John Haynes, Dane Laffrey, Lisa Lazar, Mimi Lien, Joan Marcus, Rebecca Martinez, Carol Rosegg, T. Ryder Smith, Craig Schwartz, Richard Termine, Paul Toben, Sam Breslin Wright, Yi Zhao, and David Zinn. Christopher W. Soldt of Boston College's Media Technology Services was instrumental in preparing the photographs for publication. Special thanks are due to Ron Crawford and Rebecca Martinez for permission to reproduce their portraits of Les Waters.

A last-minute scramble to secure permissions to use a number of quotations in the book was facilitated by helpful and compassionate people at numerous publishing houses, literary agencies, foundations, and other outlets, including Barbara Bair at the Library of Congress, Helene Dahl at the Ingmar Bergman Foundation, Robbie English at Round Hill Music, Jodi Fabbri at Curtis Brown, Victoria Fox at Macmillan/FSG/Picador, Louis Jaquet at DACS, Joanna Karasinska at Wisława Szymborska Foundation, Yessenia Santos at Simon & Schuster, and Derek Wright at Wordsworth Editions. Special thanks are due to Richard Long for providing a corrected and updated quotation for use as our epigraph.

Boston College provided a Research Expense Grant to defray some costs related to the book as well as Undergraduate Research Fellowships that made it possible for several students of mine to provide research support at different stages of the project. Early on, when the book was a mere pipedream, Amanda Maguire and Haley Bannon conducted preliminary research. And in the 12 months of intense work pulling the book together, Emma Thompson was there at every turn, transcribing interviews, organizing reviews, searching for photographs, corresponding with contributors, clearing permissions, proofreading, and other tasks. From cover to cover, the book has benefitted from her good work.

At Routledge, I am indebted to Stacey Walker for taking an interest in the book as an idea and to the entire production team for making that idea a material (or digital) reality, especially Senior Editorial Assistant Lucia Accorsi, who demonstrated a remarkable patience with my seemingly unending flow of questions and special requests. It has been a pleasure to work with them.

Finally, on a personal note, I want to thank Marie Clouqueur for encouragement and support, Adrianne Krstansky for wisdom and care, and Janet Morrison for a love that endures (whether she knows it or not).

—Scott T. Cummings

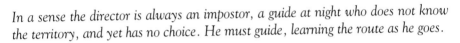

In a sense the director is always an impostor, a guide at night who does not know the territory, and yet has no choice. He must guide, learning the route as he goes.

Peter Brook
The Empty Space (1968)

As an artist I turn my ideas into long walks.

Richard Long (2021)

"Introduction: A Long Conversation"

Scott T. Cummings

Les Waters started directing plays in 1972 as a 20-year-old undergraduate at university, and he has never really stopped. There were several periods when work was put on hold for life transitions, but for the vast majority of the past 50 years, he has been engaged with some part of the directing process. After leaving his position as Artistic Director of Actors Theatre of Louisville (ATL) in 2018, he had been particularly busy in his ongoing collaboration with playwright Lucas Hnath, workshopping and then premiering two new plays, *The Thin Place* and *Dana H.*, and directing Hnath's widely produced and wildly successful *A Doll's House, Part 2* at Berkeley Repertory Theatre and the Huntington Theatre in Boston. But as the severity of the coronavirus outbreak made itself felt, his work – like that of virtually all theatre artists and millions of other working people – came to an abrupt halt. On March 12, 2020, performances of *Dana H.* at the Vineyard Theatre were suspended in keeping with the massive shutdown of theatres in New York. Other projects – see the list in this book called *Some things will be lost, maybe* – soon slowed to a halt, indefinitely postponed or cancelled altogether. Waters retreated to his home in the hills overlooking Berkeley, California. Life in Pandemic limbo had begun.

This book would not exist if not for that limbo. The tsunami of free time that came crashing in its wake reactivated a slow-motion conversation that Waters and I had been having for years. In 2014, having just seen his Humana Festival production of Hnath's *The Christians*, I approached him in the lobby of Actors Theatre and asked if anybody had ever written a book about his work or if he was thinking of writing one. He said, no. I was not at a point in

DOI: 10.4324/9781003170808-1

my life and work where I could commit to a period of sustained field research (observing rehearsals, conducting interviews, documenting productions) that would result in a scholarly study, but I offered to transcribe and edit a series of recorded conversations about his approach to directing, if he ever wanted to do that. At the least, they would yield an interesting interview-essay for a theatre journal or magazine. We agreed to carve out time to sit down with a microphone whenever our paths crossed in Louisville or New York or Boston. That turned out to be roughly once a year.

Then came 2020. In May, we began to speak on the phone two or three times a week through the spring and summer and then once a week into the fall. We did not have a precise plan or specific goal in mind. It soon became clear that Les had zero interest in channelling the wisdom of his experience into some kind of orthodoxy about how to direct a play. He did not want to write a practical handbook or articulate a philosophy of directing. He even hesitated to discuss his productions with a specificity that might come off as pretentious or conceited. But it was clear that the conversations had a value for each of us, not just for where they might lead, but for the oasis of structure and collegiality, they offered in the open Sahara of pandemic time. So, we kept talking . . . with a microphone on most of the time. Our conversations were often informed by the troubling news of the day: the bungled public health response to COVID-19; the righteous demands for racial justice stemming from the murder of George Floyd and others; the soul-searching implications of systemic racism for the American theatre; the unrelenting mendacity and protofascism of the President of the United States. It was a year of limbo and suspension, a year of unrest, a year for all manner of reflection.

Over the summer, our long conversation about theatre, art, and life led to impulses about a possible book about Waters and his work. A concrete plan took shape. A proposal was drafted. The importance of collaboration in Waters's practice – and in directing in general – suggested that it would be interesting to include the voices of some of his artistic partners in a book by and about him. After all, in and of itself, a theatre director's art is invisible; it only gains tangible, material form through the work of playwrights, designers, and actors, which makes it difficult to isolate and identify in a performance just exactly what the director did. Who better then to shine light on that work than those he did it with? So it is that half of this book consists of short essays by more than two dozen of his collaborators over the decades, not just playwrights, designers, and actors but also dramaturgs, stage managers, assistant directors, and former students.

The pursuit of this strategy brought to mind the old Buddhist parable of the blind men and the elephant. When a group of blind men learn that a strange creature has been brought to their town, they gather around the large animal to find out what it is – by touch. When each one makes contact with a different part of the beast – the moist tip of the trunk, the wiry tail, the leathery hide, the softer flesh of ears, the legs like tree trunks, the smooth ivory tusks, and so on – he forms an impression that differs radically from his fellows to the point of questioning whether they are actually experiencing the same thing. Perceptual dissonance and possible argument aside, combining their individual subjective perspectives yields a composite portrait of a complex and amazing being.

Les Waters is the elephant in the room here – the rehearsal room, that is. The contributors to this book were not assigned specific topics or productions to write about. Each was simply invited to write a short essay that captured something particular and essential about their experience of working with Waters as a director or about the work that they created together. I asked them to avoid simple valentines and concentrate on describing in vivid detail the point of contact between their work and his. The composite portrait of Waters that emerges here is perhaps more consistent than the divergent impressions of the blind men standing around the elephant. Efforts have been made to avoid redundancy, but there are definite traits, impressions, and preoccupations that run through multiple essays, thematic dots that can be connected to form a clear Waters silhouette.

One of those themes is his laconic nature. It is a virtual Les Waters cliché. As these accounts make clear, Waters is a person who chooses his words – and when he says them – carefully. He is comfortable with silence and feels no need to fill a vacuum with chatter or noisy ego. Some find him Sphinx-like – in a manner that can be beguiling or intimidating. He gives the impression of having a lot on his mind. And he is circumspect about holding forth, about claiming an authority that goes much beyond his personal experience, and so we faced the challenge of getting his voice into the book in a way that felt honest and genuine. Our summer conversations actually began in writing with me jotting questions on a shared document online and him answering in real time while I hung on every keystroke. But he's a slow typist (and he does not particularly like to write out extended lines of thought), so we switched over to talking on the phone. After some trial and error, transcribing and editing those conversations into a conventional question-and-answer format felt fabricated and forced and that led to pulling out nuggets of conversation that could serve as the nucleus for more extended prose statements touching on some aspect of his artistic practice, his life and career, or directing in general. I dubbed these "stems" – on the notion that they might be a verbal stalk or trunk from which other shoots of thought might grow or to which other paragraphs from different days could be grafted.

In one of our early, 'on paper' conversations, I asked Waters, who is approaching the age of 70, if he had a bucket list of plays and projects yet to accomplish. He mentioned a few things – more Chekhov, *King Lear*, Caryl Churchill's *Far Away*, a play about Vikings ("obsessed with them as a child"), a production of *A Midsummer Night's Dream* with older actors playing the fairies in torn cardboard wings – and then he added, "I'd like to do things I don't know how to do." This talk of bucket lists prompted us to discover that we were both inveterate list-makers and quite passionate about the practice, which led me to ask him now and again over the summer to share other lists. Some of these were simple, 'naked' lists and others came with comments or explanations for some or all items on the list. It became clear that making lists was a meaningful way for Waters to organise and reflect on his experience.

And so, it is that the other half of this book consists of a series of casual writings by Les Waters that take the form either of lists or "stems," observations, reflections, diatribes, and anecdotes that came out of our running Pandemic conversation. Both are diaristic in nature, candid, concise, sometimes cryptic or incomplete, always honest. These jottings are interspersed and juxtaposed with the ruminations of Waters's collaborators in a way that is more associative than systematic, more elliptical than linear. This is in keeping with Waters's preferred forms of engagement with the world around him. Together, supplemented by this introduction and a directing history and biographical time line at the back of the book, these short pieces offer a lively and impressionistic portrait of an important and influential theatre artist whose accomplished body of work sits at the heart of American theatre in the 21st century. Through Waters's example, the book aspires to provide object lessons, provocations to thought, and maybe even a few tiny epiphanies about the nature of theatrical collaboration and the complex artistry involved in directing for the stage.

* * * * *

Les Waters does not care for the word career. There is something linear, almost planful, about it that does not embrace the vicissitudes of life. Still, by any measure, he has had a remarkably steady and successful career as a theatre director, first in the United Kingdom and then in the United States.

He came of age in the 1970s as a young man in the north of England wanting to direct plays. That's what he did, more or less on his own, at university and for a couple years after. At age 25, he began to work at the legendary Royal Court Theatre, the premiere venue for new writing in London; there he found a supportive mentor (for a time) in Max Stafford-Clark and earned the opportunity to direct, first in the studio Theatre Upstairs and then on the mainstage below. He also connected with the innovative Joint Stock Theatre Group where he met among others, the playwright Caryl Churchill. When his successful premiere Joint Stock production of Churchill's *Fen* made a splash on a 1983 tour to New York, invitations to direct at the Public Theater in New York and at institutional theatres around the US became regular. He worked back and forth between the two countries until 1995, when he was recruited to head the MFA directing program at the University of California San Diego and permanently shifted his career to America. He directed the world premiere of Charles Mee's *Big Love* at Actors Theatre of Louisville's Humana Festival of New American Plays in 2000 and again a year later at an alliance of regional theatres, including Berkeley Repertory Theatre where artistic director Tony Taccone invited him to become the associate artistic director. He directed 18 plays all told at Berkeley Rep, including Sarah Ruhl's breakthrough play *Eurydice* and her *In the Next Room (or the vibrator play)*, which he later restaged on Broadway. In 2012, at age 60, he became artistic director at Actors Theatre of Louisville, where he began a collaboration with playwright Lucas Hnath. He remained in Louisville until 2018, when he left his position and resumed an independent career as a freelance director.

That's it in a nutshell. That's the general outline. Of course, as lived in the flesh, it was not as straightforward as all that. Along the way, there were professional setbacks and sidetracks, disappointments, lost opportunities, blowups, unrecognized triumphs and outright disasters, and strained or fractured relationships, plus a personal and family life with its own rewards and challenges. But it is a career path that would be the envy of any aspiring theatre director. Waters has directed more than 100 different plays in 50 years, many of them at multiple venues over a span of years, some of them in altogether different productions of the same play staged years apart. In the UK, in addition to ten productions at the Royal Court, he directed at the Royal National Theatre, the Almeida, Hampstead Theatre, Bristol Old Vic, Liverpool Playhouse, Leicester Haymarket, and the Traverse Theatre in Edinburgh. In the US, in addition to Berkeley Rep and Actors Theatre of Louisville, he has directed at many prestigious large institutional theatres, including the Public Theater and Playwrights Horizons in

New York City, as well as the Guthrie, Arena Stage, the Mark Taper Forum, La Jolla Playhouse, the Goodman Theatre, American Conservatory Theater, Steppenwolf, and others around the country. He has staged Shakespeare, Sheridan, and Shaw as well as such classics of the American canon as *Our Town*, *The Glass Menagerie*, *Long Day's Journey Into Night*, *Buried Child*, and *Glengarry Glen Ross*.

Waters is best known for his work on new writing with contemporary playwrights, first and foremost among them Caryl Churchill. He was assistant director for Max Stafford-Clark on the original Joint Stock production of *Cloud Nine* in 1979 (and then co-director of its Royal Court revival a year later). In addition to *Fen*, he directed the world premieres of Churchill's *Three More Sleepless Nights*, *The Skriker*, and *A Mouthful of Birds*, her freewheeling response with David Lan to Euripides's *The Bacchae*. This book includes portions of the diary he kept when he directed *Top Girls* in Tokyo in 1992. And in June 2021, as the Pandemic loosened its stranglehold grip on theatre, he co-directed (with Jared Mezzochi) a live-streamed production of a brand-new, 20-minute Caryl Churchill piece called *What If If Only*. In addition to his work with Churchill, he directed world premieres in the UK of plays by Timberlake Wertenbaker, Rona Munro, Paul Kember, and Terry Johnson, among others. For part of the time he was on staff at the Royal Court, he was in charge of the Theatre Upstairs, an incubator for emerging playwrights and developmental projects. When *Fen* brought Waters to the US and the attention of producer Joseph Papp, he was invited back to The Public to direct more Churchill, *Romeo and Juliet*, and the 1986 world premiere of Keith Reddin's *Rum and Coke*, the first of three new Reddin plays he directed in five years.

Over the past 25 years, Waters has had ongoing partnerships with a number of prominent and important American playwrights – Charles Mee, Sarah Ruhl, Lucas Hnath, Anne Washburn, Naomi Iizuka, and Jordan Harrison – and he has directed world premiere productions of plays by Rebecca Gilman, Will Eno, Mark Shultz, and Jorge Ignacio Cortiñas. He has a knack for connecting with playwrights on what turn out to be watershed productions in their careers – Mee's *Big Love* at Actors Theatre of Louisville in 2000, Ruhl's *Eurydice* at Berkeley Rep in 2004, Hnath's *The Christians* at ATL in 2014 all come to mind – and his collaborations with these playwrights invite comparisons to the historic theatrical partnerships between Robert Woodruff and Sam Shepard in the 1970s, Lloyd Richards and August Wilson in the 1980s, or more recently between Sam Gold and Annie Baker. Would Caryl Churchill be Caryl Churchill without Les Waters? Would Sarah Ruhl still be Sarah Ruhl? Yes, absolutely. Would she be the same Sarah Ruhl? Maybe not quite.

The influence of a director on the first production of a new play and the "value-added" of a director to a playwright's career are notoriously difficult to pinpoint. It depends on who you ask. Churchill, Reddin, Mee, Ruhl, Iizuka, and Hnath all weigh in on their work with Waters in the essays that follow.

On a broader level, Waters's position as Artistic Director of Actors Theatre of Louisville from 2012 to 2018 made him a national leader in new play development as the chief curator of the famous Humana Festival of New American Plays, a career milestone for any playwright who has a play showcased there. His influence on the careers of contemporary playwrights has been less visible in his role as a panelist for major (and lucrative) awards, including the Donald Windham-Sandy M. Campbell Literature Prizes at Yale University and the Harold & Mimi Steinberg Charitable Trust's Distinguished Playwright Award.

In July 2020, in recognition of his successful career and his recent New York productions of Hnath's *The Thin Place* and *Dana H.*, Waters received an Obie Award for Sustained Excellence in Direction from the American Theatre Wing and the *Village Voice*. The citation that accompanied the Obie read as follows:

> For moving fearlessly and skillfully between the naturalistic and the fantastical,
>
> For his ease with both the delicate and the spectacular,
>
> For his mastery of the borderlands where emotion and reality are equally slippery,
>
> For his significant collaborations with actors and designers and for his advocacy for new writers and young directors, and
>
> For his exquisite work this season with two beautifully troubling and eerie plays by Lucas Hnath,
>
> The committee is very pleased to award Les Waters an Obie for sustained excellence in direction.

The citation evokes the breadth of Waters's accomplishment. A scholarly examination of his body of work might take these items as touchstones and trace these themes and relationships over the decades in systematic fashion. But this book is something else, something more amorphous, more open-ended. The word "sustained" in the name of the Obie Award draws attention to Waters's age. So did the prolonged nothingness of the pandemic shut-down, which was already stifling when he turned 68 in April 2020. Do you remember how we all thought at that point that theatre would surely be back up and running by the fall? The mind-numbing year that followed imposed an unrequested preview of retirement and even an intimation of mortality. Aging is a subject that surfaces several times in Waters's writings in the book.

The Pandemic made it clear to Waters that he is not ready to call it a career. Early on in our conversations, I asked him what he missed, if anything, about making theatre. On June 24, 2020, when it already felt like the shutdown had gone on forever, I received this answer:

> What I really miss is chaos.
> There's always chaos in theatre making. Or the potential for chaos.
>
> There's chaos in a rehearsal room.
> There's chaos in previews and opening nights.
> There's chaos being out of town, particularly in NYC.
> To deal with it, my life is ordered.
> I read, I eat, I go for long walks. I'm solitary.
> Now there is no chaos.

* * * * *

In 1998, when he was head of the graduate directing program at UC San Diego (UCSD), Les Waters contacted his friend Caryl Churchill in London to see if she would be interested in contributing to a project with his students based on the work of Belgian symbolist playwright Maurice Maeterlinck. She responded with new versions of three short Maeter-linck plays – *The Intruder*, *Inside* (often translated as *Interior*), and *The Death of Tintagiles* – which were rehearsed by students in his site-spe-cific theatre course and performed in different spots around the mansion home of his UCSD colleague Marianne MacDonald. Each play centers on the specter of approaching death. In *The Death of Tintagiles*, a child prince is summoned to the decaying castle of a mysterious and dreaded queen, where he is trapped in a dungeon cell and eventually has the life choked out of him. In *Inside*, an old man and a stranger stand in the garden outside of a house looking in through the windows at a family of four gathered around a table near a fireplace. The two men have come to inform the family of the drowning death of their daughter, but they hes-itate as they peer inside at the quiet domestic scene – until the murmurs of a crowd of locals bringing the girl's body home drive the Old Man inside with his tragic news.

The Death of Tintagiles (1894) and *Interior* (1895) were conceived by Maeterlinck as plays for marionettes, part of his effort to create a metaphysical theatre that evoked the operation in the material world of powerful unseen forces beyond. *The Intruder* (1891) used a different technique. It takes place in a dimly lit room in an old country house where the family of an ailing woman – her husband, brother-in-law, three daughters, and the Grandfather, her elderly blind father – await the arrival of her sister-in-law, the Mother Superior in a convent. On doctor's orders, the sick woman is recuperating in bed in a room offstage left, attended by a sister of mercy. Her newborn son, whose birth nearly killed her, lays in a nursery offstage right; he has not cried since birth, lying there "like a wax doll."

As the characters wait, the stillness and anticipation seem to heighten their senses, especially the blind Grandfather. They take notice of a series of simple events going on around them. Outdoors, the nightingales in the lane go silent. The swans in the pond are frightened. The wind in the garden causes the rose petals to fall. The door to the terrace outside won't shut. The gardener – or somebody – sharpens a scythe outside. Footsteps are heard on the stairs; either the sister has arrived or there is an intruder, but the maid says no one has come. The Grandfather awakens from dozing off and feels that somebody has entered the room and is sitting at the table beside him – in a chair the others insist is empty. The oil lamp flickers and goes out. They sit in near darkness. The Grandfather panics. The clock strikes midnight. Quick and heavy steps are heard in the mother's room. Cries of terror come from the baby's room. Then silence. And the attending nurse comes out of the sick room and makes the sign of the cross.

Of course, the unseen intruder getting closer and closer is recognized by the audience as the figure of Death coming to claim the life of the woman stricken in childbirth. What is relevant here about Maeterlinck's dramaturgy – and about much of Waters's directing – is the way that the activation of the senses heightens attention to detail and thereby invokes presence by virtue of absence. In a once radical manner that we might now experience as obvious or insistent, Maeterlinck conjures death – as an ominous, autonomous force – out of thin air by tracing its material ripples in the realm of the characters' perception. At one and the same time, the "intruder" is there by virtue of what the characters see and hear and feel (almost like a vibration) and not there by virtue of having no actual, concrete, material form.

The theatre of Les Waters demonstrates a similar interest in this paradoxical simultaneity of the there/not there. It challenges the audience's perceptions in an effort to get them to see more than first meets the eye and to hear beyond the threshold of audibility. His body of work is too large and diverse to say that this is what all of it is about – far from it – but variations on the technique of invoking the there/not there can be found in many of his productions. Let me describe two examples from productions I have seen.

For the 2017 Humana Festival, Waters staged the world premiere of Jorge Ignacio Cortiñas's *Recent Alien Abductions*, a play set partly in the living room and kitchen of a simple family home in Bayamón, Puerto Rico. There is a strong political undercurrent in the play and a sci-fi element stemming from a major character's preoccupation with *The X-Files*, but the second act plays like a realistic domestic drama. It includes a scene in which a woman and her neighbor chat while they change the adult diaper of her elderly mother-in-law, who has dementia and is confined to a wheelchair. The incidental dialogue follows this toileting process step-by-step – "I'm going to turn you on your side now ok Olga?" – "Is that a bed sore?" As staged by Waters, the characters came and went through a door off the living room, fetching necessary supplies, wheeling the elderly woman around the furniture and out of the room, moving back and forth until one or two and then all three characters were out of view but still chattering away about how to get the woman's husband to sign an important document central to the plot. The scene continued like this with no actor in sight for three or four minutes, long enough for the audience to become self-conscious about sitting there looking at an empty stage. The characters were there vocally and textually but not there physically or visually, and this lasted long enough to become uncomfortable (for me, anyway) and to advance an underlying tension in the action.

The empty stage was conspicuous, but it might simply have been a convenient solution to a delicate staging challenge written into the script. Two years earlier, when Waters directed the world premiere of Charles Mee's *Glory of the World* at the 2015 Humana Festival, he went out of his way to invoke this absent-present paradox. The play was commissioned from Mee to commemorate the 100th birthday of Thomas Merton, the influential theologian and Trappist monk who lived for years in a monastery near Louisville. The project was part of Waters's effort to generate work at Actors Theatre that connected with the life, culture, and history of Louisville. And that effort became personal during a 2014 workshop to develop the play at the Colorado

New Play Summit in Steamboat Springs, Colorado. That was when Waters decided to append a prologue and epilogue to Mee's script that featured him coming out at the beginning and the end of the performance and sitting in a chair motionless for a prolonged time while simple but cryptic sentences were projected on the walls of the set behind him. He did not move, he did not speak, and, in the appearance at the beginning, he sat at a table with his back to the audience in a way that it might be perceived that he was reading these projections just as we were or that they represented thoughts emanating from his mind and manifesting in type on the walls. He was *there*, physically present and not at all anonymous; that is, he was present as Les Waters, instantly recognizable to many ATL patrons and theatre professionals and conspicuous to others given his unique personal appearance. And he was *not there*, by virtue of remaining silent and denying the audience a view of his face. Even at the end when he sat facing out, he did not contact or acknowledge the viewer; he was expressionless, serene, without affect.

It would be difficult to exaggerate the magnitude of this gesture in the context of Waters's body of work. While he appeared in several of the projects he created with graduate students at UCSD, this was the first and only time that he put himself on stage in one of his professional productions. Essays by Lila Neugebauer and Amy Wegener in this book will look at this revealing sequence from *Glory of the World* in different contexts, as will Waters himself. My point here is that it represents another manifestation of presence-in-absence in his work. Yes, on a practical or pedestrian level, all theatre directors could be seen as there and not there at the same time. They conceive a production; collaborate with designers, actors, and others; shape the play on stage to have the desired tempo and tone; and then withdraw, leaving their work behind for an audience to experience night after night when they are gone. They are present in the many choices and decisions they made that are manifest in each and every performance, and they are absent by virtue of having left town after opening night to get going on their next project. Waters is doing something more than that. He is using the there/not-there dynamic – and other types of contradiction – to open up gaps in the audience's perception, gaps that invite them to pay closer attention and sometimes perhaps to experience the presence of something that is literally not there. In other words, he is making the subliminal liminal, summoning thoughts, sensations, phenomena from beyond the level of conscious perception and bringing them forward, like Maeterlinck's intruder, so that they push against the threshold of consciousness and make their presence felt. In this way, Waters's sense of theatricality is always metaphysical – regardless of the subject or tone or style of the play.

Another figure, also from Maeterlinck, suggests this dynamic. In an essay called "The Tragical in Everyday Life," published in his collection *The Treasure of the Humble* (1896), Maeterlinck articulated a vision of what he labelled "static drama," by which he intended a theatre that set aside the intrigue, adventure, and passion of classical tragedy and went "beyond the determined struggle of man against man, and desire against desire" in order to focus on the presence of the eternal in ordinary, everyday life. Famously, Maeterlinck wrote:

> I have grown to believe that an old man, seated in his armchair, waiting patiently, with his lamp beside him; giving unconscious ear to all the eternal laws that reign about his house, interpreting, without comprehending, the silence of doors and windows and the quivering voice of the light, submitting with bent head to the presence of his soul and his destiny – an old man, who conceives not that all the powers of this world, like so many heedful servants are mingling and keeping vigil in his room, who suspects not that the very sun itself is supporting in space the little table against which he leans, or that every star in heaven and every fiber of the soul are directly concerned in the movement of an eyelid that closes, or a thought that springs to birth – I have grown to believe that he, motionless as he is, does yet live in reality a deeper, more human and more universal life than the lover who strangles his mistress, the captain who conquers in battle, or "the husband who avenges his honour."[1]

Les Waters has directed a hundred productions, many of them full of sound and fury, some of them animated by silliness or bravado, all of them representing as best he can the play as he understands it. It would be reductive and misleading to paint them with too broad a brush. But metaphorically speaking, his theatre, in some collective or aggregate sense, can be seen as akin to Maeterlinck's old man in an armchair, still, silent, awake, surrounded by – and maybe fleetingly attentive to – the forces and motions that exist beyond the threshold of perception.

* * * * *

When I first approached Waters – who from here on in this book will be known more familiarly as Les – in the lobby of Actors Theatre in 2014 and again when we began our pandemic conversations in May 2020, I was curious what was on his mind about his craft, how he made artistic decisions, how he communicated with his collaborators, how he engaged with so many amazing playwrights, and how he came to create some particular images on stage that I found spellbinding. I learned that these are not his favorite topics of conversation. He is not inclined to analyze his creative process or to articulate a step-by-step method for "how to direct a play." As our dialogue stretched from spring to summer to fall, I came to understand that the key to his practice is preparation on at least two different scales. He comes to each rehearsal process abundantly ready. That readiness includes a penetrating familiarity with the script at hand and a period of visual, historical, and topical research related to the play. Most plays he directs are brand new, so there is no critical history trailing behind them, but even when there is, he does not read reviews of previous productions or consult the exegeses of scholars. He practices analysis by immersion. He steeps himself in the text and related materials so that when he begins to interact with his designers and actors, he has the play within and can take a reactive position to what they are offering. He can trust that his responses come from a subliminal knowledge of the play and its reverberations for him. One benefit of this practice is that it makes room for the creative contributions of his colleagues and channels all that into his vision for the production.

There is also the preparation that goes beyond a specific project to a broader scale that involves the self-care and feeding of the artist himself. From an early age, as many of the lists and anecdotes that follow will detail, Les has taken an interest in the history of art and aesthetic experience more generally. He likes to look, he likes to listen, and in the natural course of pursuing his interest in theatre, he has attuned his senses to various expressive vocabularies. He is an aesthetic being: an avid reader, a film buff, a museum goer, an aficionado of fine art photography, as well as a theatregoer. This practice endows him with a heightened sensitivity to formal composition and to his own affective experience of the art object. It prepares him on a more general level to engage in the creative process himself. In short, he is an artist.

On Wednesday, May 20, 2020, Les wrote the following in our shared online document:

> A quote from a hero.
> "It's less like an object, more like the weather."
> John Cage.
> Not sure what he is referring to. I could look it up but I prefer not to know.
> Explains my distaste of labels.

I did look it up. And when I mentioned that to Les, he did want to know. (Maybe.) In the spring of 1981, composer John Cage and choreographer Merce Cunningham, twin giants of postmodernism in the arts, were interviewed during a residency at the Walker Art Gallery in Minneapolis. By that time in their careers, they had been collaborating for almost 40 years and each had changed the fundamental perception of their respective art forms. In the process of describing their creative process and the nature of their collaboration, Cage said:

> It's less like an object and more like the weather. Because in an object you can tell where the boundaries are. But in the weather it's impossible to say when something begins or ends. We hope that the weather will continue, and we trust that our way of relating dance and music will also continue. It's not starting from an idea, not starting even from an expression of the same feeling nor an exposition of the same idea but rather simply being together in the same place and the same time and leaving space around each art.[2]

In trying to agree on an evocative subtitle to follow the simple title *The Theatre of Les Waters*, we considered a number of possibilities (some only for a millisecond), including:

Working Things Out in Public
Trust in Silence
Directing as Collaboration
Something Unspoken
A Line Made by Walking
Shaping Time

But we kept coming back to More Like the Weather. Les favored it, I think, for its enigmatic quality, especially out of its original context. Less like an object, more like the weather. What does *that* mean? (He is attracted to the mystery of incongruity and probably wishes that it was not spelled out here.) I favored it because the phrase was coined in reference to a collaborative partnership, perhaps the most consequential artistic collaboration of the 20th century, and collaboration is one of the principal themes of this book.

The Theatre of Les Waters: More Like the Weather is an idiosyncratic work about directing. Part diary of a plague year, part group portrait of the artist, part memoir, part miscellany, part theatrical festschrift, it is a book by Les Waters as much as it is about him – to the point where he might well have been credited as author or co-editor. It has definitely been a collaboration. It offers an impressionistic introduction to a major theatre artist looking back on his life and his work at a historical (and biographical) moment that compels reflection. It skips a stone across the stillness imposed by the Pandemic and watches the ripples as they radiate. While the sequence of the individual pieces here is intentional, they might just as readily be read by flipping open to a random page and starting there. The book is neither comprehensive or conclusive. It does not have an argument and its truest subject is never directly in view. It is best glimpsed out of the corner of your eye, a bit low and off to the left, shadowy, elusive, maybe even ominous at first but actually safe and generous and caring.

Oh, and if you are reading out loud, it's "Lez." Rhymes with fez. Probably should've mentioned that earlier. The name appears so often in these pages, better to get it right in your mind's ear at the outset. "Lez" has worked exclusively in the US for more than 25 years, but he was born and raised in the north of England and the way to say his name comes from there. That pronunciation is one of the first things you learn when you get to know him, an experience that for me has been an unmitigated pleasure over the year of making this book. I hope that you feel the same by the time you finish reading it.

Notes

1 Maeterlinck, Maurice. "The Tragical in Everyday Life." In *The Treasure of the Humble* (trans. Alfred Sutro). New York: Dodd, Mead & Company, 1910. p. 105.
2 "Chance Conversations: An Interview with Merce Cunningham and John Cage." 1981. https://www.youtube.com/watch?v=ZNGpjXZovgk&t=19s (consulted on March 30, 2021)

1. *Our Town* at Actors Theatre of Louisville (2014).

2. *At the Vanishing Point* at Actors Theatre of Louisville (2015).

Early theatre experience

I don't remember any HA!! moment when I thought this is it, I know what I'm going to be, I'm going to be a theatre director. I can remember exactly where I was when I decided I was an atheist but not a director. Both choices involved long walks through local woods on Sunday afternoons as a brooding teenager. The decision to reject God and Christianity was a form of shattering. With directing I just started walking and many miles later I arrived back home, a director.

The first show I ever saw was the panto *Dick Whittington and His Cat* at the theatre in Cleethorpes (I was born there) one Christmas. Going to the theatre was a major event. We couldn't afford the theatre. We couldn't afford much of anything. I remember cats dancing on the roofs of London at midnight and it was snowing. I was 3, maybe 4, and slightly scared of the whole thing and was sitting on my grandpa's lap and I thought the cats were real and I thought I want to make things like that. It was that clear. But I was 3. Then, it's a blank till my last two years at Grammar School, and by then I knew that I needed to be in the theatre and I didn't want to be an actor. Being looked at can be difficult for me and that tends to be a major stumbling block for any performer. I was very influenced by two teachers – Enid Pittwood who taught history and directed the school play, and Jim Hawkins who taught English and made events with the students. He introduced me to John Arden and the work of the Royal Court. So, by my Junior year at High School, I was regularly disappearing to London to see plays.

I was a teenager in the 1960s. Everybody knew something big was going on and it wasn't going on in the town where I was growing up. I became involved

DOI: 10.4324/9781003170808-2

with the Scunthorpe Youth Theatre. Mike Bradwell – who started the theatre group Hull Truck and was close friends with the film director Mike Leigh and went on to run the Bush Theatre – was from the same area as me. And he directed a production of John Whiting's *The Devils* in Scunthorpe one summer. Quite a radical choice for a youth theatre. But it was the 1960s. I played Cardinal Richelieu. I think I had one scene and I don't remember anything that I said. I must have been 15 or 16. It was amazing. We were a bunch of arty, snotty, deeply opinionated teenagers, and Mike would say you should listen to this music, or you should read this, or there's a play by so-and-so, or you have to see the work of this director. I remember lying in a medieval sarcophagus in Thornton Abbey graveyard at midnight and believing this was improvisation. I remember listening to Pink Floyd's *A Saucerful of Secrets* at all hours of the day and night, waiting for revelation. My world suddenly became more expansive and more interesting. A sense of connection to an imaginative universe.

School report

I found a box in the garage the other week filled with old school reports and photographs of me as a child. The box had collapsed. I think in the past I would have moved it over to a sturdier box, not looked at it again, but these being pandemic times and in a sense a time of contemplation, I took them out and thought, "Oh look, here's a school report from 1963." I was 11 years old, and now I'm 68. I found I was very vulnerable to the report. I found it upsetting. What did it say? It said, "After a term here, it is very clear that Leslie is not a leader, but he's happy to follow others. This will be his path in life."

And I thought, "I'm 11 years old and I've just been thrown on the scrap heap." And it made me angry. I was wounded. And then – and I can get to this emotion very, very quickly – I thought, "I hate fucking England. I just fucking hate England." I remember the teacher who had written it, who seemed to be upset all of the time because she was middle class and she was teaching predominantly working-class children. We were an embarrassment to her, a drop in social status. It took a couple weeks to get over this school report. And if we weren't in a pandemic and I was as usual getting on planes to go somewhere to work, I would've thought, "Oh, fuck that," and just moved on. But now, I'm haunted for weeks by something somebody wrote about me when I was 11. In the end that school report went in the shredder. It's gone, that one's gone.

DOI: 10.4324/9781003170808-3

"My Les"

Annie Smart

I met Les in April '74 when we were undergraduates at Manchester University Drama Department, and we have lived and worked together on and off ever since. Now that we have 3 grown children (most admirable human beings), a mortgage, a dog and cat and the rest, and have worked together on more than 30 productions, the task of trying to sum up what I think about Les seems daunting, almost ridiculous.

Our first theatre collaborations were (on my part) as student stage manager and reluctant actor, for Les, as the director. The first show was Les's thesis production of Edward Bond's *The Sea*, with some extraordinary fellow students, including Clare McIntyre, Mick Ford, and Roger Allam among others. My job was to provide set dressings and props and choreograph and control the many set changes. I remember feeling completely inadequate as I was only a first-year student, and all those involved were my seniors. Les very purposefully gave me both permission and the courage to be in control, and the changes went well. Later, with many of the same group, we performed John Antrobus's *Captain Oates' Left Sock* to some acclaim at the Edinburgh Fringe. That was the last time I acted in public, playing the almost mute Dorothy. Les performed too, but I was so lost in Dorothy's great shyness and inarticulacy I barely registered what anyone else was doing and have little memory of the performances, only of us all regularly eating fantastic cauliflower cheese at Henderson's Restaurant.

I designed several shows as an undergrad (in the UK tradition where scenery, props, and costumes are all considered the Designer's purview/job) and found ways to extend the experience and eventually train at the Motley (also

DOI: 10.4324/9781003170808-4

known as the English National Opera and the Lindbury) design course. Since then, I've designed sets and/or costumes for dozens of Les's productions, from Mike Weller's *Loose Ends* at Hampstead Theatre in 1980 to, most recently, *A Doll's House, Part 2*, in Berkeley and Boston in 2018. I have nothing but gratitude for all those opportunities and experiences. Given the hit-and-miss nature of all theatre-making, comparatively few went awry. I treasure them all, even the disasters.

Before starting to write this, I listened to the Zwirner Gallery podcast *Dialogues* featuring an artist I've been obsessed with for a few years, Mamma Andersson, talking with her also-artist husband Jockum Nordstrom. It seemed a useful place to start, with another artistic married team, but also because Les (who first showed me Andersson's work) is a director who thinks visually like a painter – in frames. He is entirely in love with painters and photographers and over the years has built his own, rather wonderful and eclectic collection of contemporary art. With any production design for Les, the frame of the stage picture is critical, which means his forays into in-the-round or deconstructed stages are rare. He also reads voraciously and collects books like an addict. But two-dimensional imagery is invariably the basis of his research, his approach, for any show.

Les has a complex relationship with two-dimensional art, he always and only as the viewer. As he says himself: "I can't draw. I drew a Christmas Robin once." And he drew one for me long ago, the shaky outline of a fat bird with a pipe in its beak. This is one of Les's essential choices as an artist himself – to be ignorant, inexperienced. He believes (rightly!) in his own expertise as a theatre director. Outside of that, he allows and respects other people to be experts in their own fields: painters, photographers, writers, actors, designers. So working on any show he is helming always means taking full responsibility for your own craft. He isn't going to tell you how to do it. He much prefers, I think, the mystery of the "other."

We were both born in 1952 and almost daily thank the gods for the old UK, post-war era gifts we've built our lives on – totally free education and health care. Les is the only child of working-class parents, with a stay-at-home mum and a steelworker dad. He was brought up in Scunthorpe, Lincolnshire, an area where his ancestors can be traced back well over a thousand years. Such communities are rooted, sure of their place and who they are. This manifests in Les in many ways but the one it took me years – as a gabby, cityfied, anglo-saxon/celt – to understand is his lack of need to explain, to theorize, to formulate cause and effect. (Which is what I'm doing here now, so Les will probably hate it.)

Nobody could make me laugh like Les's mum Phyllis. Her way was never to explain but to make the driest, surprising statements, that made me bark and choke on my tea. She could have me weeping with laughter over the saddest of stories – "Jim down the road. He's really getting on but won't admit it. Your father told him not to go climbing ladders. Anyway, he fell off doing his gutters only last week." Pause for effect. "Is he ok?" I ask. "Oh he's *fine* . . . Broke both his ankles." Adept, economical storytelling. Laughing in and at pain. Never explaining. It seems to me these are essential to how Les engages with his own art.

The first publicly acclaimed show I designed for Les was Caryl Churchill's *Fen*. We (Joint Stock Theatre Company) researched the play content together, staying in the area, visiting Fenland homes, listening to stories, taking photos. When, a few weeks later, the first script draft arrived from Caryl – missing the last quarter of the script, but barely in time for a design to be created and processed for build – I read it, thought about the intrinsic necessities, and asked Les, "Do you want a house in a field or a field in a house?" His reply, "A field in a house." constituted our entire concept conversation. Of course, afterward, images were checked over, practicalities discussed, but the essence of the concept was never analyzed or formulated or theorized. It was enough to have contracted together for this simple choice, this visual statement.

The work we both loved to go see at this time was profoundly visual, rather than narrative or didactic, Pina Bausch, IOU, Welfare State, Hesitate and Demonstrate, Forced Entertainment. Always work that showed rather than told; embodied work rather than literary. This despite him working at that center of literary excellence, the Royal Court, where he was always developing and thinking about new plays.

Looking back at those first 20 years of our careers, I was deeply involved in feminist activism, and I worked whenever possible with women directors, producers, and writers. At the same time, Les was a recognized champion of women's writing, and he has always supported and encouraged women writers, such as Timberlake Wertenbaker, Caryl Churchill, Sarah Ruhl, and Naomi Iizuka, among many others. With that background, the fact that women here in America have continued to struggle for parity, for an equal share of the platform and resources, has been a strange and depressing experience for us both. In the recent great wave of new American Artistic Director appointments, things at last feel like they are genuinely shifting and improving as more women (and women of color) take over more of the reins of power. However, now that COVID-19 has compromised venues and jobs, and is destroying audience attendance habits, one wonders what these new women in power will in fact inherit in the long run. Very troubling times.

A 'Les essential' I think I must include is walking, as it affects his work in myriad ways. He has always walked simply to think about things, and to process, removing himself from work and home and their distractions. He is an 'escaper,' choosing to leave difficult situations to find himself a physical and mental space to objectify and review things before returning. Of course, it's a form of meditation as much as an act of claiming space.

So art, writings and mysteries that focus on walking, or are structured like it, such as Richard Long's walks and photographs of British footpaths and ley lines, the writings of W. G. Sebald, or Knausgaard, pilgrimages, flâneurs, and the essential unpredictability of journeys, all these make sense to him, reflecting the human condition more truly than moral certitude or conventionally structured story-making.

And in ways I haven't fully formulated for myself, the walking links with making lists. Les is a list keeper. His hardback diaries and notebooks go back decades and record movies seen and to see, books read, people and places visited. He loves lists and art about lists – all the various recordings of the journey.

*   *   *   *   *

ANNIE SMART *is a set and costume designer who studied Drama at Manchester and Nottingham Universities and took the Motley Theatre Design Course at English National Opera. A native of Birmingham, her work in the UK includes designs for the National Theatre, the Royal Court, Leicester Haymarket, Liverpool Playhouse, Joint Stock, and others; and she was Chair of the MFA Theatre Design Course at Wimbledon School of Art. At this time, she also designed regularly in the US, including for The Public Theater, Arena Stage, and The Guthrie. Her work shifted permanently to the US in 1996, mainly to California, where she has designed for La Jolla Playhouse, American Conservatory Theater, Magic Theatre, California Shakespeare Theater, Berkeley Repertory Theatre, and others. She currently teaches theatre design at the University of California, Berkeley. She is the partner in life and art of the subject of this book.*

Some things will be lost, maybe.
Some things will be found, maybe.

Due to the 2020–2021 Pandemic, some projects were postponed/cancelled. Others are still in development. Who knows what their life will be?

Here's the list.

Dana H. at the Vineyard, NYC. Shut down due to COVID-19 on March 12 after 31 performances. The set sits ready and waiting in the theatre. In limbo. Maybe Dublin? Maybe London? Maybe Broadway? Maybe Berlin? Scheduled to reopen October 2021.

The two Pinter one-acts – *A Kind of Alaska* and *One for the Road* – for National Asian American Theatre Company, NYC. Originally May-June 2020. Production cast. Design in progress. March 18 postponed or cancelled. NAATCO would like to produce.

Abe Koogler's *Aspen Ideas* at Studio Theatre, Washington, DC. Originally June-August 2020. Postponed or cancelled March 23. Studio would like to produce. World premiere. A play about a wealthy middle-aged couple who think they are part of the answer. A play about a young couple who think the other couple are the problem.

Wintertime by Charles Mee at Berkeley Rep. Originally January-February 2021. Now October-November 2021.

New Sarah Ruhl commission for Berkeley Rep. We talked about an adaptation of Euripides' *Alcestis* – a play that I have a thing about (death, fear of

DOI: 10.4324/9781003170808-5

death, what would you do for the someone that you love) – who knows what will happen?

Black Mountain Women. Music by Martha Redbone and Aaron Whitby, book by Naomi Iizuka. Public Theater, NYC. An epic play with music about the women in Martha's life in the former mining community of Lynch, Kentucky. In March, we were about to set out on a research trip but the Pandemic stopped that. We are still working.

Eurydice by Sarah Ruhl. Signature Theatre, NYC. Part of the Sarah Ruhl residency there.

Out of Time. Five 30-minute monologues for actors over the age of 60 by five Asian American writers – Jaclyn Backhaus, Sam Chanse, Mia Chung, Naomi Iizuka, and Anna Moensch. NAATCO. Writers are commissioned and working. Conceived by Mia and myself in the weeks leading up to the lockdown. Inspired by the extraordinary Anne Teresa de Keersmaeker's *Mitten Wir Im Leben Sind.* When? Where?

Witch by Jen Silverman. MCC, NYC. Based on the Jacobean play *The Witch of Edmonton* by Rowley, Dekker, and Ford. New York premiere.

What If If Only by Caryl Churchill. A play about grief and possibilities and the future and hauntology. Six pages of Churchill brilliance. Co-directed with Jared Mezzocchi. Produced by NAATCO. Live-streamed, June 2021.

The Dinosaurs by Jacob Perkins. Commissioned by Clubbed Thumb. A play about time and disease and the need for structure. We met during *Dana H.* in 2020. Maybe developed 2021? Maybe produced 2022?

The Character Actor by Sarah Ruhl. The ghost of a character actor returns to the back stage of Berkeley Rep. Ten-minute audio play. Part of Place/Settings: Berkeley series. Produced March 2021.

If all this happens – and who knows how much theatre will be produced post-pandemic – I'll be a lucky man. It's three years of work. And then, I'll be 72. And then what?

Postcards

At one point in my life, before I decided on theatre, I wanted to study the history of art. Before the history of art, it was archaeology. How many theatre directors wanted to be archaeologists? I know at least 3. Anyway, I have a substantial collection of art, architecture, and photography books. I have lived most of my life with a designer, with Annie, so we have an ever-growing art library. And I collect postcards at whatever museum or gallery I visit. I have 100s and 100s of postcards. These postcards are kept in shoeboxes. On a shelf in my office at home are eight or ten shoeboxes of postcards. I wear Chuck Taylors – most of the time – and it turns out Converse shoeboxes are very good for holding postcards.

As preparation for the design process and the whole process of making a new production, I take out these boxes and go through them, pulling out postcards and thinking "Is there anything about this postcard that connects the play to me?" I try not to worry about it or obsess or overthink it. I am trying to hold the idea of the play very lightly in my brain and free associate around it. To shunt the play to the sidelines of my thought. To de-center it. And I gather together the postcards and I pin them to a large cork board and edit them and move them around and assemble and reassemble them in ways that I find interesting. This will go on for weeks or months. I usually keep the board up through the entire rehearsal process.

And I stare at it. It ignites my energy at the beginning of the process, and during the rehearsal process, it provides focus when I have lost track of the project and I feel I'm losing the company because I cannot communicate in any compelling way why I wanted to do the play in the first place. I will just

DOI: 10.4324/9781003170808-6

stare at it. And think, "Oh, there's a connection." Or it might be that the production has actually become something else and I am still trying to hold on to early things.

Sometimes, I find two or three particular images on the board that I am fascinated with and when I have a meeting with a designer, I will take these postcards along and say, "I have been looking at these two things or three things," or "I am interested in this or that." And I find it very pleasing to do and very rewarding to do. I like being able to do it physically. I like being able to pin these postcards and move them around physically.

Sometimes, it is surprising what's up there. When working on *Long Day's Journey Into Night*, I read biographies of O'Neill and articles about theatre of that period. I read a lot of material, and I went through the postcards and I thought there would be images of Victorian rooms or houses or things to do with theatre in a general sense because *Long Day's Journey* is a play about a theatrical family and it is set in a particular period and in a particular house. And I have postcards of Ellen Terry and Sarah Bernhardt and the Barrymores striking these extraordinary theatre poses. Not so. What appeared on the corkboard was hardly any architecture and very few Victorian photographs but a series of portraits of people. The Elizabethan painter Nicholas Hilliard made portrait miniatures of Elizabeth I and her Court, and they were up there. And I thought, "Oh, this is interesting. I thought it was a play about a certain time and place and a particular profession that I know well and now it seems to be a play about close-ups of people." Antje Ellerman's set reflected this – a wooden platform, a props table, and a house with no walls, no doors, no windows.

I wasn't taught this. I cannot remember exactly when I started. It certainly was in full play by the time I was at UCSD. I remember arriving there and asking the good people in academia who provide office materials for a corkboard as big as possible.

"The Next Phase"

Mia Katigbak

I caught it. Les did that slight recoil of delight followed by a glance to my friend, the playwright, Jorge Ignacio Cortiñas. I was auditioning for Jorge's play, *Recent Alien Abductions*, which Les was going to direct for the 2017 Humana Festival. I'd never met him before, and I remember thinking, "Cool. He gets my sense of humor." The part was Olga, a woman in the late stages of Alzheimer's, and I went for the funny rather than the pathetic.

After I booked the job, I heard from colleagues:

> "Oh, he's so hard to read; he doesn't say anything and you don't know what he's thinking."
> "I kept wishing he'd tell me if I was on track or not."
> "I never knew how I was doing."
> "He lets everyone just do their thing and you don't know what's going on."

Well, this should be fun, I thought. But contrary to what I'd been led to believe, Les was rather forthcoming, even occasionally (very occasionally) loquacious. During the first week of rehearsals, typically given over to "table work," Les was an active participant as we discussed the difficult themes of the play around the rehearsal table. We considered the meanings of "alien"; the violent manifestations of colonialism; violence itself, its perpetrators and victims; disease, metaphorical and literal; fraternal sexual abuse; suicide. Les and Jorge communicated effortlessly, with intelligence, insight, and humor,

DOI: 10.4324/9781003170808-7

and that dynamic allowed the rest of the company to navigate and explore the demanding terrain of the play safely.

After this preliminary phase of the process, we got on our feet to begin to stage the play. I was called to rehearse my first scene in the play, a short one. After two passes at it, I got a nod from Les, a "Good," and that was it. We were done in 12 minutes. The stage manager cited it as possibly the shortest rehearsal call on record. This was the first time I encountered the reticent, hardly verbal Les I had been warned about. While I appreciated the efficiency, I wondered if he was being dismissive or inattentive. Regardless of experience and confidence, we actors cannot ever completely overcome all insecurities.

There can be something disconcerting about Les's neutral affect. There were times I wasn't quite sure if what I was saying was making any sort of impression. During tech, I asked about a staging issue: my character was wheelchair-bound, but during a transition, I had to walk to the next setup. Would this be distracting? I got the nod, followed by "I'll watch." I thought it was only a courteous gesture because it was a relatively minor thing. I only had to take a few steps in semi-darkness. I was only doing my due diligence, and there were other more pressing issues. I wouldn't have been surprised if my query hadn't registered, but after we ran the sequence, Les quietly came up to me and said he didn't think it was a problem, given the choreography of the scene change and the light and sound that accompanied it. The response was succinct, deliberate, and attentive. I clocked it, my actor-self giving my artistic director-self a mental nod.

Later, we were standing at the back of the theatre during a break, and I impulsively asked Les if he would consider directing for my company, National Asian American Theatre Company (NAATCO). I'd spoken to him about NAATCO's work on behalf of Asian American theatre practitioners and my life-long mission to battle the persistent stereotypic and limiting representations of Asians and Asian Americans onstage. Trying to replicate his telegraphic style, I elaborated: "All Asian American cast. Your choice of playwright. Hardly any money." After ever so slight a pause, enough for me to start to get embarrassed, he nodded and said: "Sure," and we shook hands on it.

Back in New York after the run in Louisville, I was too timid to follow up. Les is a fancy director after all, it was only a handshake agreement, and NAATCO operates on a fraction of the Actors Theatre of Louisville budget. So, I was amazed when I got his email in October the following year, after he'd stepped down from ATL, asking if I was still interested in having him direct for NAATCO. He wanted to do Pinter with us and asked that I consider either *Landscape* or *Silence*.

I was not sold on either play and suggested we keep looking, but the choice of Pinter was spot on for NAATCO. We present plays by White people with all Asian American casts. "Classics" written before the 20th century seem to be more readily accepted by our critics. The closer we come to modern times, the more transgressive we seem to be. Our productions of William Finn's *Falsettoland* and Clifford Odets' *Awake and Sing!* were met by grumbling about Asian Americans portraying Jewish Americans, despite the fact that both shows were critically acclaimed and received all sorts of recognition and awards. I welcomed Les's choice of plays written by a British playwright in the last quarter of the 20th century. The interrogation of what we do as some sort of whiteface or upholding white culture is important to me. Challenging the preconceptions and misconceptions of who we are, what we are capable of, and what we represent as Asian Americans is a key element of NAATCO's mission.

Our correspondence during this time was true to character: I emailed in paragraphs and Les responded in haiku. He eventually suggested Pinter's *A Kind of Alaska*, which I really liked, and I proposed *One for the Road* as a companion piece. In October 2019, a year after Les had gotten in touch, we set production dates for April-May 2020. By February 2020, we were completely cast, design and technical teams were confirmed, and the graphic design for postcards was done. Then, on March 18, 2020, following Governor Mario Cuomo's mandate to close all places of public assembly in the state of New York for at least the next six months, we sadly cancelled the Pinter one-acts.

Thankfully, another opportunity for Les and NAATCO presented itself. In late February, days before theatres shut down, Les had come to a show I was doing at LCT3. We went for drinks after, and he told me about a dance concert he had just seen, *Mitten wir im Leben sind/Bach6Cellosuiten*, by Anne Teresa De Keersmaeker. In this suite of pieces, five older dancers performed long solos accompanied by a live cellist. Les described these solos as brutal on the dancers, requiring great stamina, and expressed a desire to create a similar work for older actors. He spoke about what a disgrace it was to relegate older actors to characters of decreased capacity in spite of the richness their lives and experience could bring to any performance. He had a defiant idea to commission a marathon of monologues, each one at least 30-minutes long, written by a different playwright, and performed by an actor at least 60 years old. He wanted no set, only one chair, and a maximum of one prop per monologue. He said he didn't care if it took five hours, eight hours, half-a-day.

I'd come to appreciate this "fuck you" stance against traditional strictures that Les would sometimes take. He was probably also saying "fuck you" to aging, rebelling against the perceived limitations and often undignified portrayals of the elderly. His idea appealed to me because I was essaying something similar in my work. In addition to my life-long commitment to the increased and more enlightened representation of Asian Americans in American theatre, I had begun a project in 2017 through TCG's Fox Foundation Resident Actor Fellowship to support actors facing the double whammy of being older and being Asian American. Actors like me.

Into our second round of drinks and snacks post-LCT3, we compiled a wish list of playwrights and actors, wondered about a venue, and Les casually asked if it was something NAATCO would consider taking on. I replied that as long as Asian Americans were predominantly featured, I definitely would. That February night, we decided we'd focus on it after the Pinter production. Then came the Pandemic.

Early in June, heavy-hearted from the George Floyd killing and the unrest that followed, fighting to keep a deep civic depression from immobilizing me, I suddenly remembered something about the De Keersmaeker piece that Les had vividly described to me. After one solo, the dancer collapsed on the floor, breathing heavily. For what seemed an endless span of time, all that could be heard was the dancer's labored breathing. The audience, rather than becoming restless, held *its* breath, suspended in the kind of tension that makes for great theatre.

The memory was resonant: age, isolation, effort, endurance, breath. Antithetically, it extricated me from a darkening vortex. I contacted Les, circling back to his monologue marathon idea. I proposed commissioning five Asian American playwrights instead of the group of writers we had originally envisioned, which included non-Asian Americans. He readily agreed and we have commissioned monologues from five Asian American women playwrights: Jaclyn Backhaus, Samantha Chanse, Mia Chung, Naomi Iizuka, and Anna Moench. In the wake of the pestilences of virus and of government, despite personal and professional challenges, their first drafts are in. Our work will continue, even as we hear of violence against Asians around the country. The project will test the physical, mental, and emotional stamina of the actors, it will test the perceptions of our audiences about age, aging, and

Asian Americans, and it will ask us to contemplate what lies ahead. Les has brilliantly entitled the project *Out of Time*.

* * * * *

MIA KATIGBAK is the co-founder and actor-manager of NAATCO. She has acted extensively in New York and with NAATCO, receiving an Obie Award for her portrayal of matriarch Bessie Berger in NAATCO's 2013 revival of Clifford Odets' Awake and Sing! She is a 2021 USA Fellow, a TCG Fox Foundation Resident Actor Fellow for Distinguished Achievement, and she received a 2019 Special Drama Desk Award in recognition of sustained achievement and being "the backbone of the Off-Broadway scene." Born and raised in Manila, the Philippines, she came to the US when she was 11. She holds a BA from Barnard College and an MA from Columbia University.

I love lists

I love lists. I find them comforting. Both to write and to read. If I am in somebody's apartment, I usually gravitate towards the kitchen. The lists live there. Often on the fridge. "Eggs, bread, so-and-so, finish reading Heidegger." Those are the ones that I love.

I make endless lists. I used to keep notebooks in which I listed everything I read/saw/listened to. Many are in a box in the garage. There was a great exhibition of lists at the Morgan Library in NYC about 10 years ago (2011). And of course, Georges Perec's *An Attempt at Exhausting a Place in Paris*. That's a list.

Lists come easy because they are both factual and fragmented. They convey information succinctly. They are about the past and the future. What we have done and what we hope to do. They can be surprising. Often baffling after the event.

On Friday May 4, 2007, I made this list:

> Pack
> Chalfant's key
> Order cab
> Activate OA
> Nancy – $$$?
> Email Valerie

A trip to New York.
Yes.

DOI: 10.4324/9781003170808-8

Stayed with Kathy and Henry Chalfant.
Yes.
What is OA? Office assistant?
Maybe.
Nancy is my older daughter.
$$$ for her approaching birthday?
Maybe.
And who is Valerie?
I have not a clue.

Do most people think of lists as brief and perfunctory?
I think of a list as revelatory. A coded message from an unknown person.

Theatres I have known

The Royal Court Theatre, London.
Proscenium. A wonderful relationship between the stage and the auditorium. Epic in an intimate way. So many memorable productions – Max Stafford-Clark's *Top Girls*, *The Glad Hand*, Bill Gaskill's *The Sea*, Nancy Meckler's *Curse of the Starving Class*, Peter Gill's *Small Change*, Ian Rickson's *Mojo*.

The Almeida, London.
What was the original function of the space? A meeting hall? A warehouse? Its curved, brick back wall. Its height. Its intimacy. The sense of being inside the production with the performers. Joint Stock's production of *Fen* opened here in February of 1983. A frigid winter. No heating. Seeing the actor's breath on stage.

The Traverse Theatre, Edinburgh.
I'm thinking of the old Traverse in the Grassmarket. I'm not sure I even remember the space with any clarity. I do remember interviewing on two occasions for the position of Artistic Director and being rejected. A numbing heartbreak at the time. I feel that my career would have been very different if I had been accepted. "Career" makes me cringe. Sounds like something planned, something well thought out. Now I did want to work at the Royal Court. And I did want to work in the States. And I achieved both things. I have had a life. I am having a life. I don't want to say "a life in the theatre" because that is so love-y. And also a David Mamet play.

(The challenge in writing this list is that it is about memory. I intended to write about physical space. Or mostly about that. But it's become very

DOI: 10.4324/9781003170808-9

quickly about my emotional connection to the space/theatre. I directed one show at the old Traverse. Rona Munro's *Fugue*. I remember so little about the play. I don't remember the design at all. I don't think it was a "bad" production. But the experience of being there working on that show is firmly lodged in my mind. Traverse/*Fugue*/Edinburgh/Artistic Director Interviews/Disappointment. Proust and his madeleine.)

The Public Theater, NYC.
I've seen shows in all of the spaces there and worked in the Newman, the Anspacher, the LuEster, and the Shiva. My American career (that word again!) started here with *Fen* in 1983. I didn't really know how important the institution was. Joe Papp, his generosity, his cruelty. My youth, my self-importance. I can't really describe the actual spaces and how they work. Like being inside a monument, a monument called the Public Theater.

The Roda Stage, Berkeley Rep.
The larger of the two stages. The Proscenium. I understand prosceniums. The disconnect between the seats downstairs and the seats upstairs. Too separate experiences. No wing space. Wide enough to feel epic. And yet two people standing on that stage in its emptiness can feel intimate. I love working there – *Fetes de la Nuit*, *In the Next Room*, *The Lieutenant of Inishmore*, *Concerning Strange Devices from the Distant West*. I think of this place as a home.

Soho Rep, NYC.
I have probably seen more productions here than any other theatre in NYC. I love what they do. Sarah Benson. Hero. It's small, it's cramped, it shouldn't work but it does. It transforms. I have seen great plays here – Branden Jacobs-Jenkins's *An Octoroon*, *Fairview* by Jackie Sibblies Drury, *Is God is* by Aleshea Harris – in great productions, but the place sings design to me. I think of Soho Rep as design. The transformation of space. Think Louisa Thompson for *Blasted*, David Zinn for *10 out of 12*, Mimi Lien for both *An Octoroon* and *Fairview*. Geniuses. Heroes.

The Lyceum Theatre, Broadway, NYC.
Where the good people at Lincoln Center produced *The Vibrator Play*. Perfect alignment of play, design by Annie Smart, and theatre. A play set in the Victorian era living in a Victorian theatre. I don't like watching my own work – I know that is a problem – but I was happy sitting in those cramped seats amongst a puzzled audience watching this. During the many weeks of previews, I got to know the space well. I watched from up top and loved the layers of velvet dust on the sculptures. I watched from the wings, and when

I couldn't watch anymore, I listened to the show from the dressing room within the proscenium arch itself. A magical place.

Brooklyn Academy of Music.
Beautiful. Important. Honored to have had two shows in the Harvey. Both by Chuck Mee. Both originating from ATL. *Big Love* and *Glory of the World*. That space carries the spectacle of the work as if it's a head on a silver platter. I've watched amazing productions there – Ivo's *Opening Night*, the dance pieces of Pina Bausch and Susanne Linke. Joe Melillo. Hero.

Actors Theatre of Louisville.
I've worked in all three spaces – the Pamela Brown, the Bingham, and the Victor Jory – and in an abandoned warehouse in Butchertown. My involvement with ATL began with *Big Love* in 2000 and ended with *The Thin Place* in 2019. I was AD from 2012 to 2018. Not so much the performance spaces as the rehearsal room, the Humana Room on the 5th floor of the administrative offices on Market Street, says Actors Theatre to me. It's not rundown and seedy like so many rehearsal rooms. It's crisp with a little bit of battered. It's not large enough to accommodate the width of the PB. It's not deep enough either. The AC system is quixotic. It has fluorescent lighting and it has windows. It can be quiet. And it doesn't feel isolated. For 6 and a half years, I both made theatre and watched others make theatre in that space. I've watched discoveries and meltdowns and revelations about plays and performance that can never be recreated. I have had seizures in that room. It is a perfect space. A space of endless possibilities.

La Fenice, Venice, Italy.
I've never been to Venice, I've never been to Italy. To be honest, I'm not really sure what the space is like. The name calls out though. La Fenice.

"Archaeology, Erasers, and Les Waters"

Sarah Ruhl

Les Waters, my dear friend and beloved collaborator, said to me once:

"I'm worried."
"Why?" I asked.
"Because my daughter said she wants to be an archeologist."
"Oh?" I said.
"Yes," he said.
"Why is that bad?" I asked.
"Because," he said, "it secretly means she wants to be a director."

He said his childhood dream was to be an archeologist and that he knew many wonderful directors who likewise fantasized about digging in the dirt as children, hoping to be archeologists. I asked him what he thought the connection was between archeology and directing. He said: "I think it's about finding out the invisible buried structure of a thing. And if you are me, after you find the structure, you erase it." I gasped. I understood, newly, why I love it when Les directs my plays.

I remember once in third grade being asked to do a painting. I made a painting. I loved my painting. Then, we were told to cover it in black paint, so that we could scratch lines into the paint and make a design. I was horrified. I had made something beautiful and I didn't want to cover it up.

The directors, designers, actors (and indeed writers) I most admire have no problem with erasing their own work. I love directors who direct and say: don't look at my directing, or designers who say: don't look at my design, or

DOI: 10.4324/9781003170808-10

actors who say: don't look at my acting. So many directors find the structure of a play and then underline it with a bold marker. But what kind of bravery is required to find the structure of a play and then erase it?

If archeology is uncovering a deep historical structure that can't be seen, and directing is uncovering an invisible structure buried in the play, then what is the difference between history and narrative structure? Between fossils and narrative moments hidden in the sediment? And what of erasure and the unfinished?

When Les was at the Royal Court, he crossed paths with the great Samuel Beckett, who would often write in the margins of his work, "Vaguen." Not "clarify," but "Vaguen." Erase the footprints. Don't underline.

I love that Les does not underline themes in his productions; instead, he lets them glow. Rather than paralyze actors by controlling what they do moment to moment, his penetrating gaze allows freedom in the rehearsal room. Les is beloved by actors because Les allows actors maximal freedom in performance. Les casts the best actors and then lets them do what they do best. Rehearsal rooms with Les remind me of the Heisenberg uncertainty principle – which argues, in effect, that the gaze subtly, almost imperceptibly, changes what is gazed at. Being watched by Les alters the actor's performance; they act "better" without him having to say a word. Watching, repetition, watching, repetition. In French, rehearsal is simply that, repetition.

Les and I do a minimal amount of talking *about* a script. Our collaboration is intensely in *relation* but not necessarily in conversation. I don't know quite how to explain that, only to say that Les does not waste words and does not approach a script with overly cognitive questions. He penetrates the mystery of a work, which often must be done in silence. And with a sense of humor. He never gives me "notes" on a play. I might lean over during rehearsal and ask him about a rewrite, and he'll nod or shake his head. Or say, "Hmm."

Les's rehearsal notebooks are works of art. In tiny script, he makes notes as he calibrates the performances during previews. Les and I have done five plays together – *Eurydice*, *In the Next Room (or the vibrator play)*, *Three Sisters*, *Dear Elizabeth*, and *For Peter Pan on her 70th Birthday*. In each case, we've done multiple productions of each play, often starting at Berkeley Repertory Theatre or Yale Repertory Theatre or Actors Theatre of Louisville, before moving a play to New York. So, there are about fifteen rehearsal scripts with Les's unmistakable handwriting documenting the process of these plays. What you might find in those notes are careful tonal modulations as we worked towards opening night.

Les understands grief and beauty. When he directed *Eurydice*, Les and each of the designers had recently had a seismic loss. A father, a lover. The set designer, Scott Bradley, dreamed the set one night, a glorious blue-tiled upside-down world, and then made a model of it. Les's deep regard for his collaborators allows their dreams and first impulses to come to life. And then, Les will say something like, I saw a painting of a gorilla on a tricycle and I think we should have *that* for the Lord of the Underworld. The story of the profound collaborations with his wife, the brilliant designer Annie Smart (who did *In the Next Room* and versions of *Three Sisters*, *Dear Elizabeth*, and *For Peter Pan on her 70th Birthday*) is one of minimalism, beauty, and theatricality.

I also happen to love Les's collaborations with other writers – Anne Washburn, Lucas Hnath, Chuck Mee. In fact, it was Chuck Mee who gave Les *Eurydice* to read before we'd ever met. Then, I met Les in a parking lot in Southern California (he was teaching directing at UCSD at the time). This Englishman didn't drive, so I drove us to a coffee shop. He seemed sunburned, and I was surprised he lived in Southern California. We had a meeting of the minds and agreed that he would direct *Eurydice* one day. A decades-long collaboration was born. We watched Kathy Chalfant fly in *For Peter Pan on her 70th Birthday*, and we watched Laura Benanti use a 19th-century vibrator on Broadway. We watched poets perch on planets in *Dear Elizabeth*, and Les once summoned an entire marching band into Actors Theatre of Louisville, just to gratify one of my crazier stage directions.

Another thing you should know about Les is that he was a choral singer as a boy. The musicality in all of his productions is as finely tuned as a chamber piece. Combine musicality with Methodist minimalism and dread of excess, a love of visual art and of actors, and you start to see how a Les Waters production functions.

I should also say, it is fun to be in a room with Les. He makes me laugh. People ask me what I look for in a director and it's much the same as what I would look for in a beloved. Do they make me laugh? Do the same things make us cry? Are they kind? In the last ensemble that Les and I worked with, *For Peter Pan on her 70th Birthday*, Les created such a familial ensemble that years later, the group still writes each other – "Dear Family . . . " – sending poetry, visual art, and other missives, and cooking up feasts for one another.

Writing about being in rehearsal with Les at a moment when theaters are shuttered gives me such an ache. I love watching him direct because he *never*, *ever* interrupts, disrupts, or derails an actor's internal motor once it's in motion. I want nothing more to be back in those rehearsal rooms – watching Maria Dizzia navigating a string room, and watching Les with his hands folded, taking it all in, his gaze subtly changing the molecules in a room.

*   *   *   *   *

SARAH RUHL *is a popular and widely produced playwright known for such works as* Eurydice, The Clean House, Dead Man's Cell Phone, In the Next Room, For Peter Pan on her 70th Birthday, *and other plays. She has received numerous awards, including a MacArthur Fellowship, the Steinberg Distinguished Playwright Award, and the Susan Smith Blackburn Prize. She is the author of a collection of 101 micro-essays, a collection of letters on friendship with her student Max Ritvo, a collection of poems, and a memoir of her battle with Bell's palsy. She is a Co-Founder of 3Views, a website created for the theater community in response to the Pandemic. She studied playwriting with Paula Vogel at Brown University, and she now teaches in the Yale School of Drama.*

Working things out in public

My father is quiet. My father is always quiet, but this evening he is very quiet. It is 1986 and we are walking back to his car after an evening performance of Chekhov's *The Seagull* that I directed at the Liverpool Playhouse. My mother says, "I liked it but it wasn't your father's cup of tea." Nothing unusual in that. I'm sure it was neither's cup of tea. My father's silence is unusually clenched. We walk and walk and he says:

FATHER: You do that therapy thing?
ME: Yes. Why?

SILENCE.
SILENCE.

ME: Why? Why, Dad?

SILENCE.

FATHER: Aren't you doing that thing? That thing.
ME: What thing?
FATHER: That thing. Working things out. Working things out in public.

Like most working-class people of their generation, my parents were both frightened by and dismissive of any kind of psychiatry or therapy. Most definitely it was not for them.

DOI: 10.4324/9781003170808-11

A middle-class indulgence. And most importantly expensive. When I told them I was in therapy, they were quietly distressed and the subject was dropped. Nothing was said. Nothing said.

In 1985–1986, my parents saw three of my productions. Georg Büchner's unfinished *Woyzeck* about abuse and desperation. Louise Page's *Salonika* about aging and love and memory. And Thomas Kilroy's adaptation of *The Seagull* – set in Ireland – about actresses and writers and the people drawn into their orbit. Where was the connection? What was being worked out in public? Almost 150 years separates *Woyzeck* from *Salonika*. The plays are different in style, different in content, different in emotional temperature, but in all three, a central character has committed or commits suicide. The connection unseen by me and yet crystal clear to my vulnerable father. Both of my parents had attempted suicide a decade earlier. My maternal Grandfather attempted suicide. My mother's cousin drowned in mysterious circumstances. There are – or were – emotionally fragile people on both sides of the family. And over the decades, the number of "suicide" plays I directed has accumulated: Caryl Churchill's *Three More Sleepless Nights*, Jordan Harrison's *Marjorie Prime*, and Anne Washburn's *The Small*.

The connections are always there, but how conscious of them am I? How conscious do I want/need to be of them? If I am fully aware of them, then what am I unearthing, what am I examining? And as a freelance director, the possibilities of exploring one's obsessions are limited because of the plays offered and what one chooses to accept. (If choice is even an option. The fees paid to most freelance directors are so low that choosing is not an option. The necessary option is survival.)

I know that work about Class is important to me. I know that Class permeates all social relationships and structures. I am interested in work that is pro-working class, that centers the working-class experience: Caryl Churchill's *Fen*, Paul Kember's *Not Quite Jerusalem*, Rebecca Gilman's *Luna Gale*, Naomi Iizuka's *At the Vanishing Point*, Jorge Ignacio Cortiñas' *Recent Alien Abductions*, Mark Schultz' *Evocation to Visible Appearance*. I am also drawn to work that features ghosts and the uneasy dead: Churchill's *Fen*, *Top Girls*, and *The Skriker*, Jordan Harrison's *Finn in the Underworld*, *Macbeth*, *At the Vanishing Point*, Anne Washburn's *Apparition*, Thornton Wilder's *Our Town*. And I am compelled towards (and I must admit slightly nauseated by the self-absorption of) the work play, the play about my own profession, about the theatre: Anne Washburn's *10 out of 12*, Eugene O'Neill's *Long Day's Journey into Night*, *The Seagull*.

Sitting at my desk looking at a list of my productions, there are themes and obsessions that appear and disappear and then reappear some years later. I'm uncomfortable with the word "theme." It reeks of the misery of Grammar School English Literature classes. Identify the key themes of Jane Austen's *Emma*. Trace the theme of love in Chaucer's *Merchant's Tale* (give examples). I have written those essays. "Obsession" is better. Overwrought but more accurate.

Questions obsess me. Answers are necessary and often a relief, but questions are at the heart of the work and really provide the connections over time. At this very moment, two questions in particular loom large on the list. I'm sure there are more – I know there are more – but they are not so present right now. Like most people I have experienced loss and pain and grieved: What is the point of suffering? Why do good people suffer? Sarah Ruhl's *Eurydice*, Chekhov's *Three Sisters*, *Our Town*, *Marjorie Prime*. I have moved many times – from the North of England to London to Manchester to London to San Diego to Berkeley to Louisville to Berkeley. I have moved countries and become a US citizen. I have lost communities and gained others: Where do I belong? Where is home? Will Eno's *Middletown*, *Fen*, *Our Town*, *At the Vanishing Point*.

At Actors Theatre of Louisville, I set out to create a series of productions linked by a question. When I first visited the city, I was struck by the number of places of worship, in particular, the number of churches. When I first interviewed for the position of Artistic Director, a Board Member unnecessarily and intrusively asked "What church did I attend?" and was disconcerted by my curt response. It seemed to me that in many ways Louisville was a faith-based city and I wanted to enter into a critical dialogue with the local community around the question "What is Faith? What do we believe?" Both *The Christians* and *Glory of the World* were commissioned and produced by Actors Theatre. *The Christians*, a performance in the form of a church service, deals with a Pastor who rejects a central tenet of his faith and the consequences of that decision on his congregation. *Glory of the World*, raucous, all male, and magnificently stupid, celebrates the 100th birthday of Thomas Merton, monk, mystic, and Louisville celebrity. I wanted to make a trilogy, or rather a triptych, of work exploring all the questions that interrogate the concept of belief. Mark Schwartz's confrontational, despairing *Evocation to Visible Appearance*, a play about the devil, not in some fabulous character sort of sense but in a palpably real sense, the devil as a sucking void, was the third part of that conversation.

What really provides the connective tissue that holds together these and other productions is a very simple existential need to know who I will be after I have directed any of these plays. Who will I be after directing *Out of Time?* Which Les Waters will be there after Lucas Hnath's *Dana H.?* Will I be damaged? What will I have lost? Will I be erased? Will anything be gained? I want to know who I will be after the process.

Will I recognize myself?

3. *Fen* at Almeida Theatre (1983).

4. *Eurydice* at Second Stage (2007).

5. *Big Love* at Brooklyn Academy of Music (2001).

6. *Macbeth* at Actors Theatre of Louisville (2016).

7. *10 out of 12* at Soho Repertory Theatre (2015).

8. *At the Vanishing Point* at Actors Theatre of Louisville (2015).

"Les Waters is an Attractor"

Anne Bogart

Les Waters creates an air of spaciousness around him. When I am with him, there is plenty of room for both of us. Perhaps this is one of the principal tools of an effective theater director: *to create space* and to hold space for others, allowing them to feel present, to be useful, to be heard, to be acknowledged, and to be seen.

I first met Les in the "smoking pit," an outdoor area between the rehearsal halls and the building that houses the Actors Theatre of Louisville (ATL). This was in the year 2000 and Les was still a smoker. He was in Louisville directing the premiere of Chuck Mee's *Big Love* for the Humana Festival of New American Plays, a successful production that would later tour widely. I was in Louisville to direct Naomi Iizuka's *War of the Worlds* with SITI Company. Immediately, I felt at ease with Les and was able to enjoy his relaxed sense of humor and his quick wit. I felt as if we were simply hanging out and catching up, gossiping a bit, and sharing struggles and frustrations from the rehearsal hall. And that basic feeling has always remained between us, a certain laid-back mutual enjoyment and also a shared intimacy. I think that many people feel this with Les.

Les is a lighthouse for young directors. One of my current MFA directing students at Columbia University, who was a directing intern at ATL when Les became the Artistic Director, still sports a Les-like beard, a long protruding visible statement. I think that the beard is the young director's way of ingesting Les, imitating and honoring him.

DOI: 10.4324/9781003170808-12

Despite these anecdotes about Les, ultimately, he is quite difficult to pin down. He radiates an inherent density-of-being. A hint of privacy and maybe even a little mystery surrounds him. What is it that makes actors and designers want to occupy the same space with a director for extended periods of time? There has to be some "there, there," as Gertrude Stein would say. Les is very present, but one can also sense a touch of darkness and a quiet emotion that is, perhaps, a link to some pain. Is this what makes him an *attractor*?

Les has two highly visible tattoos, one on each arm. Despite his mild demeanor, these tattoos suggest to me that Les can be rebellious and assertive and that he will stand up for what he believes in. His debut production as Artistic Director at Actors Theatre of Louisville in 2012 was Eugene O'Neill's *Long Day's Journey Into Night*. The marketing department at the theater became concerned when the rehearsal reports suggested that the evening would be too lengthy for Louisville audiences. Les marched into the marketing office and proclaimed, "The play's title is *Long Day's Journey Into Night*! What do you expect?"

Les is not afraid of making bold strokes or using extended moments of silence and stillness or loudness and then sudden unexpected, theatrical flourishes. He can work quickly, and he can also slow things d-o-w-n. Energy, which is the baseline of any theatrical venture, is a mysterious property that is difficult to describe and even harder to conjure. And yet, one of a director's main tasks is to nurture life and energy within the temporal and spatial container of a play. Even though, on the surface, Les does not seem like an energetic person, his laidback qualities clearly belie his belief in the explosive energy that must abound within the scaffolding of any production. Les's shows are full of life, color, and energy. Perhaps he encourages the accumulation of life and energy through nothing less than his patient and expectant demeanor.

Les embodies yet another key trait of a director, which is the ability to convince co-conspirators and collaborators to join in his enterprise, no matter how daunting or difficult. A director is in some ways like Mark Twain's Tom Sawyer, who managed to convince a whole passel of boys that painting his fence would be an honor, a privilege, and a hell of a lot of fun. Tom gave them all paintbrushes and then sat down on a barrel in the shade to dangle his legs and to enjoy an apple while the boys worked. Twain wrote, "He had discovered a great law of human action, without knowing it – namely, that in order to make a man or a boy covet a thing, it is only necessary to make the thing difficult to obtain."

Les is clearly driven by curiosity and he seems more interested in questions than in concepts. To be curious is to defy limits and boundaries, to ask questions and to maintain a commitment to journeys of exploration and discovery. Les exudes curiosity about whatever situation he is in, not only in rehearsal but in the unexpected details that arise from moment to moment, whether traveling on a bus or walking through a city. Noticing and taking interest in one's own life is a necessary condition for a theater director. With curiosity, inspiration can be found in the sounds on the streets, in the echoes of arguments coming through the open window of an apartment, in an ethereal light shining down at a particular moment on the side of a building, in the clinking of silverware, or in the sound of bells or the whistle and roar of a distant train.

Generally, a theater director must not be afraid to enter into a process that offers no guarantees. Les is a leader but he also seems willing to get lost and find pleasure and engagement in not knowing the answers, in getting off the beaten track. He does not seem afraid to follow a hunch or take a detour. Les Waters straddles this seemingly paradoxical duality with apparent ease and facility.

*   *   *   *   *

ANNE BOGART *is one of the three Co-Artistic Directors of the SITI Company, which she founded with Japanese director Tadashi Suzuki in 1992. She is a Professor at Columbia University where she runs the Graduate Directing Program. Her most recent works with SITI include* Falling & Loving; The Bacchae; Chess Match No. 5; Lost in the Stars; the theater is a blank page; Persians; Steel Hammer; *and* A Rite. *For different companies, she has staged these operas:* Wagner's Tristan and Isolde, *Ruder's* The Handmaid's Tale, *Handel's* Alcina, Dvorak's Dimitrij, *Verdi's* Macbeth, *Bellini's* Norma, *and Bizet's* Carmen. *She is the author of six books:* A Director Prepares; The Viewpoints Book; And Then, You Act; Conversations with Anne; What's the Story; *and* The Art of Resonance.

"If you have Les Waters direct your plays"

Charles Mee

I was in London, briefly, in 1982 and dropped in at the Royal Court Theatre where a friend of mine was a friend of the artistic director, and I happened to meet a young 30-year-old director named Les Waters and chatted with him a little bit about Caryl Churchill who had had several plays done at the Royal Court and who liked to go into a community and pick up chunks of text she would then make into a play, which was something I sometimes did, too, and Les had been able to work with her a bit and talked about how she did things, and I understood right away from what he said that Les was a genius. And when he came to New York the next year, in 1983, to direct Caryl Churchill's *Fen* at the Public Theater, he got off the airplane in New York and came straight to my living room, the first place he came to in New York, where we had a cup of coffee and a long conversation about the theatre and what we both loved to do. So I knew we were soul mates.

And then, because I was just at the beginning years of writing plays, it was quite a while before I had something I loved that I could ask him to do. But then, he was free, so he directed my new play *Big Love* at the University of California at San Diego, where he was teaching, and then the play went on to the Humana Festival at Actors Theatre in Louisville, and the Long Wharf in New Haven, Berkeley Rep, the Goodman Theatre, and the Next Wave Festival at Brooklyn Academy of Music, and some Broadway producers saw it and wanted to bring it to Broadway, but Les refused because he didn't want to fire some of his actors so he could hire stars to replace them for Broadway, because his actors had worked with him so hard and faithfully and beautifully. And I agreed. So then *Big Love* went on to be done here there and

DOI: 10.4324/9781003170808-13

everywhere with other directors, and Les and I started talking right away about what we wanted to do together next.

I had never been to any of the rehearsals Les had for *Big Love*, because travelling around Europe back in the 1980s and early 1990s I thought: the playwrights who get the best productions are the dead playwrights. Maybe that's because they don't go to rehearsals, so the actors and director are free to do whatever they want to do with the play. There is no one in the room to tell them, no, no, that's not what I had in mind, what this character is really thinking is x, y, z. And so, if I don't go into the rehearsal room, a production isn't inhibited, or restrained or redirected or stopped in any of its explorations down the wrong path to something even more right than anyone could have known. No. It is free and spontaneous and filled with the best ideas of the director and actors that I'd never thought of. And so I didn't – and I don't – go to rehearsals. So I don't really know how Les does it, but what he does takes me somewhere I've never been before. And that's exactly where I love to go and what I love to feel when I go to the theatre.

So I asked Les to do a play of mine called *Wintertime*, about members of a family who went off to their summer home in the middle of winter, hoping that the other members of their family wouldn't be there, so they could have their love affairs without anyone knowing. So it was a play full of intimate love relationships – until other family members did arrive, hoping they could carry on their love affairs with no one else present, so that we fell into the world of love and deception and betrayal and despair and sweet, dreamy romanticism, and Les could do every human relationship – and inability to have a human relationship – beautifully.

So, of course, I asked him then to direct a piece of mine called *Fetes de la Nuit*, which I had stolen from a piece called *Fetes de Nuit* that I had seen in the courtyard of the palace of Versailles one summer. And that piece, full of human relationships, was also full of music and dance and hunting dogs and fireworks, and, of course, Les was great at that, too. In general, I think some directors are wonderful with all the intricacies and nuances and subtleties and psychological underpinnings of human relationships. And some directors are wonderful at big spectacle. And Les is great at both. I love to write plays that don't have a story line but that are made coherent – like painting and sculpture and dance and music – by a feeling or a theme rather than a plot line. So you can give Les a crazy, wild, incoherent play full of human intimacies and spectacles and the logic of dance, and he will make it right.

And then, my great friend Stephen Greenblatt, the world's greatest Shakespeare scholar, phoned me and said the Mellon Foundation had just given him a grant he hadn't applied for that would let him do something he wished he had done with his life rather than be the author of all the amazing books he had written. And he said he didn't think he wanted to do anything else except that it would be good to watch me write a play. And I said I didn't think so, because all he would do is sit to the side and watch my fingers move on the computer keyboard, and that would be unbearable. But if he would write a play with me, that would be fun. Oh, he said, what would that be? I said, well, there must be a lost play of Shakespeare's we could make together. And he said, oh, right, *Cardenio*. So we wrote *Cardenio* together – with Stephen telling me how Shakespeare wrote a play (my personal graduate course with the world's leading Shakespeare scholar!). And who would direct such a play? Les Waters, of course. The truth is, Stephen had done a fantastic job of conceiving the whole play and letting me know what Shakespeare would have done with it, but I didn't do such a great job of trying to write a play like some other old playwright. But Les took it and put it on the stage of the American Repertory Theater where it went so well that Stephen was able to take his Mellon grant and get adaptations of our piece written and produced in nine other countries. Really, Stephen was the one who did it, but I think I would have sabotaged the whole project if Les hadn't rescued the piece from the work I had done on it.

And then, just a few years ago, when Les was the artistic director of the Actors Theatre of Louisville, he phoned me from Louisville and asked me if I would write a play for him to do in the next Humana Festival. Would I? Write a play for Les to direct? Well, for sure. What did he have in mind? He felt he should have been doing some more "local" theatre than he had been doing since he had taken over the artistic directorship of the Actors Theatre. And so, one of the outstanding figures who had once lived in Louisville was the monk Thomas Merton. And if Merton hadn't died, that year would have been his 100th birthday. So Les wished I would write a piece to celebrate Merton's 100th birthday. I told Les I was an ex-Catholic, and so I was afraid whatever I wrote would get Les thrown out of Louisville. And Les said that was ok. So I put together a birthday party – 18 people gathered to celebrate the enormous complexity of Merton the Catholic monk, the Buddhist, the pacifist, the communist, the father of an illegitimate child, a play that would need to be inhabited by enough of the rich, wonderful complexity of life to begin to give some sense of who Merton had really been, and so a play that would need to have some drinking and kissing and gigantic fighting and dancing and swimming. I thought of a few of these things, and Les thought of another 6,384 things to put on stage, including air mattress gymnastics and a life-sized rhinoceros crossing the stage.

I sent him the script quite a while before he was scheduled to go into rehearsal, and he called me and said he wasn't so sure about the men and women I had in the play, that he thought Merton was in a monastery where everyone was male, and so he thought it should be an all-male cast. No problem. I went through the script and changed the names of the characters so they were all male. And Les took it into rehearsal. And Les proved he could do everything and have it come out fantastic every time. It was called *The Glory of the World*. And it was a huge hit in Louisville and got huge rave reviews. And then, as it turned out, one of the people who came to see the production was a monk named Roy Cockrum. Some years earlier Roy had been an acting apprentice at the Actors Theatre, and then acted for a time in New York, and then he became a monk. But, while he was at the monastery, he heard his parents were not well, and so he went back to his hometown, Knoxville, Tennessee, to take care of his parents. And while he was there, he bought a lottery ticket and won 259.8 million dollars. And then, wondering what he would do with his money, what he most wanted to do was to support theatre projects that he loved and felt deserved support. And when he came to see our play in Louisville, he loved it and wanted to pay the full cost of taking it to New York to the Brooklyn Academy of Music. Of course, it was panned in the *New York Times*, but the critics of the religious newspapers and journals loved it. And some random audience members posted their reviews:

"I sobbed thru the last 5 minutes of this play."

"OH MY GOD. *The Glory of the World* OH MY GOD."

"RUN TO SEE THIS PLAY! It is not serious. And it is very, very good. The direction and performances are beautiful, and Chuck Mee has created a world unlike any other on this planet. A causes B causes rhinoceros causes lazy boy causes sprinklers indeed. Bravo. And Congratulations."

"This play is incredible. We loved it …."

"*The Glory of the World* is what would happen if Adult Swim made a play about Thomas Merton. Hilarious."

"Excellent performance of a thought provoking, complex, entertaining play."

"I imagine that decades from now, people who were lucky enough to see it will think back to… 'The Glory of the World' … as one of the finest, most startling pieces of theater they've ever seen. I imagine someone at a party, talking theater, maybe swirling a glass of wine, cultivating a cryptic smile to reel in an audience, then saying, 'The best fight scene I've ever seen was in a play about Thomas Merton.'"

So that's the kind of review you can expect if you have Les Waters direct your plays.

* * * * *

CHARLES MEE is a playwright known for adapting the Greeks and others with wild abandon, for incorporating chunks of borrowed text into his plays verbatim, and for making his scripts available on the internet at www.charlesmee.org. He has written Big Love and True Love and First Love, bobrauschenbergamerica and Hotel Cassiopeia, Orestes 2.0 and Trojan Women A Love Story, and Summertime and Wintertime, among other plays. His work has been performed in theatres large and small all over the United States as well as in Berlin, Paris, Amsterdam, London, Brussels, Vienna, Istanbul, and elsewhere. He is also the author of a number of books of history and the former Editor-in-Chief of Horizon magazine, a magazine of history, literature, and the fine arts. His work is made possible by the support of Jeanne Donovan Fisher and Richard B. Fisher.

Silence onstage

Never miss a good chance to shut up.

—Will Rogers

I am in love with silence onstage. When the script asks for a pause, my pause will be substantial. If there is a line of dialogue, followed by "Silence," another line, and "Silence" again, my desire is to make those silences incredibly long. To really push to see how long we can live in silence onstage and what that silence actually means. Often during a first run-through, I look and think, "Oh, there I go. I've done it again. I made the silence three minutes long and you cannot follow what is happening." And we start again.

There is a scene in Caryl Churchill's play *Ice Cream* where the character Jaq reads a newspaper and that is all that happens onstage. When we did it at the Public, Julianne Moore was playing Jaq, and the first time we worked this scene she sat on the floor and read two pages of the newspaper for five minutes. Then, she slowly turned the page of the newspaper and read that page for four minutes and then turned the page again and read for another two minutes. She is looking in the newspaper to see if a death has been reported. And the first time we rehearsed the scene in isolation, that long silence was interesting. It was powerful. It was tense. It made one lean in towards it. I don't remember how long it was in performance, but it was long.

A part of my job is to get people to look at things, to really look at things in the moment, to pay attention and take notice, and silences are often an effective way to get the audience in the same place, sitting in a theatre waiting

DOI: 10.4324/9781003170808-14

for something to happen. Silence creates tension. We go to the theatre to hear people talk. That's what theatre is to most people, it's talk. And often that talk is brilliant and it's delivered by very skilled, talented people, and sometimes a whole new vision of the world is created and it can change lives. It can be important. But as soon as you deny an audience what they expect, tension is created. Actors don't need to act that tension. The silence does the work for them. And the audience doesn't like it. It worries them. They don't like what is brooding within that silence. Something might happen to them.

I am particularly aware of the rhythm of a production before it encounters silence. The musicality of that is very important to me. Is the rhythm very fast, very "loud," and then everything is unplugged? And then silence. Or is it a silence that comes out of a slow build? Should it be surprising or should it sneak up on you?

And how do you recover from silence onstage? Do you want the silence to build so that it becomes intolerable and then snap into something – sounds/ lights – so that the audience jumps? As if the silence was a crystal vase you were holding in your hands, and for no reason, you suddenly dropped it and this vase violently shattered on the floor. Or do we ease out of silence? And are we aware of it? Unaware?

I would love to work on a completely silent play. Maybe I should just go into a room with my collaborators and explore. Two people walk onstage, meet, look like they are going to have a conversation, and then walk offstage? Somebody sits on a chair with their back to us and the lights are fading and . . . ? My initial impulse would be to find some heartbreaking music and play it, but what if you don't do any of that? What if you don't fill it? What if the stage is empty? What if there is complete silence? Of course, there is no such thing as complete silence. John Cage famously proved that. But what if there is silence and how long can you go before you are tempted to fill it with something? I would love to try that. I think it would be interesting.

> When I pronounce the word Future,
> The first syllable already belongs to the past.
>
> When I pronounce the word Silence,
> I destroy it.
>
> When I pronounce the word Nothing,
> I make something no non-being can hold.
>
> —Wisława Szymborska, *The Three Oddest Words*

24 things I could look at all day

When I was directing *The Glory of the World*, I thought it would be helpful to follow a prayer schedule. Thomas Merton, the play's inspiration, was a Trappist Monk so why shouldn't I too embrace a devotional practice throughout the day? Vigils 6 am, Lauds 7.15 am, Eucharist 11.45 am, Daytime Prayer 1 pm, Vespers 5.15 pm, Compline 7.15 pm. I'm not a believer of any organized religion and it would have been hypocritical to pray, so instead of prayer, I endeavored to meditate on music used in the production – Future Islands *Seasons (Waiting on You)* or *Black Moon Spell* by King Tuff, for example. Enjoyable for sure (briefly) but in no sense spiritual. I had hoped the discipline would focus and illuminate the work. Unfortunately not.

I was raised a Methodist – my maternal Grandfather was a lay preacher – and now identify as an Atheist. I might claim art is my religion. Art provides my necessary dialogue with something beyond myself. As an exercise, I tried to construct a 24-hour devotional schedule – some piece of art to look at for every hour in the day – but the effort defeated me. What is the correct hour for *This Rain* by Agnes Martin? 2 am? Noon? An intellectual game that was both puzzling and pleasurable and, in the end, futile in some byzantine manner. Instead, I made a list of 24 works of art that I could look at all day. Some are very familiar to me – I've been looking at Bridget Riley and Francis Bacon all my life – and some newer acquaintances – Edgar Heap of Birds and Karin Mamma Andersson. All worthy of contemplation.

Fragment of a Queen's Face – Egypt, New Kingdom – 1353–1336 BC – Metropolitan Museum of Art, New York

DOI: 10.4324/9781003170808-15

Untitled (Placebo – Landscape – for Roni) – Felix Gonzalez-Torres – 1993

Fall – Bridget Riley – 1963 – Tate Modern, London

Photo Bloke – Barkley L. Hendricks – 2016

Monogram – Robert Rauschenberg – 1955–1959 – Moderna Museet, Stockholm

The NewOnes, will free Us – Wangechi Mutu – 2019 – facade of Metropolitan Museum of Art, New York

When Frustration Threatens Desire – Kerry James Marshall – 1990 – The Metropolitan Museum of Art, New York

Sand Dune – Francis Bacon – 1983 – Tate Modern, London

Blackboard Tableau # 8 (Edward) – Vija Celmins – 2012

Crack Between The Floorboards – Mark Bradford – 2014 – Metropolitan Museum of Art, New York

This Rain – Agnes Martin – 1960 – Whitney Museum of American Art, New York

Swannery – Karin Mamma Andersson – 2019

Genocide and Democracy – Edgar Heap of Birds – 2016

Winter Nocturne – Matthew Wong – 2017

Complication – Lynette Yiadom-Boakye – 2013

Ghost – Rachel Whiteread – 1990 – National Gallery of Art, Washington, DC

In The World But Don't Know The World – El Anatsui – 2009

The Ten Largest, No.7, Adulthood – Hilma af Klint – 1907

Trumpet – Jean-Michel Basquiat – 1984

The Dog – Francisco Goya – 1819–1823 – The Prado, Madrid

Untitled (S.044) – Ruth Asawa – 1968–1972

Piss Flowers – Helen Chadwick – 1991–1992 – Richard Saltoun Gallery, London

Dust Motes in Sunbeams – Vilhelm Hammershoi – 1900 – Ordrupgaard Museum, Copenhagen

Black Girl's Window – Betye Saar – 1969 – Museum of Modern Art, New York

"A Story, a Whisper, a Joke"

Quincy Tyler Bernstine

I have to admit, I am where I am today, in no small part, because of Les Waters. I first met Les back in the Fall/Winter of 1995 at New Dramatists in Manhattan. He was one of three adjudicators (director Walt Jones and dramaturg Robert Blacker being the other two) sitting in the darkened (at least that is my memory of it) Lindsay and Crouse Studio at my audition for the MFA acting program at the University of California San Diego (UCSD). I auditioned on a whim. A college theater professor recommended that I audition for a few of the "top" programs just to "see what might happen." It had never really occurred to me before that I could go to school simply for acting or that I might be able to make a profession of it someday. I think Les and I might have spent a total of twenty minutes together that afternoon and spoken five or six words between us, but that time and those words would end up being life-changing for me, in myriad ways.

I have worked with Les numerous times since, both in school and professionally – we made our Broadway debuts together, in fact! – and the thing that strikes me most about working with him is his ability to create unparalleled, highly theatrical pieces of art by doing not much at all. And I mean that in the best possible way. It is truly awesome. I feel like Les is somehow able to direct via seemingly random conversations around the table or on a ten-minute break smoking (formerly!) on the sidewalk outside the theater or by whispering a joke under his breath to an actor as he wanders by while blocking a scene. I don't know how he does it. I have been fortunate to work with some of our finest theater directors throughout my career, many of whom I would call "hands-off." But Les takes that a step or two further:

DOI: 10.4324/9781003170808-16

he has an almost ghostlike presence in the room. My memories of working with him are that you never quite know where he is in the rehearsal hall or theater. That presence ends up imbuing his work with a somewhat haunted quality, a spiritual nature that I don't often find in other productions.

Working with Les, in both the classroom and beyond, opened my eyes to a whole new world of theatrical possibility. I don't think I had ever heard the term "site-specific" before him, but early in my career at UCSD, my nine classmates and I found ourselves in the midst of a sweeping and sprawling "production" (was it something Greek? I honestly don't remember now . . .) at a fellow professor's San Diego mansion involving her roaming peacocks and drained swimming pool underneath the Southern California stars. She had given us free rein to use her property as a stage and Les had given us free rein theatrically. Or at least, it felt like that. I don't remember many of the details of that first site-specific exercise I did with him, but I do remember the feeling I had while creating and performing it. It was the sense that anything and everything was possible in the crafting of it and that what we ultimately created was like something sacred, maybe even holy.

I had also never before been in a production where an audience member stormed out mid-show, in disgust, cursing all the way out the door. Our world-premiere production of Chuck Mee's *Big Love* was not everyone's cup of tea, it seemed, but I was in heaven. What an absolute thrill to hurl wedding china into the orchestra pit each night. I had never done anything quite so THEATRICAL before! I remember feeling confused initially by her exit and then appalled and devastated. Les had some choice words for her, I've no doubt, and we ultimately ended up laughing it off, but I learned an invaluable lesson that day about what effective theater truly is – love it or hate it.

And how lucky was I to make my Broadway debut with my graduate school professor. What might have seemed big and scary and overwhelming was made comfortable and familiar by his presence. He directed Sarah Ruhl's *In the Next Room (or the vibrator play)* in the same way he had our school projects and productions. I was in that majestic rehearsal room at Lincoln Center, but I could just as easily have been in that drained pool back in San Diego with Les whispering a direction disguised as a joke as he floated by, like a ghost.

Most recently, although a few years ago now, I appeared in a production directed by Les where I spent about 97% of the show offstage, another first for me. It was *10 out of 12* by Anne Washburn, and I was playing a stage manager during a tech rehearsal. I was working on a play about making a play yet found myself almost disembodied from the experience as I sat either in a tiny sound booth in the basement of Soho Rep delivering most of my lines into a microphone (heard by the audience through headsets) or on the green room couch listening to the rest of the play happening above me. I had always trusted Les and knew that what we were creating together was something unconventional and quite special. Although I couldn't really see it for myself, I knew it to be true. Another feeling, I suppose.

I am not articulate enough to describe Les's "esthetic." It's more an experience or a sense I get every time I work with him or see his work. Yes, Les has excellent taste. His productions are esthetically and aurally brilliant. His productions attract some truly outstanding collaborators because he is so beloved. Of course, I have no idea what goes on behind "behind-the-scenes." But it's been my experience that he gathers all of these elements together, tells a story or two here, makes a brilliant joke or two there, shares a passing thought under his breath and somehow, some way, some sort of theater history is made. I know that whatever Les creates will be brilliantly conceived and singular. I just don't know how he does it. It's more than magic. I truly believe it is otherworldly.

* * * * *

QUINCY TYLER BERNSTINE *is a film, television, and theater actor who has appeared in numerous Off-Broadway productions and on Broadway in* In the Next Room *directed by Les Waters. Her performances have earned an Obie Award for Lynn Nottage's* Ruined *and a Lucille Lortel Award for the title role in Jackie Sibblies Drury's* Marys Seacole, *among many others. The daughter of lawyers, she grew up in Washington, DC, played soccer and lacrosse in high school, and majored in Public Policy as an undergraduate at Brown University before pursuing an MFA in acting at UCSD. Known for being especially drawn to new work, she said in a 2019 New York Times profile, "The jobs that are, I think, in the end most worth it are the ones that almost break you."*

"A Huge Vat of Human Skin"

Steve Cosson

I consider it a great stroke of good fortune that I happened to land in graduate school during Les's time as head of the UC San Diego directing program. Fortunate on the human level for simply getting to know Les the person. He is one of those rare individuals whose whole way of being, his humor, and his worldliness without pretense are an invitation to live in a more interesting way – even if, say, you're having lunch in the soul-crushing UCSD food court. And fortunate on a professional level for Les's influence on me. He shaped pretty much every aspect of my work, from how I conduct myself in the rehearsal room to the theater company I started in 2001, The Civilians.

Les is a friend, certainly, but also a life-long mentor, even if a lot of the mentoring is now just happening in my head. When I catch myself in some of my less-than-awesome directing habits, I'll sometimes remember what I'll call the Les look. That look was key to how Les taught. He'd hang out in rehearsals sometimes while we worked on various projects or productions and either react positively or, when something was off, you'd get that questioning look that seemed to say, "Hmm. I might be curious about why you're trying to make that bad choice work?" If I'm letting my frustrations and insecurities carry over into the rehearsal room, I'll remember another aspect of Les's directing style: working in the room with humor and ease and then later venting to your assistant director. Which, on several occasions, was me. It was all instructive: you don't really need to have the equanimity of the Buddha to run a good rehearsal room, you just have to pick your moments.

I first met Les at my audition for the UCSD MFA directing program. After my formal interview, Les invited me out to the hallway to chat. He mentioned

DOI: 10.4324/9781003170808-17

that he wanted to teach a class in which the students would devise a project from some kind of interaction with the real world, a mix of a creative and a documentary process that I'd later learn grew out of his work with Joint Stock. Les mentioned that UCSD was doing some groundbreaking research on how to help burn victims and that apparently there was a vat somewhere on campus where they were growing a huge stretch of human skin. Les said something like, "Isn't that disgusting? I'd like to make a show about *that*." And I knew this was the guy I wanted to study with. I had some instinct that Les approached theater-making (and theater pedagogy) in some profoundly different way. Instead of declaring "I have a system/technique/knowledge-of-how-theater-really-works," he seemed to be saying "I'm not sure what this is. Let's figure it out and see what happens." That felt right.

And now, having known Les for decades, I think this approach – being comfortable in the not-knowing – is key to how he works and what he's able to accomplish. That said, Les is still very much the author of his productions. I'd argue he's a kind of stealth auteur. There is a deeply "Les" sensibility infused in every element of his work but without any attention-seeking "signature" gestures. How does he manifest such a strong vision with such seeming ease? I think it comes in part from how he manages to give his collaborators space but in a way that everyone is working under one roof, as it were, in the same house. And he's already envisioned its architecture. He does an enormous amount of preparation. He reads the script so many times that – and this is just me guessing – it's all in his mind as a living event rather than just a text. He has tremendous dramaturgical skill, knowing what's in the deep structure of a play so he can both build from there and cut away anything that's extra.

And he does a lot of visual research. He had (still does, I assume) an amazing collection of postcards; he loves photography; and he has a natural fluency with visual art and design. I'm sure being married to designer Annie Smart, his frequent collaborator, is also a big part of all that. So, by the time he enters the rehearsal room, a lot is already in place in his mind. But even if he's ten steps ahead, he's really good at letting everyone make their own discoveries. I remember asking him how he managed to get actors to do what he wanted without explicitly telling them what to do, and he said something about letting them figure it out while he's quietly closing doors behind them. The actor's choice is still her own (and more interesting because it comes from her), but it is a choice that could only happen within the structures that Les has prepared.

At UCSD, one significant class with Les was the "Joint Stock" class – in which all second-year actors, directors, playwrights, and stage managers participated. Les had been a member of Joint Stock, a London-based company known for its sociopolitical plays, some high-profile writers like David Hare and Caryl Churchill, and for making work from creative interactions with real life. There was no set-in-stone Joint Stock methodology. Instead, there was, in my interpretation, a kind of ethos of how to make work. So, if the company was interested in rural working-class England, then they would go there to live, work, and spend time with people who worked as farmers, gaining insight into actual, lived experience before giving that raw material to a playwright to create a play (in this case, Caryl Churchill's *Fen*). For other projects, they'd invent different methods. I was fascinated by how the company's research, interviews, and observations transformed into a play through this highly collaborative creative process.

The UCSD class focused on phase one of a Joint Stock–style process, the research workshop. Les taught us the basics of the Joint Stock approach to interviewing – which was done with no notes or recording devices. The task was to pay close attention and just listen with no agenda other than to be present and interested and then after to transcribe as much as possible from memory. We were given a subject, the very rich and the very poor of San Diego, and tasked with finding people to interview. (The "big vat of skin" idea, alas, never happened). Eventually, the interview content would be edited together into a presentation. I decided to pursue the very rich as I figured it'd be a challenge to get access to the wealthy. In fact, with just a few phone calls and a few half-truths, I found myself in the homes of some very rich strangers for hours, mostly listening.

Both of my interviewees completely upended my expectations. And something clicked that would change the course of my professional life. My preconceived ideas about a person, a community, whatever, were just a starting point, probably wrong, certainly too simple. Suddenly, the world was a more complex, more mysterious place, which is saying a lot in a place as aggressively bland as San Diego. The Joint Stock–style interview was not just about gathering content. It was an opportunity to crack open how I think about humanity. To find that place of not-knowing, being curious, listening more than talking, and waiting to be surprised was a lesson in how creativity works. And I've tried to be guided by that lesson ever since. I think that way of being may come more naturally to Les. I'm not sure. But I see this ethos in everything he does. Pay attention to what's interesting . . . and go closer to that.

At UCSD, Les directed my class in the first production of Chuck Mee's *Big Love*, and I assisted. I wasn't part of the play's 2000 premiere at the Humana

Festival, but I was able to see the production, and I went on to assist Les on multiple regional productions culminating in a run at the BAM Next Wave Festival. The show itself is a wild ride combining pitched emotions and intense physicality, all channeled through Chuck's theatrically constructed rhetoric. In Louisville, it was mounted in the Festival's smallest theater, and sitting amidst all that energy compressed in the little Victor Jory Theatre, I had that rare experience as an audience member of completely dissolving into the play. It felt like a Dionysian dissolution of ancient tragedy, mixed with some wonderful postmodern insanity, all of it growing out of a thoroughly compelling story. Chuck's plays are notable for their wonderful excess – big ideas, huge physical gestures, epic speeches. *Big Love*, for example, saw men hurling circular saw blades into a wall, actors throwing themselves around the set, a mass wedding ending in a mass murder (and a mass food fight). Under Les's direction, these events were shocking and thrilling, but they were also somehow necessary, growing organically out of the characters and the story. He has the ability to create an event on stage that seems as if it came into being of its own accord. You don't sense the choices that made it so; it just *is*.

While I was assisting Les on all these *Big Love* productions, I was also formulating the ideas for what would become The Civilians. I was fascinated by what it might mean to translate the Joint Stock process to an American context. That became the subject of many conversations with Les. He pointed out that more important than a master plan was getting the right people together and then just doing something, which is, in fact, what eventually happened. I collected a group of people, many from UCSD, others from Williamstown where I'd just met composer Michael Friedman, several from a couple years in downtown NYC theater. We booked a date at Joe's Pub at the Public for a first draft of our first show, came up with a clever (maybe terrible) idea, and then set our first rehearsal . . . for what turned out to be the week of 9/11. The planned idea got tossed out, and in every sense of the word, we winged it. The result, a piece called *Canard, Canard, Goose?*, was, I'm sure, nothing like what the Joint Stock artists would have done. We learned by doing, with no time to think. And part of what made that possible was the influence of Les – on me, and also on fellow collaborators from UCSD: Anne Kauffman, Aimée Guillot, Brian Sgambati, Damian Baldet, Jennifer Morris.

From that first show, The Civilians evolved and grew. Our second show, *Gone Missing*, created from interviews by the originating company on the theme of lost things, led to multiple US tours, a run in London, and later a one-year commercial run Off-Broadway. I coined the term "investigative theater" in an attempt to distinguish what we did from verbatim or documentary theater. Our goal is to bring the creative process into contact with life as it's actually lived in order to make something different happen. It's about hitting that point where the stories you tell yourself fall apart and you can open up to the complexities and contradictions of real life. It's more about undoing what is thought to be true than "presenting evidence" per se.

Once we began doing larger scale works, such as *This Beautiful City* about the politicized Evangelical movement in Colorado Springs, we began recording interviews. But Les's example of listening, waiting, and letting a production come into being as if on its own remained a guiding principle. It's certainly what enabled me to connect with people with very different world views and life experiences, such as an Air Force cadet who told me how he exorcized a demon from a woman and cured her blindness. And I can see the same ethos in play when I'm directing, especially a complex new work like Anne Washburn's *Mr. Burns, a post-electric play*, which originated with The Civilians. Over the past two decades, there have been many overlapping artists (both UCSD-related and not) between Civilians and Les's shows. I like to think of us as an informal community of similarly minded people, all engaged in different shows, but somehow part of a larger, shared project.

* * * * *

STEVE COSSON *is a director, writer, and the founding Artistic Director of The Civilians, the first theater company to be Artist-in-Residence at The Metropolitan Museum of Art. He has led the company in many theatrical projects that began as creative inquiries focused on such distinct communities as Evangelical Christians, the porn industry in LA, and inmates in Colombia's national women's prison. He is the creator and host of the documentary musical podcast* Let Me Ascertain You. *With The Civilians, he developed and directed the world premiere of Anne Washburn's* Mr. Burns, a post-electric play, *which in 2018 was ranked fourth by the* New York Times *of "The 25 Best American Plays Since Angels in America."*

Ten films I admire that other directors might find interesting

I sat in a chair and thought about film and over 50 years of going to the cinema and this list emerged. There is one film per director in order to keep the list under control. I love all seven films of Tarkovsky so that one film can be a hard choice.

The first "art" film that I saw was Jean-Luc Godard's *Masculin Feminin* at the Scunthorpe Film Society in 1968. I was 16. The last film that I saw in a cinema pre-pandemic was *First Cow* by Kelly Reichardt on March 12, 2020, in San Francisco. The coronavirus lockdown started a few days later and was expected to last two to three weeks. Cinemas in the Bay Area did not open again until March 19, 2021. The next day, I saw *Nomadland* by Chloe Zhao. If I had seen this film pre-pandemic, I would have loved it – it's remarkable – now it will always be the first movie I saw when cinemas reopened. Things continue.

Cries and Whispers (1972) – Ingmar Bergman. I had no idea that this kind of movie existed until I saw it. Influential in a profound way. The blood red rooms, the white costumes, the intensity of the performances. Also Bergman's production of *Hedda Gabler* with Maggie Smith in London in 1970. I was 18.

Ikiru (1952) – Akira Kurosawa

Weekend (1967) – Jean-Luc Godard. For its fuck you all and fuck everything ness.

DOI: 10.4324/9781003170808-18

Jeanne Dielman, 23 Commerce Quay, 1080 Brussels (1975) – Chantal Akerman. Saw this for the first time in 2019. A revelation. If I had seen this back in the day when I was 23, my work would be very different now.

Nostalgia (1983) – Andrei Tarkovsky. The only film I have seen three times in one day.

Wendy and Lucy (2008) – Kelly Reichardt

India Song (1975) – Marguerite Duras. The beauty of it and what Duras denies the spectator.

Do the Right Thing (1989) – Spike Lee

The Long Goodbye (1973) – Robert Altman

Nomadland – Chloe Zhao (2020)

Killer of Sheep (1978) – Charles Burnett. Extraordinary. Everybody should watch this at least once.

Daughters of the Dust (1991) – Julie Dash

Blow Up (1966) – Michelangelo Antonioni

Don't Look Now (1973) – Nick Roeg

Bleak Moments (1973) – Mike Leigh. Mike Bradwell plays a character, loosely based on a teenage me. Excruciating.

Ceddo (1977) – Ousmane Sembene. One of the great films by this genius director.

The Night Porter (1974) – Liliana Cavani

Badlands (1973) – Terrence Malick

No, that's 18 films, not 10. This list could go on and on. I've seen most of Ingmar Bergman, most of Jean-Luc Godard, most of Carl Dreyer. I adore Luis Bunuel, Michael Haneke, Jane Campion, Lucrecia Martel, Yasujiro Ozu, Spike Lee, Kelly Reichardt. All these extraordinary film directors.

I really am a child of the 1970s. Half of these films are from that decade. All have impacted my directing. Like hammer blows sometimes. At other times, seeping into my nervous system. I think I dream them into my neurons.

This list was started on June 1, 2020. I should make at least two more.

Testing for COVID-19

People had told me that the swab was uncomfortable, and for me, it was "Oh, that's a six-inch Q-tip going up my nose. I didn't know a Q-tip could go that far." But the emotional side was "Here, I am in an underground car park at Kaiser Hospital in Oakland at 2:05 pm on May 29, 2020, being tested for COVID-19. Is this the beginning of terrible doors opening?" I was very glad that I was fine, but the experience was fearful.

> I know death hath ten thousand several doors,
> For men to take their exits; and 'tis found,
> They go on such strange geometrical hinges,
> You may open them both ways: any way, for heaven-sake.
>
> —John Webster, *The Duchess of Malfi*

I love this play. These lines. The quality of a thin place. Death as many swinging doors. No clear boundary between this world and some other. I don't want COVID. I don't want it. Deep down I know that if I get it, I am not going to survive.

DOI: 10.4324/9781003170808-19

"Les(s) Is More: The Essential Artistry of Les Waters"

Tony Taccone

A woman stands alone in the middle of the stage, her face dappled in shadows, surrounded on three sides by translucent glass walls that reach upwards of 20-feet high. Huge swaths of painted green foliage cover the walls, shimmering in silvery light, threatening to swallow her completely. At once beautiful and terrifying, the entire set seems to press the woman towards us. She looks out at the audience and waits . . . letting the silence grow, daring us to come along with her . . . wherever she's going . . . and as the seconds tick away, we start to feel as if whatever is between her and us is shrinking. The thoughts and feelings and the million and one things that prevent us from fully engaging in the moment . . . those things are evaporating under the spell of her mysterious silence. A raw, psychic space is being created that she can only inhabit with us. And finally, when we are fully transfixed, when we have given ourselves over to this utterly lonely communion, when everything else has been stripped away . . . only then does she begin to speak.

The scene I've just described is from Les Waters's spectacular production of *Suddenly Last Summer*. But really, aside from particular visual details unique to that show, all of Les's work is marked by intimate existential encounters between actor and audience framed within fantastical theatrical environments . . . worlds that are both concrete and mysterious, where the air is rarefied and the landscape of the play is magnified to reveal the Essential.

It may sound incongruous, but this is the genius of Les Waters:

He gets out of the way.
He lets the play breathe,

DOI: 10.4324/9781003170808-20

stripping away everything that stands between the text and the actor,
gently propelling the actors forward,
without force,
without some overriding, overly aggressive idea or concept
of how to behave, or think, or move . . .
trusting the language, both spoken and unspoken,
visible and invisible,
to make manifest the world of the play.

It is this profound trust,
in the writer, the designer, the actor, the audience,
that is unique to his work.

For a profession built on the idea of collaboration, it is perhaps curious
that such trust should be so rare among colleagues. But it is.

Les believes that each and every one of his collaborators should be given
the time to digest the material on their own terms. Even when that process
is difficult and confusing. Even when he could provide answers that would
make everyone's life easier.

He simply doesn't. To a playwright desperately wanting him to provide answers, I have seen him respond by only asking questions. To a designer whose
sketches hadn't yet captured the world of the play, I have seen him gently
suggest a book of photographs as a source of inspiration. To an actor who was
struggling mightily to find their character, I have seen him give a single note:
"I don't think you're quite there yet."

In the mouth of another director, these actions could be interpreted as in-
different or irritating or even cruel. But in every instance, the writer, the
designer, and the actor knew that Les was being wildly supportive. That he
trusted them to find a creative solution, one that was unique to their imagination. By doing so, he let them, rather he *insisted* that they find their own
truth. And at the end of the day, when the process had led each of them to
discover self-created solutions, their sense of accomplishment was absolute
and their ownership over the project filled them with a buoyant sense of
confidence and joy. Not to mention compounding their undying loyalty to
Les . . .

 . . . which explains why he repeatedly works with so many of the same artists.
Chuck Mee, Sarah Ruhl, Lucas Hnath, Bruce McKenzie, Naomi Izuka . . .

are all members of the Les Waters Extended Family Circus . . . at the center of which is the gifted designer Annie Smart, who also happens to be the mother of his three extraordinary kids. Loyalty is a value that Les holds close to his fibrillating heart. It allows him to go deep with people, to ask them to take bigger risks, and to create a relaxed atmosphere while doing so. Over the years, he's come to increasingly rely on this network of blood brothers and sisters, as the plays he's interested in directing have only become more challenging.

Not that he was ever interested in a conventional career. Or a conventional life, for that matter.

Growing up in Cleethorpes, a small seaside town in Lincolnshire, he spent most of his time running away from home. He doesn't talk much about his family life, but he's leaked enough intel to give the impression that he was happy to get away.

I imagine him hiding in the Fens, a large marshland bordering on Cleethorpes that the Romans would traverse using stilts, listening to the locals gathered around an open fire, telling ancient folktales filled with the ghosts of those who had disappeared in the foggy bogs.

Or surely, like every other English child, on some trip with his parents to see a play where he was transfixed by the performance of some icon of the British stage in his or her last tour of some Shakespeare play . . . or maybe it was a Christmas panto. In any case, the art of storytelling seeped into Les's bones at an early age, and he took it with him on his final flight from home into the heart of London, into the world of the theatre.

And what a tribe was waiting for him there. He cut his teeth working at the Royal Court, the most prominent writer's theatre in the English-speaking world, where he had a front-row seat working with a slew of great playwrights including the great Caryl Churchill (a friend to this day). From there, he teamed up with William Gaskill and Max Stafford-Clark at Joint Stock, whose reliance on extensive workshops, improvisation, and shared research conducted by the entire company became a model for generations of theatre artists. The Royal Court and Joint Stock were at the heart of the cultural revolution in England in the 1960s and 1970s, creating plays infused with audacious imagination and political urgency. Being part of that movement cemented Les's identity as a renegade/hipster/syndicalist, and watching those plays get made began his life-long affair with new work.

And here I have to pause for a moment of clarification:

When Les refers to "new work,"
he is not referring simply to plays that will be seen by an audience for
the first time.
For him, new work refers to texts that invent a language to describe
the world.
A language that frequently dispenses with traditional narrative,
that relies on the collisions of images and ideas,
rather than a linear set of arguments.
Without neat resolutions.
That contains dialogue that might be called "poetic,"
but then again,
maybe not.
Peppered with events that seem inexplicable, absurd, or strange.
Plays without easy answers ("Bloody fucking hell no," Mr. Waters
would say).
That can get messy ("Well what did you expect?").
That the uninitiated might call weird ("Wonderful, isn't it?")
That make no sense . . .
. . . except that they make total sense.

Les likes work that other people can't understand or respond to when they
read the words on the page but which feel oddly and profoundly comprehen-
sible when staged. At least when he stages them.

The man is walking to a different drummer.

Which is blindingly obvious when you meet the guy . . .

He stands well north of six feet tall, is skinnier than your average broomstick,
and sports a beard that is the envy of orthodox priests the world over. His
arms are rife with tattoos, patterns of thick lines that curl around the skin
(the ones I've seen anyway), and he wears his (now fully grey) hair in a kind
of post-hippie pompadour. I'm not sure he takes off his high-top sneakers.
Ever.

The entire look is a celebration of Oddness. If you didn't know the man you
might be a little wary, maybe think about crossing the street if you saw him
approaching from a distance. But as he gets closer, you get a better read. The
body is lax, almost invitingly vulnerable. The gaze in the eyes is soft. He's
just shuffling along in a kind of meditative wanderlust. Now you think to
yourself: "Who is this intriguing fellow?"

And when he manages to sit down, when he somehow squeezes those arms and legs into the safe confines of a chair, he starts to speak.

And you notice that when thinking through a problem, he extends his syllables, stopping just short of singing.

And that he's quick to laugh. A kind of chortle that's spit-laced with mischief and self-deprecation.

That he can talk as easily about Wittgenstein as he can about the art of flatulence.

That he prides himself on having read every play by some kid you've never heard of.

That he loves photography . . .

Loves photos of any kind,

as they strike him as windows into the real world,

the one right in front of us and the one we can't see,

that we pretend is not there,

swirling all around us with a velocity that is terrifying and containing everything we don't know.

Because a great photograph makes you look at the world differently.

It strips away everything around it, and

reveals something special,

something essential.

"It's right there," he says. "Can you not see it?"

Les spent eight years at Berkeley Rep.

From him I took the value of looking. And listening. Deep listening.

I can think of no higher compliment than to say that the man influenced the way I direct plays.

What he took from me I have no idea. That's his problem.

We've both left our jobs as an Artistic Directors and are now untethered, roaming the earth, trundling through the dark forests of the free-lance world. We meet now in poorly lit bars in various cities and talk about the value of a good nap, the list of people who no longer return our phone calls, and the completely fucked state of the human race.

Oh and yeah . . . how excited we are about our next show.

I can't wait to see his. I know I'll see something I've never seen before.

*   *   *   *   *

TONY TACCONE *was raised by a large family of artists who believed that "art is the highest calling of mankind." His dad was Italian, his mom Puerto Rican, which made for a lot of very loud Sunday dinners. He was heavily influenced by the counter-culture movement of the 1960s, developing a progressive political perspective and a love for rock n' roll that remain strong to this day. He toyed with the idea of becoming an archaeologist, until he discovered that he'd have to take courses in statistics. He met a group of actors at a bar, and thought, "Hey, these people are really fun." Acting on this profound insight, he made a long and lucky life for himself in the theatre.*

Some productions I saw that made me the director I am

Peter Brook's production of Seneca's *Oedipus* adapted by Ted Hughes. National Theatre at the Old Vic, London 1968.

I was 16. How did I know about this? Probably from the Ken Tynan review in the *Observer*. How did I get there? Did I hitch? At 16? Did I catch the bus? Certainly not the train as that would have been too expensive. I saw a matinee on my own. What do I remember? The gold cube of the set that slowly revolved. The chorus tied to the columns and balcony of the theatre. How they groaned and hissed like rockets. Irene Worth's mask-like face. Being aware that I was witnessing great actors, not just Worth and Gielgud but also the young and the beautiful of the London theatre scene. The cart with the giant phallus and the band playing "Yes we have no bananas." It was 1968, you know. The silence that followed the end of the play and preceded the unveiling of the dick. Also, a sense of tension and excitement in the house. As if this was wrong, this was transgressive.

Trevor Nunn's production of Middleton's *The Revenger's Tragedy*. RSC at the Aldwych, London, 1968.

The production seemed to live in two worlds simultaneously – Jacobean England and my schoolboy's fantasy of London in the 1960s. I thought it was decadent. The strange "singing" quality of the actors' voices. Not "speaking" but "singing." Both fascinated and repulsed. I like the cynicism about ruling elites, I like the excessive cruelty. I'm a big fan of Jacobean splatter plays.

John Barton's production of *Twelfth Night*. RSC, Stratford-upon-Avon 1968.

DOI: 10.4324/9781003170808-21

I remember hitching 130 miles to get there. I remember getting there just in time. I remember standing at the back during the performance. I remember having enough money to buy a drink at the intermission. For much of my childhood and early teenage years, I was an Elizabethan history-culture freak, and this production satisfied that deep need. I remember candle light and a wicker box set. I remember audience members complaining it was slow and I remember its pace seeming perfect and comforting. I remember Judi Dench's voice and thinking she isn't "singing," this language sounds as if it's coming into her head for the first time. I slept the night in a bus shelter in Stratford-upon-Avon. Who was I then? What kind of boy was I? Sometime, soon I need to take this old boy back to England to revisit these sites that meant so very much so many years ago.

Jane Howell directs Edward Bond's *Bingo*. Northcott Theatre, Exeter 1973.
I wrote my undergraduate thesis on the plays of Edward Bond. *Bingo* is the play about Shakespeare that most people don't know and a play that I love. A play about age and achievement and social responsibility. Does anybody produce Bond in the US anymore? Too harsh? Too bleak? Too political? Probably, the first time I saw a production with a Brechtian aesthetic. Only the essentials in both acting and design. In my memory, it was all under bright white light. Is that correct? Jane Howell is one of the great unsung directors of the British Theatre.

Max Stafford-Clark's production of Caryl Churchill's *Light Shining in Buckinghamshire*. Joint Stock Theatre Group at Royal Court Theatre Upstairs, London, 1976.
More 16th- to 17th-century history. The Putney debates. When the future of England was decided. Socialism or capitalism? Liberation or property? Freedom or restriction? Ecstasy or repression? Somewhere between Jane's production of *Bingo* and Max's production of *Light Shining*, it began to make sense. A glimmering of light. Only the essentials. Concentration. Clarity. Making demands on an audience. Questions. Questions. Less isn't more. Less is enough. You have to need to make the work. And then how do you make the work? What are the conditions you need to make the work? How do you protect/maintain the urgency of the need? Whose history, whose story are you telling? Why had this working-class narrative been hidden from history? Who owns the narrative? High up there on my list of plays that I want to direct. I want to work with Caryl again. It crushed me when NY Theatre Workshop didn't follow through and ask me to direct their production in 2018.

Nancy Meckler's production of Sam Shepard's *Action*. Royal Court Theatre Upstairs, London, 1974.
I've directed this twice and would be happy to work on it twice more. How this play would sing now. Four characters try to celebrate a holiday meal after some "crisis" has happened, a post-apocalyptic meal. The life-draining ordinariness of boredom. The production was scrupulously real whilst being totally enigmatic. Like lifting the lid of a box, and inside that box is a whole other world that is happening without you. So much mystery. The kind of a play I like to think of happening somewhere without anyone watching.

Komachi fuden or Tale of Komachi Told by the Wind written and directed by Ota Shogo for the Tenkei Theatre Company. Institute of Contemporary Arts, London, 1981.
My obsession with silence and stillness on stage starts here. A woman slowly – oh so very slowly – crosses an empty stage; the only movement is her flexing and contracting her toes. The company builds and furnishes a room in total silence. All is precise and ordered and yet loose and dreamlike. The beauty of observing unadorned actions. The excitement of seeing something new for the first time.

And the very big one was Peter Brook's *A Midsummer Night's Dream* which is the greatest production I've seen. RSC, Stratford-upon-Avon 1970.
One of the most famous productions of the 20th century and certainly one of the most written about it. In my own work, I am proud of the fact that audience members often screamed when the lights went out in *The Thin Place* and very proud that a man fainted when Frank hit Val with an axe in *Fen* at the Public, but Brook's *MND* was the one and only time that I have heard an audience scream with excitement. Totally alive. Totally present. Totally of its time. Totally in the moment. An incredibly sexy cast. Sally Jacob's white box set. Richard Peaslee's music. A game changer. Electricity. Radiance.

And then the grown-ups arrived. Patrice Chereau's *La Dispute* by Marivaux. Théâtre National Populaire at the National Theatre, London, 1974. And Gorky's *Summerfolk* directed by Peter Stein. Schaübhne at National Theatre, London, 1977. Who knew that work of this beauty and subtlety and to use an old-fashioned word excellence could be achieved with such resources and on this scale. Who knew that socialist principles could co-exist with such loveliness. The extraordinary brilliance of these acting companies. The dreamy sensuality of Riccardo Peduzzi's set for *La Dispute*. The real trees and real earth of the set by Karl-Ernst Hermann and seemingly real light for *Summerfolk*. The attention paid to detail. Unlike anything I had seen before and truly in a league of its own.

All of these were in my teens and 20s. It served me well being in London and having the opportunity to see work like this.

Sometimes

I have never hallucinated a person. As far as I am aware. There is the "thing" that lives close to the ground, always on the periphery of my vision. Greasy. Dirty. Oily. A pinguid mass. Always on the left-hand side. But it is a "thing," not a person. No moments for me "overflowing with unbounded joy and rapture, ecstatic devotion, and completest life," as Prince Myshkin describes the beginning of a seizure in Dostoevsky's *The Idiot*. No religious fervor for this atheist.

Sometimes, the floor will tilt up 45 degrees and then slowly return to its original position.

Sometimes, a wall that I know is 20 feet away will rush toward me and suddenly stop 6 inches in front of my eyes.

Sometimes, I hear feet walking along a hallway.

Sometimes, a kettle whistling.

On a rare occasion someone calls my name, Leslie. My father's voice calling me. Only my father's voice.

Sometimes, people are speaking a language I know but have never heard spoken before. English but with all the vowels removed?

Sometimes, something I just said or something I heard will loop in my brain. During rehearsals of *The Christians* in Louisville, I heard Marvin Gaye's *Mercy Mercy Me* – a song I love – playing in a store on 4th street. The phrase

DOI: 10.4324/9781003170808-22

"Whoa, oh, mercy mercy me/Oh, things ain't what they used to be, no no" continuously looped inside my head for 24 hours.

Sometimes, my limbs seem too big as if they've suddenly thickened.

And always these blanks, these absences, I am conscious but not there. My school reports comment that I am a good student when I am there. Not a reference to any physical absence from school but rather a brief, unexpected lapse in attention. "Leslie's mind likes to wander." It glitches. It pleats and folds for tiny moments in time. With the true perspicacity of childhood, my daughter Madeleine once said as I stared at something unseen, "Dad, you've come untethered from life."

On a couple of occasions, a vile stench. The smell of rotten eggs. And immediately a seizure.

Monday, March 27, 2006 – It's the day off. I'm running across the courtyard of Berkeley Rep. I climb the first of the concrete steps up to the stage management office on the second floor to collect my script that I left behind after Sunday's rehearsal. I am stressed. Rita Moreno, who is playing Amanda Wingfield in *The Glass Menagerie*, has missed several days of rehearsal due to illness. We begin tech on the Tuesday and are not sure if Rita will have recovered enough to attend. So, I'm stressed and about to climb the

Johnny van Chang, the Maintenance Technician at   , finds the bottom   and helps to   where

am   to ER   Kaiser Hsp   Oklndndthyrn nd

She s n t sre   thnksthtwhtmght

I am 54. I have just had my first seizure. My mind is full of blanks. My mind is blanking. My mind is a blank . . .

Let It Go

It is this deep blankness is the real thing strange.
The more things happen to you the more you can't
Tell or remember even what they were.

The contradictions cover such a range.
The talk would talk and go so far aslant.
You don't want madhouse and the whole thing there.

—William Empson

Thursday, July 2, 2020 – I'm sitting in the garden of Cafenated, corner of Vine and Shattuck in Berkeley, talking with Jim Carpenter. Jim is a wonderful actor and we have worked together on several productions in the Bay Area. We talk about keeping busy and our partners eccentricities and wearing masks and I'm looking at him and I'm thinking, "Are you the only other epileptic I know working in the theater? How can this be?" According to the Epilepsy Foundation, 1 in 26 people in the US will develop epilepsy during their lifetime. I know of some famous epileptics in the arts – Danny Glover, Neil Young, Prince, Tennyson (fellow Lincolnshire "yellowbelly" and writer of long woozy looping lines of verse that smell of seizure), Ian Curtis – but where are the rest of us? Are we "invisible" because we fear people will not employ us? Do we frighten people? Is it Shame? That thick queasy emotion, Shame.

I must admit I am not the most reliable narrator of my own epilepsy.

I have no overview of my seizures. I do not know what my body actually does during an epileptic episode. I am my own seizure. What I do feel afterward is an acute sense of shame. Shame that maybe my face contorted, that my limbs stiffened and jerked, that I might have said something, that I might have soiled myself. Shame of my involuntary vulnerability.

I have had absence seizures of some kind from about the age of ten. No physical jerking, just moments of blankness. Fairly common in lots of children and often disappears with adulthood. My BIG seizure came out of the blue. I had never had one like this before – blackout/collapse/spasms. I had no feeling at all that it was about to happen.

Do I identify as disabled? Sometimes. Certainly, when the seizures are frequent and my mind is foggy and my memory is diminished and the ground is thin ice beneath my feet, then my neurodivergence makes life and work challenging. Strong light, flashing light, light bouncing into my left eye, repetition, unnecessarily long hours can make technical rehearsals daunting. During these periods, I constantly check where things are. If I were to fall in the kitchen, what would break my fall? What objects in my immediate vicinity could cause me harm? What would happen if a seizure took me in the bathroom? I am acutely aware of the edges of things. But for the most part, despite the visual shunting and the bangs and the beeps and the chuntering voices, I can focus, I can hold conversations, I can direct. I don't feel broken in any way, I feel like me.

Does my epilepsy make my work different? Is there even an answer to that question? Maybe I am not the one who can answer that. I had big seizures during both the workshop in Colorado and rehearsals in Louisville of *Glory of the World*. The ice felt very thin during that time. The stillness/contemplation was there to anchor myself/the production and the chaos built by the guys was very much how my neurology was functioning then. Images strung out like beads on a string, sudden jumps, and collisions. A certain kind of logic happening just ahead of the thought process. I do know that I have no difficulty with material where things happen for no apparent reason. In *Glory of the World*, a man leads a rhinoceros across the stage on a leash whilst two men in speedos dance in a water sprinkler all to the sound of two other men playing a slowed-down version of Britney Spears' *Oops . . . I Did It Again*. That makes sense to me.

9. *The Glory of the World* at Actors Theatre of Louisville (2015).

10. *Girlfriend* at Berkeley Repertory Theatre (2010).

11. *10 out of 12* at Soho Repertory Theatre (2015).

12. Portrait of Les Waters with bowling pin by Rebecca Martinez.

"Les. Fragments."

Anne Washburn

SET DESIGNER

Do you love it Les?

DIRECTOR

I think it's the ugliest thing I've looked on in a while. (*Beat.*) I think that's a compliment.

Before there was internet all the time, everywhere the period of technical rehearsal – lasting several days, up to a week – was particularly tedious for a playwright; your opinion will generally be called upon maybe once or twice in the day, it's often too dark to read, mainly you'd sit there, in the dark, as the strange discombobulation of the world of the play went on around you – lights flicking on and off, strange sounds at random, actors appearing half in costume, reappearing in a different version of that costume, people around you springing into action with great focus or bored and snacking, quipping, muttering into headsets, the play flickering in and out of life. I fell in love with the dreamy weirdness of it and in 2005 began taking disconnected notes.

DIRECTOR

Hey Garret?

GARRET

Yeah.

DOI: 10.4324/9781003170808-23

DIRECTOR

Will you muck your hair up so you don't have the parting?

GARRET

So I don't have the part?

DIRECTOR

That's right.

GARRET

You mean craziness?

DIRECTOR

No, I think it should just look like it usually does.

GARRET

You mean really cool and sexy?

DIRECTOR

(A beat.)

That's right.

Eventually, these notes became a play. A play which takes place over days, and is often in the dark, and partly on headsets, and which needs to have moments that are visually extraordinary, and moments which are incredibly strange, and moments which are deeply pedestrian. It's a hard play to do. I brought it to Les.

Assistant Stage Manager goes offstage.

After a long while she returns and continues to sweep and vacuum.

There is a low muttering hum coming from all the speakers in the space, an utterly unintelligible murmuring.

Electrician 2 crosses, holding a bundle of electrical cording.

Gradually, we do hear the LIGHTS, a faint but distinct intermittent stream of instruction and SOUND, ditto – we will continue to hear this, steadily, evenly, until the play begins.

2. OUR PLAY BEGINS

> *At once, the muttering hum rises in volume: all conversations are audible for a second or two*
>
> *Then*

LIGHTS

Going dark!

> *Darkness. Babble ceases. After a moment, Vacuuming stops.*

ASSISTANT STAGE MANAGER
(*Slight sarcasm.*)

Thank you dark!

LIGHTS
(*Quietly.*)

And 332 – Go.

> *Lighting does something incredibly vivid and comprehensive.*

SOUND

14 – Go.

> *As does sound.*

There is a Director in this play. Some of his lines are pulled from those actual tech rehearsals, two of which were for plays Les had directed, some from other productions. So, the Director is kind of an amalgam person, also a character I went on to create, who in bits and pieces and moments sounds an awful lot like Les.

SOUND DESIGNER
I've seen people not only text during shows but hold up the cell phone to see it better.

DIRECTOR
I grabbed a cell phone out of a teenager's hands, she was texting during the entire show, I grabbed it and I placed it under my butt.

(All of these excerpts, some of which appear in *10 out of 12* and some of which do not, are taken from my notes during shows directed by Les.)

Bruce McKenzie played The Director; Bruce has been in a number of Les's productions. Over the rehearsal period, Bruce's director became just a bit more Les-like, and from time to time you could see Les catching Bruce observing him.

DIRECTOR

The horns are lost in the mail?

Unrelated crash from somewhere in the auditorium.

COSTUME DESIGNER

Uh huh.

DIRECTOR

Do you want *my* horns? The ones I put on when I come home to the apartment, have a gin, do a little dance, and roast babies on the stove?

The cheeriest I've ever seen Les: in Louisville, directing *Little Bunny Foo Foo*, a stage adaptation of the children's song in which field mice negotiate a tricky power relationship with a rabbit, often while singing and dancing. A sizable chunk of the rehearsal was devoted to the field mice, played by a squad of eight-year-olds led in dances and frisks by choreographer Barney O'Hanlon, to the perfect be-bop inflected music of Dave Malloy. How do you address a group of eight-year-olds? "Friends," Barney would say, gathering them to him, and they would rough out some series of maneuvers, and then Dave and his band would start up in the corner, and the field mice – talented and innocent and ambitious and joyful and fraught, in the way of eight-year-olds, and every one of them cute as the cutest possible button – would come roaring out in unison to frolic and caper in a totally pure and successful bid for our entertainment while Les beamed from ear to ear.

(During that same rehearsal period, in a bitter Louisville January, in a city where people drive places, Les would walk the several miles from his home to the theater; his beard was long, he wore a heavy grey tweed coat; one day, he came in looking very pleased: a car had pulled alongside him and an earnest do-gooder, mistaking him for a homeless person, had rolled down the window to offer him a sandwich.)

The difficulty of bringing Les into a character or into the character of a director is that playwrights often well I do default to language as communication,
and though Les is a verbal person, his superpower as a director is that he is
always and very acutely observing. Les directs by giving his attention. How
do I describe the quality of his attention? And the result of the quality of his
attention? And how do you unearth what lies beneath an attention?

STAGE MANAGER
Maria please hold while we relight you.

Lights up bright on Maria.

Then brighter.

Then some other change.

We're also hearing toggling.

MARIA
This light is so bright.

....

I feel that it's judging me.

DIRECTOR
The light is just doing its job. I'm judging you. Judging you, and finding you
wanting. (MARIA *sticks tongue out.*) Oh that's nice. There will be one more
light, right in your eyes.

MARIA
Excellent.

DIRECTOR
And small spikes, right in the stage.

MARIA
Excellent.

We were rehearsing *The Small* for Clubbed Thumb Summerworks (a series
of plays presented for a week each over the summer) in 2010 in its last year
in the venerable Downtown venue, The Ohio. Les had assembled a dreamy
group of people to work on what was, at the time, a more or less unpaid gig
which most of them were doing for fun. We rehearsed at night; the actors

were awesome, the play was delightful, we were all enjoying ourselves; every take of every scene was a pleasure; it was going great. After rehearsing steadily all the way through the play we headed into our first run-through a few days before the brief tech period. This was our first time showing our work to the producer and we were all sunny confidence. The play was dreadful, however – nothing was wrong with the production, the acting was great, but the play was incredibly boring. I thought, as I was watching it, that maybe I'd just seen it too many times, was weary of it, jaded, but no, the producer confirmed that it was really dull. Well, these things happen, and we assumed the second run-through would straighten out the problem but the second run-through, also, was super tedious. I was in an elevator with Les, on our way down from the rehearsal, feeling downcast, and, seeking reassurance, I said well, Les (Man of the Theater; Ye of Vast Experience), this is just . . . part of the process . . . right? I was wanting something reassuring and showbizzy. He looked at me in muted despair: "I don't know, I just don't know."

The third run-through was also dreadful and the first performance was very tedious *and* shaky, and then it shook all its gears into place somehow and was, again, the rather wonderful thing we had all been making together, only more so. It often happens that way. But it doesn't always happen that way. Every single play ever is a bewildering and unknowable beast; if you take your relationship with it for granted, it will eat you; if you are wary and careful, it may also eat you. Les never pretends otherwise.

18. END OF DAY/END OF PLAY

STAGE MANAGER

Ladies and gentlemen, we've come to the last five minutes of the day, please stay alert as we are going to push through to the very last second available to us, and as a reminder, please be sure to be here at ten sharp tomorrow bright eyed and bushy tailed and ready to go as we're going to have a very long day's work ahead of us.

All the actors are on stage while something major is adjusted.

There is a stream of technical information. Maybe all departments at once.

Paul stands alone, his expression is remote.

Eva and Siget are singing softly.

Ben is talking with Jake while Richard listens.

Jamie is on a ladder messing with a light. Electrician 2 is holding the ladder and passing something up to her. His hand is almost mummified in olive green electrical tape.

Paul is on stage in full costume, sitting to the side. PAUL IS THINKING; WE CAN HEAR IT.

During Paul's thought, the other people on stage have slowly started to take up the melody, humming it, or singing it along.

The stream of technical information starts to come in that melody.

The Electricians start singing the German song to that melody.

Then, everyone is singing all at once.

A new song continues which mingles the words and melody of the song with the words and melody of the German Song and Goddesses and a lot of Technical Chatter.

And casual gestures have become a dance. Everyone on stage is dancing.

And the lights and sound and set do something very beautiful and initially strange but at the end complimentary.

STAGE MANAGER
Ladies and Gentlemen, that's it for the night. You can all go home.

Darkness.

Those are the words from which Les made the ending of *10 out of 12*. I don't think there's any video of this but it wouldn't matter if there was.

The walls peeled back, the light changed, everyone was onstage, Barney O'Hanlon had composed a dance: complex, and very simple, and everyone on stage danced with each other, while the lights changed while the lights stayed the same, they danced, warily, then more in it, but never quite lost in it, eyes connected, grave.

There was something ragged, and joyful, and brave, and broken, one of my favorite moments ever, and I can't describe it in words, and Les made it by patching together words, and watching, a spirit, and the souls of many in the kind of ragamuffin spell which is most powerful.

I wish I could tell you how he did it.

DIRECTOR

It's that hundred years war. Unforgivable. They – (*Illegible.*) – in 1342.

>   *Gesture.*

Fuck that!

*   *   *   *   *

ANNE WASHBURN is a West Coast playwright who has been a New York playwright for a while. Les Waters has directed four of her plays: Apparition, The Small, 10 out of 12, *and* Little Bunny Foo Foo. *Her plays also include* Mr. Burns a Post Electric Play, Shipwreck, The Ladies, Antlia Pneumatica, The Internationalist, I Have Loved Strangers, A Devil at Noon, *and* The Communist Dracula Pageant.

Room control

For many young directors, the focus of a rehearsal, whether they admit it or not, is control of the room. And it's not easy. It's a complex social and political negotiations of status, age, race, gender, class, all the things that make work so challenging and interesting. But the struggle to be in control of the room can lead one to think, "I want this to be MY production, and therefore I must be right about everything." Impossible. Our job is to do the prep and to be present to the energy in the room. And you cannot be present to the energy in the room if all you are thinking is "I have to be in control of the room, and whenever anybody asks me a question, I have to have the answer, and the answer has to be right, and the right answer is what I want it to be." I have observed this when I was teaching at UCSD, sometimes at Berkeley Rep, sometimes at Actors Theatre, the Humana Festival in particular. The number of directors I have watched who are really themselves in a rehearsal room is small. And who you are – what makes you "you" and nobody else – is what you have to work with. That's the major thing. If a director plays the role of being in control or is constantly indicating "I'm directing the way I was taught to direct in college, and this is correct and you must respect that," actors pick up on that. And suddenly, they are no longer rehearsing. They're playing the role of an actor acting like they think you want them to act. And then the real trouble starts.

DOI: 10.4324/9781003170808-24

A good rehearsal room

Somewhere that is part of the theatre and not miles away.
Somewhere quiet.
Somewhere where people can enter quietly.
Somewhere with good lighting.
(Sitting under fluorescent light all day is not good.)
(Staring through a window at the sun all day is not good.)
Somewhere above ground.
(I don't want to have to join the Miner's Union in order to work.)
Somewhere the same size as the playing area of the stage.
Somewhere I trust everybody I am working with.
Somewhere where everybody has an appetite for the project.
Somewhere with an endless supply of coffee.
Somewhere we can fail and nobody will snicker or titter or roll their eyes.
Somewhere I feel safe and there is a sense of possibility in the room.

DOI: 10.4324/9781003170808-25

"Les in Space"

Amanda Spooner

I have been a Stage Manager ever since I was introduced to the idea. I cannot unsee it. The very act of it tugs on all that makes sense to me. The more life I live, the more I realize there are people who see the world in words and colors and mechanics and movement. I see the world in the infrastructure that holds it all up.

Les sees the world in the space in between. Like me, he cannot unsee it. He deals so much in space that he has mastered creating it and letting thoughts hang inside it, chaos swirl within it, and emotions seep into it. Sometimes, he lets it just sit quietly. You would think that someone like me, in the business of building girders and understructure, would be at odds with someone working in all that negative space. That someone like Les would make me nervous.

And maybe he did, at first. But only because I experienced his work before I met him. I am the product of suburban San Francisco – close enough to the city to have had everything pierced in the 1990s but just far enough away that I was about three years behind the trend. When I was accepted at the Yale School of Drama, I had no interest in going. Yale was cold, self-important, and exhausted with contrived decadence. But I ended up accepting their offer because it made me uncomfortable. It made me feel out of control. It made me feel small. It forced me to see the weak spots in my intellect, the holes in my own plot. That excited me. And let us face the facts here: I was raised by loving parents but also on Pop-Tarts and reruns of *Mary Tyler Moore*. One of the professors who wrote me a letter of recommendation for Yale agreed to do it but only after telling me I was under-read and illiterate.

DOI: 10.4324/9781003170808-26

But when I saw Les's production of *Eurydice*, during my first month at Yale, I understood every tiny detail. All of the decisions in that production aligned perfectly. I felt everything all at once, watching that play, so much so I had to sit in my seat for a long while after the house lights had come up. When I talked about it with classmates, they were intimidated by how much I understood, how much I received from the story. These were people who played violin for the Pope when they were three. I could name all of the QVC hosts from 1995 through 2002. But somehow I was innately fluent in *Eurydice*.

So of course, years later, when I was scheduled for an interview with Les Waters to stage-manage a show called *10 out of 12*, it felt a little like having to look the universe in the eye. Like I was meeting a myth. Although we were on the phone, I had dressed up for the conversation. I believed it would help me say smart things, but really he just asked me about scheduling production meetings and that was it. We would be embarking on a partnership, building an Anne Washburn play about a tech rehearsal in a theatre. It was not more complicated than it needed to be.

Trying to curate a 2.5-hour experience of a technical rehearsal, for an audience all wearing headsets, is a meta-fantastic apogee for a woman who loves aligning tiny details and infrastructure. Because of all the recorded sound cues, we were basically in a constant state of technical rehearsals ourselves. Les would show up for meetings, ask concise questions, and share brief, elegant responses to what Anne had written. Brilliant responses that would take me six months to craft. I was simply hanging on every succinct offering his imagination floated into the conversation. Until he turned to me and said, "What do you think?"

This is a complex moment for a Stage Manager. We are trained in the currency of what *other* people think. And this was not a question about where our tech tables would be erected or the way the script would be printed. He was asking me about what should be included in the preshow that would be staged with actors portraying crewmembers. He was asking me about the storytelling.

This was Les making space. He was tapping into my resources, skills, and experience. And he was not just being polite – sometimes, people do that. But not Les. He is a kind person, do not misread me, in fact, he is so thoughtful it becomes dangerous to think his brand of consideration and humanity is normal. Sadly, most people will disappoint you if you calibrate your expectations according to your partnership with Les. But when Les is finished talking or does not want to hear from someone, he says so. It is refreshing and I wish more people just said exactly what they mean. Because people such as Les, when they ask you what you think, they mean it sincerely. And you do not feel undereducated or intimidated or as though you are an impostor. Even when he tells you that you are being daft. Because sometimes I am daft. We all are.

And that is how we work on everything. I get really quiet and still. So does he. I track his every word. He will ask me for my opinion when he wants it; he often does. Some people say Stage Managers should be seen and not heard. I get what my place is in the production process. But I would also point out, I am one of the first people around and one of the last to leave. And I do not mean on a daily basis – although that is true, my days are like that – I mean for the whole process. As a Stage Manager, I am around for the early brainstorming meetings and I am the last one on the island with the cast at the end of the run. I listen to *everything*. That is my job. One thing we know for certain about Les, he is no fool when it comes to collaboration and resourcefulness. He knows who is in the room, what they brought with them, and how long they are going to stay.

Stage Managers do not get to take a lot of breaks. The second I announce we are on a ten, an actor is asking me about an audition they are trying to schedule for themselves. And I will never begrudge them that. They love their job too and they are just trying to secure more of it while also working on the gig they already have. I am guilty of ruining my own breaks, anyway. I often like spending my lunch with my co-workers . . . because I usually have questions to get answered and I get drunk off productivity. Les Waters, when he is finished for the day, he is finished. When it is time for a break, we break. When we go to lunch, we eat. He does not feverishly fill hours and minutes. The first read-through of *10 out of 12* took about three hours of a seven-hour rehearsal day. This was our second rehearsal together, ever, and he turned to me and said, "Okay." And I said, "Great, should we take our lunch now?" and he said, "No, the day is over." Most directors would have an anxiety attack at the thought of giving up four hours on the second day of rehearsal. For Les, things take the time they take and then we are done.

And he never runs out of time in his process. Ever.

I have a child, he is five and his name is Jack. I have heard everything from "Stage Managers do not have babies" to "You should not tell people about your child because they will stop hiring you." I will admit it is hard being a freelancer in a field that is not built for parents. And it does not get easier, even after sleep regression passes and they are in school. In fact, I think it gets harder. And frankly, I am tired. And the quarantine made me fall so deeply in love with playing Hot Wheels and "fashion show" that I thought I would never leave the house again. But when Jack was a baby, I would do foolish things like have him come for a visit during meal breaks at the theatre. I think I was trying to be an advocate and a good mom. Instead I was being a subpar, distracted Stage Manager covered in spit-up. Les loved having Jack around. In fact, when I would try to send my child home, Les would demand he stay for notes with the actors. Once I was trying to run a tech rehearsal for our production of *For Peter Pan on her 70th Birthday*, and somehow I ended up holding a crying Jack while trying to talk on the god mic. Les thought it was the best thing he had seen – and heard – all week. Aside from the play, of course, which was breathtaking.

Les Waters is the kind of leader people are afraid to be. A true collaborator. A visionary. Hilarious. Serious. Normal. Too smart for us all. The friend we do not deserve. And Jack thinks he is Santa Claus. I will forever feel accomplished when I make Les laugh. I adore him, always will. For all the things he gives the world and for all the space he makes for me to do the same.

*   *   *   *   *

AMANDA SPOONER is a Stage Manager and educator based in New York. She has worked on Broadway and throughout the country. She is the founder of the grassroots campaign Year of the Stage Manager, the Vice Chair of the Stage Managers' Association, an ambassador for the Parent Artist Advocacy League, and on council at Actors' Equity Association. Amanda received her MFA from the Yale School of Drama and serves on faculty at Ithaca College. Among many other productions, she has stage-managed three directed by Les Waters: 10 out of 12, For Peter Pan on her 70th Birthday, *and* Glory of the World. *(All of this was true at the time of writing; by now, she might be stage-managing Tuesday Night Bingo in a warmer climate.)*

"Hearing Things"

Bray Poor

I met Les at a critical point in my life and my career as a theater artist. I had a new baby and I had only recently made the change from actor to sound designer. I knew my way around plays, but I was still finding my voice as a designer. Our first project together was Sarah Ruhl's *Eurydice* at Berkeley Rep. I had flown out to Berkeley to be in residence for rehearsal. And that was where I first saw Les's great gift in action: his patience. He has an ability to wait for story, character, or collaborator to emerge. He creates an atmosphere of deep support, winking humor, and profound empathy. He is a champion for outsiders and broken people. His deep love for the lonely – and of loneliness – allows him to wait for the fragility of his sometimes shy, judgment-scarred collaborators to peel open so that they can make art that is their own.

The climax of *Eurydice* centers on Eurydice and Orpheus's walk back from the Underworld. Choreographing and scoring that "walk thru hell" involved every department and every actor in the company. For days and days, the actors walked the circumference of the stage, timed their lines, hit marks, listened for music, stepped in and out of light. Maria Dizzia and Joseph Parks, who played the lovers, were put through the wringer. But we all took our cues from them. We watched and listened to Maria and Joe and designed around them. How they spoke to each other across the chasm, when she made her fateful turn and looked at him, and how we all sank as they said their long wrenching goodbye was guided by Les, as he watched his actors play a love scene between two Demi-Gods from Greek myth that was really just a quiet, tragic ending to a relationship between two people who love each other.

DOI: 10.4324/9781003170808-27

Les made that big theatrical machine feel like the inside of a young couple's apartment on the saddest day of their lives.

Les is remarkably kind while he works. He cares for the play and for the company with a wide-ranging and protective eye. He guides gently. This tenderness comes out despite his best efforts to remain caustic and British and hilariously sarcastic. He exudes a kind of prickly warmth that he battles against lest he become too maudlin. So he undercuts it at all times. But there is no mistaking his true feelings for his creative partners. This feeling of safety, of casual humor, of quiet appreciation even for the mistakes means that nothing is out of bounds for him. He has a wide embrace. This is not to say he is not discerning or rigorous. He knows how to steer you toward what he wants. But never ever have I seen or heard someone try something, no matter how raw or off-center, and feel vulnerable or bad after showing it to Les. It's that gift of patience.

About 10 years after *Eurydice*, Les and I worked together again on Anne Washburn's *10 out of 12* at Soho Rep in New York. It's a play essentially about a tech rehearsal of a play, one of the most tedious, patience-testing, unendurable phases of making a piece of theater. In fact, as theaters seek to create more humane work environments, 10 out of 12's may become a thing of the past. But this *10 out of 12* was one of the most holistic collaborations I have ever been a part of. The script of Anne's play stipulates that every audience member be given an ear piece. The dialog of the play takes place on two planes: the live actors performing on stage (playing actors in period costumes in the middle of a *10 out of 12*) and the actors performing over headset (playing technicians and designers commenting on the action on stage or doing their work or living their own dramas).

The project was a sound designer's dream: an ear piece for every audience member, half the script prerecorded, music that combined live performance, speakers, headsets, secret click tracks, hidden voice-over booths, and more than 800 sound cues. This required an incredibly complex coordination between me, Anne, Amanda Spooner – the Stage Manager, Sam Kusnetz – my associate, and Les (who had to wear an earpiece for all rehearsals in order to hear half the dialog). Each time the script changed, we had to make changes to our running sound design. It was like working on a recorded radio play and a live performance on stage at the same time. And, no surprise, it was like being in "tech" from the moment we began rehearsal until opening night.

This would have driven many directors mad. But not Les. Throughout rehearsals, while the cast was waiting for us in sound-land to make changes or adjustments, Les seemed always to be scanning the room for tableaux of actors in repose, or boredom, or eating a snack, or otherwise killing time. He would observe a person when they thought no one was watching. And just as Anne made the script by sitting in tech rehearsals for her other plays, writing down overheard scraps of dialogue, Les watched and listened to the company in moments of quiet and privacy and then recycled those stage pictures in the final production. And so a play about making plays was created out of the process of making that play.

Making any piece of theater with a group of strangers thrown together for a few weeks is difficult and paradoxical. It requires an ability to toggle back and forth between the public and the private all the time. Les makes you feel that every idea you have is valuable. And that makes people brave. He has an affinity for the private, the personal, the hidden-away in people while being driven by a great sense of showmanship. He loves a spectacle. He's not afraid of noise. But his plays often have long moments of quiet while a character simply exists on stage. He hears fragile, delicate, strange, and often overlooked frequencies. He encourages them. In fact, I would say he draws them out of all of us.

*   *   *   *   *

BRAY POOR is a sound designer and composer. His work has been heard on Broadway, Off-Broadway, and at numerous regional theaters around the country, including Actors Theatre of Louisville and Berkeley Rep. He has created sound designs and/or music for Les Waters's productions of Sarah Ruhl's Eurydice, In the Next Room, Dear Elizabeth, and For Peter Pan on her 70th Birthday, as well as his productions of Red, Luna Gale, Gnit, 10 out of 12, and Little Bunny Foo Foo. He earned an Obie for Sustained Excellence of Sound Design in 2016.

Learning to direct

I went to the University of Manchester to study English and Drama in 1971. Once there, I immediately dropped English. The Theatre Department had a studio space in a converted church. It was a good venue to rehearse and perform in. And we could put on our own shows. The faculty were supportive, but I don't remember any training at Manchester in being a director. We were left to our own devices to make theatre. I directed two Howard Brenton plays, *Magnificence* and *How Beautiful With Badges*, John Spurling's *In the Heart of the British Museum*, and Edward Bond's *The Sea*. I don't remember any faculty ever coming in and watching what I'd done and saying, "You know it would work better if you did this," or "It would be more interesting if you did that," or "Why are they where they are in this space?" or "Is this scene change part of the production or is it not?" I don't remember any of that kind of practical advice.

Where did I even know how to begin? I made it up. I read books about directors. There was an English theatre magazine, *Theatre Quarterly*, and it had long articles about theatres in Europe, and directors like Roger Planchon, who ran the Théâtre National Populaire, or Peter Stein and the Schaubühne in Berlin and his production of Ibsen's *Peer Gynt*. These articles had an enormous effect on me. Or I would look at *Plays and Players*, the monthly magazine, which would occasionally have articles or studies of a director working on a particular play and that's how I began to put it together. There was no grad school for directors. There was nowhere in England at that time. So, self-producing was the thing to do.

DOI: 10.4324/9781003170808-28

The year I graduated from Manchester, maybe it was the year after, I directed John Antrobus's *Captain Oates' Left Sock*, first produced at the Royal Court Theatre Upstairs in 1969. It is a play about an encounter group at a psychiatric clinic, and it had a large cast and a circle of chairs and people sat in the chairs and talked about themselves. I did it with a group of friends and colleagues from Manchester, and we performed it late at night at the Edinburgh fringe festival. And it was good fun to do. It was more than good fun. I'd left university, and what else was I going to do. My life was a mess, a complete mess. I broke up my first marriage to my childhood sweetheart, Gill, and times were turbulent. I lived in a village outside Cambridge with a close friend and his wife from high school. I worked in a factory that made soft drinks in Cambridge. I was a lost boy, completely lost. And directing gave me a focus.

I wanted to do more. Somebody from the Belfast Arts Festival had seen the show in Edinburgh and said, "If you want to do a show with us, bring another show, let us know." I had seen Nancy Meckler's production of Sam Shepard's *Action* at the Royal Court Upstairs and I had loved it. I found a copy of the play, and it has a cast of four sitting around a table and there's a Christmas tree, and a turkey, and a bucket, and a broom, and a fish, and it looked producible. We rehearsed it in Manchester, I think, in the converted church, and took it to the Belfast Arts Festival. By this point in time, the Royal Court had its hooks in me. This was the theatre that produced the kind of plays that I wanted to see in the kind of productions that made most sense to me.

Friday, August 28, 2020

Johanna Pfaelzer and Russell Champa come round for snacks and drinks and to pay homage to Gus. Johanna is the newly appointed (September 2019) Artistic Director of Berkeley Repertory Theatre, and Russell is a friend and lighting designer of shows such as *Eurydice* and *In the Next Room*. We eat and drink (socially distanced) and Gus rockets around the garden and begs for food and is as charming and slightly deranged as any other four-month-old puppy. We talk of family pets and childhoods and gardens, and I look at Johanna and think:

How cruel.
How cruel to be one of the many extraordinary people who took over the leadership of theatres in the 2018–19 season,
who had their first season with all the usual bumps and triumphs and miscalculations, who had planned their next season with more knowledge of their community and theatre and audience,
and now everything has stopped.
Not slowly eased to a halt but abruptly stopped.
Their theatres have closed their doors, they are empty.

What is a theatre if it is empty?
Is it even a theatre?
Of course, they will find a way to keep some of their staff on board, provide some work for some artists,

create something online for their audience,
but what is the role of an Artistic Director if they cannot say

DOI: 10.4324/9781003170808-29

"Come inside and see what we have made?"
What is a theatre if it cannot invite the community to engage in conversation, to challenge, and to debate?

Theatres are places of education, of discourse. Sites of encounter and knowledge. They are celebrations of the arts, palaces of pleasure. For many of us, going to theatres, concert halls, museums is more than a leisure activity, more than entertainment, visiting these public spaces is an integral part of urban life and contributes to its cohesion. Participating in the arts in any way nurtures democratic societies. Being at the theatre amongst others, witnessing the lives of others, is a crucial counterbalance to the relentless pressure of social isolation. Now in particular. Not only can theatre offer explorations and critiques of past and present social systems and cultures, but it can reveal visions of worlds to come, revelations of the possibilities of new futures.

And what will our new theatre be in response to the demands of We see you White American Theater?
How will we make an equitable theatre?
What will the role of a director be post-pandemic?
How will we lead rooms without taking up too much space?

I've never spiritually aligned myself with the image of the controlling director
(although I enjoy telling people what to do,
manipulating them through time and the frame,
as much as any director)
that's never held much attraction,
but I am trying to think imaginatively about new possibilities,
about new and more attentive listening,
listening with more intention about racial and economic justice.
The making of theatre is the invention of temporary communities.
How will I participate in this new landscape?

All of this I am thinking as we talk and eat and drink and watch Gus on a summer's night in Berkeley.

50 works of fiction that I love

Maybe in order. Maybe not.

Silence by Shusaku Endo
Moby Dick by Herman Melville
Disturbances in the Field by Lynne Sharon Schwartz
Woman at Point Zero by Nawal El Saadawi
Villette by Charlotte Brontë
The 392 by Ashley Hickson-Lovence
Lolly Willowes by Sylvia Townsend Warner
My Struggle by Karl Ove Knausgaard
The Half-Life by Jonathan Raymond
White Teeth by Zadie Smith
Invisible Man by Ralph Ellison
The Rings of Saturn by W. G. Sebald
Wolf Hall (the trilogy) by Hilary Mantel
Middlemarch by George Eliot
Great Expectations by Charles Dickens
The End of Eddy by Édouard Louis
Heat and Dust by Ruth Prawer Jhabvala
Briefing for a Descent into Hell by Doris Lessing
The Book of Disquiet by Fernando Pessoa
Madame Bovary by Gustave Flaubert
Independent People by Halldór Laxness
The Diary of a Country Priest by Georges Bernanos
My Year of Rest and Relaxation by Ottessa Moshfegh

DOI: 10.4324/9781003170808-30

There There by Tommy Orange
The Bloody Chamber by Angela Carter
A Kestrel for a Knave by Barry Hines
They Came Like Swallows by William Maxwell
A Little Life by Hanya Yanagihara
From the Hilltop by Toni Jensen
To the Lighthouse by Virginia Woolf
The Sun Also Rises by Ernest Hemingway
Then We Came to the End by Joshua Ferris
The Corpse Washer by Sinan Antoon
The Master by Colm Tóibín
The Tale of Genji by Murasaki Shikibu
Silence among the Weapons by John Arden
The Vegetarian by Han Kang
Waterland by Graham Swift
Annie John by Jamaica Kincaid
Ulysses by James Joyce
The Perfect Nanny by Leila Slimani
Agnes Grey by Anne Brontë
Mephisto by Klaus Mann
That They May Face the Rising Sun by John McGahern
The Buried Giant by Kazuo Ishiguro
The Buddha of Suburbia by Hanif Kureishi
The Lazarus Project by Aleksandar Hemon
The Third Life of Grange Copeland by Alice Walker
The Story of Lucy Gault by William Trevor
Upstate by James Wood

Some of these I read decades ago, and for various reasons, they have stuck. I read Lynne Sharon Schwartz's *Disturbances in the Field* in Feb of 1987 whilst working at Arena Stage in DC. Before the children were born. At the beginning of my American career, the start of my American life. I haven't looked at it since but the reading of it is firmly embraced by my memory as a book of significance.

> I think the hardest thing for anyone is accepting that other people are as real as you are. That's it. Not using them as tools, not using them as examples or things to get over or under. Just accepting that they are absolutely as real as you are.

> —Zadie Smith (2019)

"The Power of Contradiction"

Anne Kauffman

For me, what is extraordinary about Les as a director is his command of the theatrical gesture. He can go big and create large, intense theatrical events, and he can also go very, very small. He can put an actor's performance or a fraction of a moment under a microscope, or he can stand at the back of the theater and make a broad visual statement with a simplicity that gives it extraordinary impact. In my opinion, this juxtaposition is what his work is all about. But it's not just that. He displays the big and the small in an unusual way. He can use the smallest gesture to have a huge effect or he can use a huge, insane physical representation to point at something very small and pedestrian. It's this extraordinary talent that left a strong impression on me as his student. Now, as one of his colleagues, I remain in awe of it.

Les, I think, gets a kick out of contradiction, out of things colliding with one another, and out of revealing how contradictory and violent and insane and lacking in understanding of the world human beings are. This quality does not feel overwrought or overdetermined in his work. It's meticulous but effortless. He doesn't come at it with a torturous "This is the meaning of life in all its gravity, and I'm putting it onstage" attitude. It's more playful, more like an inside joke that Les shares with his audience. And the playfulness has a very particular undercurrent to it. It's sly, sort of wry. Like he's getting a kick out of pain. Not in a masochistic way at all. Well, actually, it might be slightly masochistic.

Juxtaposition, contradiction, opposites are things that I think about a lot in my own work because of Les's mentorship. From the moment I interviewed with him, I was struck by how Les treated me as a colleague rather than

DOI: 10.4324/9781003170808-31

a student. He was like that with everyone. More of a collaborator than a teacher. It was an empowering dynamic. It built confidence. There was a reciprocity in our education. He taught by sharing. He would share exercises and methods he had practiced at the Royal Court. We would experiment with a text, he himself was engaged with on some level. He was a practicing director first, a teacher second. Every time he shared something with us, or when he was critiquing our work, I could sense that his comments were based in something he was wrestling with himself. It felt very immediate. Like we were in this experiment together.

Maybe it had something to do with the fact that UCSD was the first time he had really taught full time. And it was graduate school. He wasn't necessarily teaching us basic skills so much as helping us to expand our creative practice. He had a way of leading with curiosity rather than objective knowledge. His particular curiosity involved approaching linear stories in nonlinear ways, pulling from various and unrelated sources to create layers and contradictions and depth in narratives that appear straightforward. I would say his curiosity also extended to his relationships and his work with his grad students.

There were two classes at UCSD that were especially impactful. One was a site-specific class that challenged our sense of what is possible theatrically and how we accessed imagery in our work. We worked on Heiner Müller's *MedeaMaterial*. We each chose a scene and then created a three-minute performance art piece around that piece of text. The goal was to dig into a particular image in the work that was provocative but simple and make a narrative from that image. I was exploring the image of burning flesh. I wore a leotard and tights that I cut holes in so I could expose fruit roll-ups that I put on top of my own skin. The fruit roll-ups were supposed to be burnt skin that I then started to peel and eat! We edited down the series of images first presented in class and performed them in various rooms and locations around a mansion that stood on an expansive piece of property. It was a powerful exercise in mining the underbelly of a story to create visceral theatrical imagery.

The other course, in fact, inspired the creation of our theater company started by my classmate Steve Cosson called The Civilians. The class was called "Joint Stock" and was based on a method of theater making and a company that began at London's Royal Court Theatre. The process began with picking a topic of interest, researching it, and then identifying subjects to interview with knowledge or experience of that topic. For our Joint Stock project at UCSD, the topic was the very, very rich and the very, very poor. Each member of the class had to identify at least one person to interview in the San Diego area. We did not record or take notes during the interviews.

We then returned to the group and delivered a monologue in which each of us would "play" the person we had interviewed – based on what we remembered from our interaction. Driven by what individuals found interesting and memorable, a character *based* on the real person but not actually representing that person would begin to emerge. At the end of each monologue, others were free to ask questions of the subject, and the one performing the monologue would answer based on their limited familiarity with the interviewee, thus continuing to develop the character.

When the process works well and the investigation of the topic proceeds without a predetermined goal, the collection of interviews can be used to build a narrative that is not what you might at first expect. Inevitably, connections, themes, and common emotional and psychological terrain pop up that often have nothing to do with the original topic. For *Gone Missing*, one of our most successful pieces for The Civilians, the company interviewed people about objects they had lost. It had to be a physical object, not something intangible like losing one's mind or losing one's faith. What started with a focus on the small and seemingly insignificant ended up as a piece about loneliness, longing, and the mechanics of memory both technically and emotionally. The piece ended up being quite epic and profound.

Les introduced us to this huge and radiant way of making work. There was a truthfulness to that approach that settled in my bones. It has to do with his effort to teach us to listen in a particular way. In the act of observing and absorbing how others create their own narratives, my perception of language and character was profoundly changed. It was liberating, fruitful, and allowed me to feel like I could make work with a particular kind of breadth and depth.

* * * * *

ANNE KAUFFMAN *is a director based in New York City known for her work with contemporary playwrights, including Amy Herzog, Lisa D'Amour, Jordan Harrison, Anne Washburn, Tracey Scott Wilson, among others. Her productions have been seen at many prominent Off-Broadway theaters, and she made her Broadway debut with Roundabout Theatre Company, where she is a Resident Director, on the revival of Scott McPherson's Marvin's Room. She is a founding member and associate artist of The Civilians. She co-created a directing fellowship with Clubbed Thumb where she is an Associate Artist. She has received numerous awards, including three Obies, a Lucille Lortel Award, and the Alan Schneider Director Award. She grew up in Arizona, majored in Slavic Language and Literature at Stanford University, and received her MFA in Directing from UC San Diego.*

"Inside and Outside"

Kathleen Chalfant

The most striking thing to me about being both a fan of Les's work and a colleague is how very different those experiences are. Les and I have been friends for 20 years and so I feel as though we've worked together many, many times. In fact, we've only done two plays together: Marguerite Duras' *Savannah Bay* in 2003 in which Les directed Marin Ireland and me and Sarah Ruhl's *For Peter Pan on her 70th Birthday* which we did together three times from 2015 to 2017. The plays had in common that they were about family and involved grandparents, but where *Savannah Bay* was meant to be opaque, *For Peter Pan* (except for the flying, of course) was meant to be accessible in a realistic way and a tribute by the playwright to her family.

The hallmark of Les as a director from the actor's point of view is that you don't notice that there is much directing going on. Les manages to convince the company that we are all setting off into the unknown together. I have never known a director who listens so much and speaks so little about what is going on. Marin Ireland recently reminded me that Les told us not to tell him or each other who we thought our characters were in *Savannah Bay*. His notion was that the text would reveal that. Or maybe not. In the end when we performed the play, the audience was equally divided between those people who were completely baffled and those people for whom the play was kitchen sink realism. The latter group, usually elderly European women, came back three and four times, often with their granddaughters in tow.

Les is very interested in silence on stage and how it makes the audience lean in. In both the plays we worked on together, the playwrights called for long silent periods. In *Savannah Bay*, at one point, Marin and I, wearing

DOI: 10.4324/9781003170808-32

our gorgeous red dresses, walked slowly around the nearly empty stage for I think five minutes – which is a very long time especially in a play that is only 65 minutes long. I don't remember what he told us, but I do remember walking and walking and walking in rehearsal and then previews until he told us we had it right and that's how we did it for the rest of the run. It was very scary because we are not taught "Don't just do something – stand there (or in our case walk there)" either in life or in acting school, but Les is very good at making you feel brave. He has a way of convincing you that if he says it's okay, then it is. In *For Peter Pan*, there are two silent periods that function in a much more traditional way to signal time passing. From the audience point of view that is made clear by the lights and the sound and things, but from the actors' point of view, it is still two long periods of not talking or anything. But he made us feel brave.

I just want to say a little more about the listening part. In *Savannah Bay*, there were only two of us and Les was a little more prescriptive about what we talked about, but in *For Peter Pan*, we were six people and a dog and while there were a couple of different versions of the cast, in every case, everyone had views about all sorts of things and like the characters in the play we talked a blue streak to and over each other and while we did that, Les mostly listened and now and again said one or two things that were always illuminating and then we'd all talk more about our families or Les's family or Sarah's family. There were all sorts of technical issues to do both with flying and, in a number of cases, the vagaries of stage dogs, so it sometimes felt a little chaotic. There were sword fights too and after one wound (I have a very fine scar to show for it), we switched to wooden swords, and on the dog issue, we finally realized that professional dogs were better than beloved amateurs. And Les solved all those kinds of outside problems – addressed them and solved them but still, for us, the play just seemed to take shape.

So that is the experience from the inside. But here is the great and wonderful mystery: when you see a play directed by Les, it is a beautifully sculpted shining work of art in which each element seems perfectly chosen and perfectly placed and inevitable. This is as true for deceptively simple incarnations like *Dana H.* as it is for wildly complex works like *10 out of 12* or *In the Next Room* or *The Thin Place*. I insist on that sense of the inevitable because Les's choices seem right and necessary and oh so satisfying. There is at least one moment in every play when you say "oh, he isn't going to do that, is he?" and at least one where you say "HOW did he do that?" and why does it make me so happy???? The plays are often funny and scary and baffling and infuriating all at the same time. What is on the stage seems dangerous and/or impossible, but it is done in such a way that you want to go on the trip wherever it is going. I read this description now and it sounds as though I am describing something "noisy," but the other thing that is always true when you see a play Les has directed is that you hear the writer. The text is what we are all riding on. In *10 out of 12*, for example, there were sometimes 14 people talking at once or at least that's how it seemed, and the thing was so beautifully orchestrated that you heard every word.

My favorite kind of acting is when you can't see how it is done or even that anything is being done – the two ways of experiencing Les as an artist fulfill that criterion – from the inside you can't tell what if anything is happening, and from the outside you only know something wonderful has been made but for the life of you, you can't tell how.

*   *   *   *   *

KATHLEEN CHALFANT *is an actor with a long and distinguished career on Broadway, Off-Broadway, in the regional theater, and in film and television. In 1993, she was nominated for a Tony Award for Best Actress in a Featured Role in a Play for* Angels in America: Millennium Approaches, *and in 1998, she earned multiple awards for her performance as Vivian Bearing, a scholar battling cancer, in Margaret Edson's* Wit. *She is a founding member of the Women's Project and sits on the boards of The Vineyard Theatre, Broadway Cares/Equity Fights Aids, and the advisory board of the New York Foundation for the Arts. She once said that "playing Ronald Reagan was the hardest thing I've ever done." In 2018, she received a special Obie Award for Lifetime Achievement.*

Actors and notes

What are the useful notes for a director to give to an actor? And when? How do you time notes? Which notes do you give right away and which ones do you save for later or back off from altogether? It's complicated.

As a director, your job is to focus and refocus what is happening in the rehearsal room from day to day. You're responding to the actors all the time, and you have to be able to say if what they are doing belongs in the world of the production you're making. Sometimes, I will say to actors, "I cannot hear it," which does not literally mean I cannot hear. It means that what they are doing is buried under stuff. Something that I think is important does not have the emphasis that it needs. It's getting lost. I could say I think you're moving around too much or it's too busy or I think you have to make this not that the focus of the scene or look at it this way or it's too emotional and your emotionality is telling me how I should feel and I think you should just tell it to me and I will feel whatever I am going to feel.

Not everybody rehearses at the same speed. Some actors are off book and have made valuable decisions before rehearsals start. Some suddenly pull it all together at the last moment. And some make huge strides in the beginning and then spin their wheels and cannot move forward. The timing of when you choose to talk to people is crucial. It has much to do with instinct. I have worked on shows where I felt that I should have talked to somebody earlier and didn't, or I did talk to them earlier and I fucked them up or made them self-conscious about what they were doing or they started acting in a way to please me. Sometimes, an actor will do a series of things in a rehearsal and I will say, "I don't like that" or some such words, and afterwards, I think,

DOI: 10.4324/9781003170808-33

"Oh god, what if I'm wrong?" or "What if they were developing something and I just stomped on their instinct in that moment?"

I am much more comfortable now saying, "Ignore what I said," or "Ignore bad direction," or "I am sorry, this is entirely my responsibility, I got this wrong, I got us all going in the wrong direction, I think we need to try this instead." As a young director, I would have been terrified to do that. As a young director, so much energy goes into trying to control the room. I have got better at it with experience, but boy, have I got it wrong in the past. Really wrong.

The list of films goes on . . .

The Passion of Joan of Arc (1928) – Carl Dreyer. Silence and the glory of Falconetti's face.

Au Hazard Balthazar (1966) – Robert Bresson. A donkey. Suffering. Godard said "this film is really the world in an hour and a half."

The Headless Woman (2008) – Lucrecia Martel

Wanda (1971) – Barbara Loden

My Life without Me (2003) – Isabel Coixet

Moonlight (2016) – Barry Jenkins. The beauty and strength of Mahershala Ali's face.

Apu Trilogy (1955–1959) – Satyajit Ray

Tokyo Story (1953) – Yasujiro Ozu. Generational conflict. Heartbreaking. What is that Italian term for effortlessness? Total command with no apparent effort? From Baldassare Castiglione's *The Book of the Courtier* (1528): " . . . a certain nonchalance, so as to conceal all art and make whatever one does or says appear to be without effort and almost any thought about it." The thing is that *Tokyo Story* is a film by Ozu shot in a very particular way and it is obviously directed by him but the control is so total that it is not asking for anyone's approval and it is almost as if whilst he was directing, he was also erasing himself. I think many of the films on this list have that quality. Some literature has it. Certainly Chekhov's short stories do. Caryl's *Far Away* has it.

DOI: 10.4324/9781003170808-34

Teorema (1968) – Pier Paolo Pasolini. The bourgeoisie and the divine. Transcendence and desolation. The beauty of the young Terence Stamp. I saw it when I was 19, and it has stuck.

Hunger (2008) – Steve McQueen

Safe (1995) – Todd Haynes. Julianne Moore and Julianne Moore.

An Angel at My Table (1990) – Jane Campion. Based on Janet Frame's autobiography. Poverty. Working-class life. How tired I am that depictions of middle-class life jam the airwaves? The shock of the movie is that the actors look like people. I am all for the beauty of actors but it's a distorting view of humanity. Kerry Fox's face.

Orlando (1992) – Sally Potter. Tilda and Quentin Crisp and Tilda and Sandy Powell's costumes and Tilda and Jimmy Somerville's voice and Tilda and Virginia Woolf.

Selma (2014) – Ava DuVernay. Crushing.

Beauty and the Beast (1946) – Jean Cocteau. The most beautiful of all films.

The Discreet Charm of the Bourgeoisie (1972) – Luis Bunuel. I must have seen this ten times. Essential viewing for directing comedy.

In the Mood for Love (2000) – Wong Kar-Wai

Boogie Nights (1997) – Paul Thomas Anderson

The Mourning Forest (2007) – Naomi Kawase

Henry Fool (1997) – Hal Hartley. The beauty of Thomas Jay Ryan's face.

The Birds (1963) – Alfred Hitchcock. How strange and perverse this is. How dramaturgically incorrect.

Uncle Boonmee Who Can Recall His Past Lives (2010) – Apichatpong Weerasethakul. I wish I had directed this.

How interesting and depressing to work in a medium (theatre) where there is no true record of the event. There's a script and sometimes photos taken for particular reasons and sometimes a recording but nothing equates the experience of the performance of the production. I used to think that was great. We perform. It's gone. There is only memory. Now I'm 68 and no longer such a fan of the transitory nature of things. Fuck the Clock! Thank you, Patti Smith.

13. *The Christians* at Mark Taper Forum (2015).

14. *Evocation to Visible Appearance* at Actors Theatre of Louisville (2018).

15. *A Doll's House, Part 2* at Berkeley Repertory Theatre (2018).

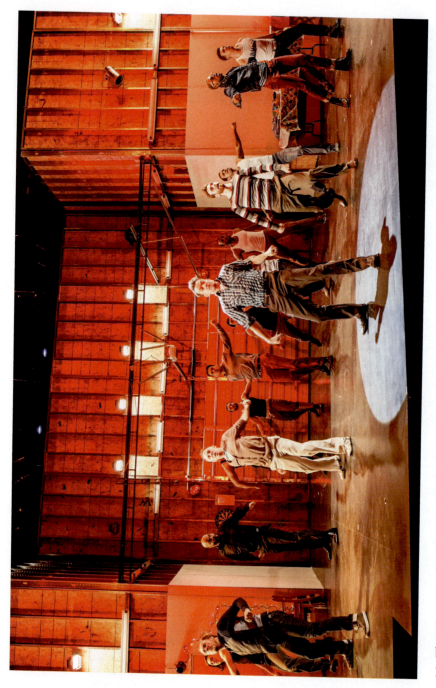

16. *The Glory of the World* at Actors Theatre of Louisville (2015).

Thin places

My mother's family in Lincolnshire were farm laborers, sometimes servants in the big house, very Methodist, and deeply superstitious. You couldn't bring certain flowers into the house at certain times of year. You couldn't cut your toenails on a Sunday or the devil would get you. A spirit of some sort called Raw Head and Bloody Bones lived under the stairs in my grandparents' house. The Wesley brothers who founded British Methodism were from Epworth near Scunthorpe where I was brought up. Methodism was very strong in my family. I spent a lot of time with my maternal grandparents growing up. I remember them as storytellers. They were first-generation town dwellers and would tell stories of what it was like in the village where they were born. I thought they were living history.

My Grandma Carrie would talk about thin places. I am an only child but I am the youngest and the smallest – I stand at 6′ 2″ now – of four male cousins. I was the little one, the baby. We never really knew what the term meant, and it was probably her way of keeping us in line but there were these thin places and she would warn, "Leslie, if you go there, you're going to be in trouble." A thin place is where the membrane or boundary between this world and some other world – I have often mistakenly said between this world and the next world but it definitely wasn't the next world – is very thin. And you could slip between one and the other. There was a thin place in a field close to the village where my grandparents were born – Kirmington, Lincolnshire. It has a population of about 300. We were told to keep away from there because it was dangerous. And why it

DOI: 10.4324/9781003170808-35

was, I don't know. Maybe somebody disappeared there a hundred years ago. I don't know. I have no information.

I lived the first 18 years of my life at 30 Lincoln Gardens in Scunthorpe. And at the corner of Lincoln Gardens and Laburnum Grove, there is a tree. Not a big tree. A medium-sized rather scrappy looking tree. And that tree, for years I believed, walks at night. I sound like a Thomas Hardy novel when I talk about this. But that tree walks at night and it's not wise to walk by that tree late at night.

It made an impression on me as a child. These places where you could walk through and be in some other world. But what horrified me as a child is that something from that other world could pass through into this one and grab me and take me back. What the other world was I don't know. At one point, I imagined it as a thick wet fog. I was worried by thin places as a kid, and then I forgot about it or it turned into yet another strange story about my mother's family's rural life.

When we were workshopping *Dana H.* at the Goodman, Lucas said he wanted the play to change gears very suddenly, for something to happen that was unexpected that shifted the play into different territory. And I said, "Oh, it sounds like a thin place." I explained it to him. And he thought it was an interesting title for a play, and then there was a play called *The Thin Place.*

Do I experience it personally? Thin Places? I don't know. In some way, it may be tied to my epilepsy. Or is it a way for me to visualize my epilepsy? I don't know what happens to me during a seizure. I have no memory of the event. Or when I have a memory of it, is it because I am reconstructing something that other people have told me? Am I unconscious during a seizure or am I in some other consciousness? I have a notion that I've gone somewhere else. But I have no knowledge of where that somewhere else is. I have gaps in my memory that are bigger than the actual event. The seizure could be only two or three minutes long, but it may eradicate several hours of memory. So, there could be a three-hour gap, and then I find myself sitting in a chair having a cup of tea, talking to people, telling them I'm all right, asking can they get me home, and I have a terrible headache and do they have something for it.

And everything else has been erased. Or rather there's a very, very faint blur of the experience somewhere. As if I had drawn or written out the experience on a sheet of paper, and then I or my rogue neurology had erased it. Maybe this is what attracts me to Rauschenberg's "Erased de Kooning Drawing" in San Francisco Museum of Modern Art. Rauschenberg asked the Abstract

Expressionist painter Willem de Kooning – near the height of his fame – for a drawing, and then he erased it and put it in a gilded frame. I could look at it for hours. For hours. I am fascinated by the traces of things. I find the idea of destroying something – the idea that the destruction of one thing is the act of making something else – profoundly interesting. Its blankness is compelling.

Max and the Royal Court

I began my career – I hate the word "career" – at the place where I wanted to work. The Royal Court Theatre. What are the chances of that? I was incredibly fortunate.

At University, I saw Bill Gaskill's production at the Court of Edward Bond's *The Sea* and thought it was amazing. When I read the plays that came out of there – Caryl's plays, Howard Brenton's plays – they made sense to me. So, I started writing to the Court when I was at college. After college, I wrote to them again. I wrote to Max Stafford-Clark and to Stuart Burge, the then artistic director. I have no idea what I wrote. It was just a fan letter, I suppose. My first job at the Court was assistant director to Charles Marowitz on Peter Barnes' play *Laughter*. I was taken on for just that show, but I went from that to assisting Max on *Cloud 9*. I stayed for three-and-a-half or four years. It was an amazing period for me.

I was happy there and very unhappy there. It had glamour – drinks with Jack Nicholson, bumping into Ingrid Bergman at the stage door, being publicly insulted by John Osborne in the newspaper, standing next to Beckett at the theatre's lunch bar, watching from the booth David Bowie watching my production of Shepard's *Seduced*. All the glitter you could ever want. What I loved most about being there was that it felt as if I had landed in the center of the theatre universe. If that happens to you when you are young, it's fantastic. I remember the absolute delight of sitting in the middle of the dress circle watching the first preview of some new production.

DOI: 10.4324/9781003170808-36

The Court believed that the way they did things was the only way they should be done. A magic certainty. No hesitation. No doubt. And that was great. And great to be embraced by that community of artists. On the other hand, I was out of my depth. I didn't have any real training. I was an undergraduate at the University of Manchester between 1971 and 1974. 1971 was really the tail end of the 1960s, so there was deep suspicion of educational institutions. I don't remember ever taking a course in directing. And somehow, I ended up in my 20s at the Royal Court making work with these swanky and very talented people and thinking, "I don't know how I got here. I feel like a fraud because I am being given opportunities to do stuff that I don't really know how to do." It was both exhilarating and terrifying.

Leaving the Royal Court was bad. Traumatic. Max used to say that I walked out and I would say that he fired me.

Sometimes when I am directing, I talk with Max in my head. And sometimes when I am stuck, I think, "What would Max do? What would Max do in this situation?" And that's helpful. That's why you have mentors. But a time comes when you have to get the mentor's voice out of your head. I was under his shadow for a long time. Eventually, that began to change. One night after rehearsals with the American cast of *Fen* at the Public I found myself thinking, "Oh, I feel a bit more like myself." That was a sign that I was beginning to shuffle him off.

Then, in 1989, I was in Los Angeles working at the Mark Taper Forum on Timberlake Wertenbaker's *Our Country's Good*. The Taper wanted to produce the play but they wanted the original director who was Max but Max wasn't fully available so Max reached out to me – he and I were talking at that point – and I went to LA and I cast the play and I rehearsed for the first three weeks and then Max arrived for the last week of rehearsals, tech, and the first couple of previews, and then he left. A crazy way to rehearse. When Max arrived and took over, I remember watching and thinking, "Oh, I am really not him." So, by that time something had changed. I no longer felt like a junior version of Max. I didn't feel overwhelmed by him both professionally and personally. I felt I owned my identity as a director.

Ten key productions for me

Marie and Bruce by Wallace Shawn, Theatre Upstairs, Royal Court Theatre, London, 1979.
My first professional production. I was 27. Aggressive, confrontational, fun, despairing. My first trip to the States to meet Wally. Probably, the show was cultural tourism but it marks a beginning and a collaboration with a major writer at a very important theatre.

Three More Sleepless Nights by Caryl Churchill, Soho Theatre, London, 1980. First collaboration with Caryl, although I was the assistant director on the world premiere of *Cloud 9*. Beginning of fascination/obsession with silence/tension/compression on stage. The question for me is always "how little do you need?" The architect John Pawson says, "Minimalism is not defined by what is not there but by the rightness of what is and the richness with which this is experienced." How does one judge this?

Fen by Caryl Churchill, Joint Stock Theatre Group, UK, 1983.
I can't write, don't write, and most importantly don't need to write, but I feel as if I wrote this. My mother's life on stage. My mother wasn't an agricultural farm worker and as far as I know, she didn't have a lover and she certainly wasn't murdered. However, this is my mother's life. The glory of creating over a long period of time. A total commitment from all involved to the work. Came after the split from Max Stafford-Clark and the Royal Court, so an intense need to prove myself. British production came to the Public Theater. And then began my American life.

DOI: 10.4324/9781003170808-37

A Mouthful of Birds by Caryl Churchill and David Lan, Joint Stock Theatre Group, UK, 1986.
A miserable experience. Failure. David Lan writes about it in his recent memoir *As If by Chance*. All my fault. One of the things that Methodism teaches is that if anything goes wrong, it is your fault. This one is all my fault. I still dream about it. Guilt. Humiliation.

Big Love by Chuck Mee, Humana Festival of New American Plays, Louisville, 2000.
Realism and spectacle. The big and the little. Creating work that gets at the nervous system before the heart and the intellect. Learning from Chuck principles of collage. A great company. The explosive choreography of Jean Isaacs. Annie Smart's squishy set. On the road with this one – Berkeley Rep, Long Wharf, Goodman Theatre, Next Wave Festival at BAM.

Eurydice by Sarah Ruhl, Berkeley Rep, 2003.
First collaboration with Sarah. Everything was exactly as it should be. Not straining, not trying to be, just being. An extraordinary group of designers and stage managers and actors lead by a fearless Maria Dizzia. A production designed to fuck you over and then fuck you up.

The Glory of the World by Chuck Mee, Humana Festival of New American Plays, Louisville, 2015, and then at BAM, 2016.
When I took over ATL, I said I wanted to make work *about* Louisville. Now I would say that I wanted to make work *for* and *by* Louisville. But this production was about Louisville and faith and spirituality via Thomas Merton. I wanted to create an event. I wanted to direct myself into the production. To create a holy noise and celebrate Thomas Merton. Meditation and NOISE. A very strong desire to overwhelm an audience with too many images and too much event and too much maleness. I'm hugely indebted to Barney O'Hanlon (choreography) and Ryan Bourque (fight direction) and the guys in the company for making this. It's also a love letter to my friends, Andrew Garman, Bruce McKenzie, and Conrad Schott for supporting and caring for me. Too many epileptic seizures on this one.

10 out of 12 by Anne Washburn, Soho Rep, NYC, 2016.
One of the best plays about work that I know. What are the others? Arnold Wesker's *The Kitchen*. What else? Anyway, this one is about technical rehearsal. The work the audience never gets to see. A hymn to the absolute beauty and total idiocy of making theatre. Brave. Unique. Ridiculous.

The Christians by Lucas Hnath, Humana Festival of New American Plays, Louisville, 201?

Was it 2014? 2015? Louisville is so blurry for me. It was in many ways a very rough emotional time. A lot of ghosts, a lot of seizures, too much distance, too much pain. Many times, I felt as if I had lost my skin and my nerve endings were hanging out, fully exposed. The work was very personal and uplifting but a price was paid. I had a religious upbringing for a while. Not the same as Lucas but it was religious and I'm interested in faith and would like to have faith but that is not going to happen. It felt like talking to Louisville, which seems to me a faith-based community. Extraordinary conversations in the lobby after performances. A performance as public event. I remember, it was 2014.

Dana H. by Lucas Hnath, Kirk Douglas Theatre, Los Angeles, 2019.

Concentration and reduction at a cruel compressed level. Both simple and complex. Uncompromising. Virtuoso acting by Didi O'Connell lip syncing to Lucas' mother's voice. Nothing is there and everything is there. Directing with one's hands tied. The most controlled piece I have ever directed and also the wildest. Rigor and a ferocious discipline and beneath that a sense that everything is about to fuck up and people will be hurt.

"Les Waters at the Royal Court"

Rob Ritchie

"Everyone from the Royal Court get into the back room!"

It's a raw April night in 1982. The owner of the Alibi club, a cramped watering-hole near the Royal Court theatre in London, is losing his cool with the cast and crew of *Not Quite Jerusalem*. Paul Kember's comedy about four English 20-somethings on a kibbutz premiered at the Court two years ago but is being revived in an attempt to transform a solid success into a sell-out hit. The director charged with this task – and the director of the original production – is Les Waters. Having staggered through rehearsals with a painfully bruised big toe, Les is doubtless wondering if his destiny is to spend the rest of his life directing the same play. Not Quite Over Yet. More pressingly, on the matter of the big toe, he is discovering that a mix of vodka, champagne, and painkillers is a gateway to the kind of grinning abandon that annoys nightclub owners.

I think we were thrown out. It's a long time ago. You could smoke on the Underground.

Manchester, 1971. I first met Les when we both enrolled as drama students at Manchester University. He was wearing an Afghan coat and dungarees. "Hippie. Cleethorpes." would be a suitable caption, except few people know where Cleethorpes is or what happens to people who are born there. [They move to Scunthorpe, 25 miles away. Read *Fen* if you want a fuller sense of the options.] Les wanted to be a director and spent the three-year course directing as many contemporary plays as he could persuade his fellow students to rehearse. Several – Howard Brenton's *Magnificence*, Edward Bond's *The*

DOI: 10.4324/9781003170808-38

Sea – were plays recently premiered at the Royal Court. Les had a crush on the Court.

Unless I missed the memo, there was no formal training in directing at Manchester. Les simply sat on the floor, hugging his knees, making the occasional suggestion. "You look depressed," he would say to an actor, looking depressed, or "Try it standing up." He never did any acting to illustrate what he was after. He wasn't a show-off. If you've worked with Les you'll know he sometimes makes a face, a pantomime of jaw-dropping astonishment. It's as if, being very tall himself, he's just noticed everyone else is short. I hope that face has survived the acquisition of The Beard. Things always got interesting when the jaw dropping started. Whatever it was he was trying to convey – shock, outrage, confusion, amazement – words alone wouldn't do the job. Theatre wasn't just about dialogue. There had to be image, music, dancers.

His big break came when Max Stafford-Clark – co-founder of Joint Stock and soon to be artistic director of the Court – hired Les as an assistant director. Joint Stock was a highly regarded touring company that shared the Court's passion for new plays but evolved a different way of creating them. Actors, writer, and director would workshop a subject – sex for example – the writer would digest the experience and write a play, the company would reconvene, rehearse, and tour the result. Les was assistant director for the original production of Caryl Churchill's *Cloud Nine*, an iconic play about sex, gender, and colonialism, and co-directed the revival. It would be hard to overestimate the impact Max and Caryl had on Les's career. Max became mentor and Caryl a regular collaborator and confidante. Somewhere along the line, thanks to a tip-off from Les, I got hired as the Court's Literary Manager. The brief was to find new plays and new writers. The roll call of trainee directors joining the hunt was impressive: Roger Michell, Antonia Bird, Danny Boyle, Simon Curtis. Unlike Les, they all moved on from the Court to work in film and television.

Before making his main stage debut with *Not Quite Jerusalem*, Les had to prove his talent directing shows in the studio space – the 80-seat Theatre Upstairs. To do that he needed a play. When *Cloud Nine* played in New York, someone – was it Les? – saw or read Wallace Shawn's *Marie and Bruce*, a dark comedy about a married couple trapped in mutual loathing. Scale, tone, and theme were perfect for the Theatre Upstairs. The play went into rehearsal a month or two after Margaret Thatcher shot to global fame as the first British Prime Minister to carry a handbag. [I know, Gladstone had a bag, but it was more a modified suitcase.] No one thought Thatcher would last. A few foresaw urban riots; Howard Brenton was planning a scathing satire, but no one predicted the Falklands war. For Les – or *"Less"* as Wally and most of North America pronounced it – there was the nagging thought that as the nation lurched to the right nobody would be going to the theatre. The fear proved unfounded. It turned out Wally had a cult following thanks to the simulated orgy in his previous play, *A Thought in Three Parts*. Directed by Max for Joint Stock, the production's attention to detail – yes, they were completely naked – prompted a visit from the police that ensured Wally's latest effort would be greeted by something of a rush for front row seats.

One of the actors in *Marie and Bruce* was Paul Kember. He'd written *Not Quite Jerusalem* on spec, inspired by his experience of volunteering on a kibbutz. The play nailed all that's truly awful about the Brits abroad. Since the Court usually did plays about how awful the Brits were at home the change of location and weather was refreshing. After much discussion, it was decided to give the play a rehearsed reading. Public readings were often regarded as a graveyard for dead and dying plays, especially if there was an audience discussion afterwards. People felt entitled to put the boot in or make insane suggestions. ["Maybe you should set it on a pirate ship?"] Paul was having none of that. He worked with Les on rewrites and revisions, a cast was assembled, and the reading revealed something that had been missed. *Not Quite Jerusalem* wasn't just funny, it was *really* funny. It was agreed the play should have a full production with Les directing. The only outstanding issue was where: upstairs or down?

Before this was resolved – how much money are you prepared to lose was the basic question – Les directed a second American play in the studio space. Sam Shepard's *Seduced* was the story of a dying American icon, a Howard Hughes-like recluse whose wealth has driven him mad. Shepard had had a spell living in London and had several plays produced at the Court. He was in a sense a local writer. With limited funds and a fresh round of cuts on the way – the Arts Council was actively considering closing the Court – some argued he wasn't local enough. New British writers should take priority. No one was shouting at Les in the street: "If you like American plays so much, why don't you go and live there!" Nor did he shout back: "You want me to direct your play? Write a better play!" But there was a feeling the Court had been failing in its core business of finding new voices and letting them sing.

To remedy this, Max encouraged directors to think like producers and come up with ideas for plays and writers who might write them. The commissioning system was overhauled, writers' fees increased, and a new rule imposed: a play would only be commissioned if there was a director attached. This was to ensure the cupboard wasn't filled with plays nobody wanted to direct.

The approach eventually led to a run of plays on topical issues: immigration, police corruption, the Falklands war, city traders, the Yorkshire Ripper. Some began with a workshop, one had an underlying book, others were developed in a more conventional way. Les worked with writer Louise Page on a play about old people. This became *Salonika*, the story of an 80-year-old widow who visits the beach in Greece where her husband was killed in World War 1. Scheduling problems meant the play was eventually directed by Danny Boyle, but he inherited a script that would have one critic reaching for superlatives. The appearance of the husband's ghost, playwright David Edgar wrote, "was the greatest entrance in post-war drama."

Les has often said a director doesn't just interpret a new play; they collaborate in its creation. That's the fun part. This way of thinking has its roots in Joint Stock, and some regarded it with suspicion. "Plays written by committee" was the usual charge. This doesn't survive scrutiny. There was nothing in the *Cloud Nine* workshop about colonial Africa, the setting for the opening act. That was Caryl's invention. The legendary writers agent Peggy Ramsay used to claim she could spot a commissioned play a mile off. There was something manufactured about it. "Obviously a *commission*," she would say as she left the first night of the latest production. "He had no reason to write the play except you asked him to." Peggy had a romantic view of writers. If they had a play in them, it would get written. It was pointless trying to accelerate the process by offering commissions. That's just television.

Not Quite Jerusalem finally opened on the main stage on a windy December night in 1980. Like most theatres, First Nights at the Court are a tense, nervous affair. Few directors sit in the front row of the circle beaming with pride. If they do, they are either heavily medicated or have found the key to the drinks cabinet. Les was a lurker, occasionally peering at the stage from behind a curtain before wandering the foyers with a wholly bogus sense of purpose. I like to think he was remembering his teenage years when he used to hitchhike from Scunthorpe to London to see plays at the Court. After the show, he would sleep on the platform at Euston station before hitching a ride home – a 360-mile round trip. Imagine being in a truck for three and a half hours trying to explain to a lonely haulier who Edward Bond was. ["What? They stone a baby to *death!*"] Surely, this commitment would be rewarded. It was. Paul got the Most Promising Playwright Award and sold the film rights for a screen adaptation that appeared five years later; the actors attracted a lot of flattering adjectives; and Les – well Les got to do it all over again two years later. With a bruised toe.

A successful first play doesn't make it any easier to write a second. The same is true of directing. Until you've directed a play on the main stage of the Court, you don't really know what a tricky space it is. Les's second production on the main stage was a British play about Americans: *Insignificance*, Terry Johnson's imagined encounter between Einstein, Marilyn Monroe, and Joe DiMaggio. I bumped into Terry in a pub toilet and, like two spies bungling a handover of secret information, he gave me a copy of the play. I read it, was impressed, and immediately gave it to Les. He'd given Howard Hughes a thorough workout in *Seduced*, Marilyn Monroe demonstrating the Theory of Relativity would be a doddle. Marilyn was played by Australian actress Judy Davis, recent winner of the Best Actress BAFTA for her performance in *My Brilliant Career*. She had stage experience: she had starred opposite Mel Gibson in *Romeo and Juliet*. And now, she paid her own air fare to fly to London to play Marilyn. For obvious reasons, there was no question of an audition. It was a blind date.

Which didn't go well. Actress and director didn't get on. By the final week of rehearsals, Les was looking like a captured partisan about to be shot. Judy Davis announced she was having the worst time of her life. She would stay for the previews but then wanted to go home. The stage crew were in open revolt. It was horrible. Max took over rehearsals and steadied the ship. When the play opened to enthusiastic reviews, there was no evidence of the turmoil that attended its production. Terry was nominated for Most Promising Playwright, the film rights for *Insignificance* were bought by Nicolas Roeg – the film was made and released in 1985, the same year as the film of *Not Quite Jerusalem* – and Judy Davis was nominated for an Olivier Award.

No harm done? Not quite. The immediate casualty was Les's relationship with Max. Les needed a show of support and a shot of confidence from his mentor. He didn't get it. Max told him he would have to remove him from the next play he was slated to direct. Les said if that happened, he would leave.

And that was it. It's hard, at this distance, to convey how devastating the break with Max was for Les. Max was brilliant at giving young talent opportunity and, in exchange for commitment, responsibility. Les had risen from Assistant Director to Associate Director – effectively Max's deputy – in rapid time. At the Court back then, you could burn brightly but you could also burn up fast.

Les didn't immediately pack his bags and head for the hills. Instead, he headed for the flatlands of Lincolnshire with Caryl Churchill to begin researching what would become *Fen*. The play was created in the usual Joint

Stock way: writer, director, and – a new departure – designer [Annie Smart, Les's partner] went with a company of actors to live in the Fens. The play was written in response to the people met, the stories and experiences shared. The production at the newly converted Almeida Theatre was wonderful. Les hadn't finished with the Royal Court. He would return with *A Mouthful of Birds*, a collaboration with Caryl, writer David Lan, and choreographer Ian Spink [yes, the dancers finally turned up]. And he directed another Caryl Churchill play *The Skriker* at the National Theatre. Les made his American debut when Joseph Papp brought *Fen* to New York. Many British directors head for New York or LA to see what they can do there. Some are frequent visitors. Les stayed.

When I think of Les's work in London, I always think of *Fen*. It has a double jaw-dropping moment that elicited screams on the first night. Not the axe-murder scene. That was like being punched in the face by somebody you've just met. It got gasps and one very audible "Oh my God . . . " The screams were a different matter. The screams were at the sudden appearance of the victim's ghost, seconds after the body was locked in the wardrobe. A proper *coup de théâtre*. A moment beyond words.

*   *   *   *   *

ROB RITCHIE is a screenwriter and script consultant who was the first ever full-time literary manager at the Royal Court Theatre. After leaving the Court, he wrote and developed film and television projects for Channel 4 Television and the BBC before becoming Head of Screenwriting at the National Film and Television School and a visiting tutor at the University of East Anglia. He has devised and run writing workshops and seminars around the UK and in Europe, the Middle East, India, Nigeria, and New Zealand. He is the author of The Joint Stock Book: The Making of a Theatre Collective.

Off a cliff

My desire to go into the theatre was a mystery to my parents. I don't ever remember discussing it with them. I do remember saying that I wanted to go to university to study Drama and English. I am one of those typical working-class kids from the north of England who wanted to leave their small town and go somewhere else, somewhere exciting. I just wanted to get out. I wanted to go to London from a very young age. Access to the arts in my home town was limited. My parents were avid readers. They were supporters of the local library. But they did not take me to the theatre as a child. There was no tradition of theatre going in my family. My dad was a steelworker and my mum was a stay-at-home mother. Money was very tight. Financial insecurity was a major issue in my childhood, as it was for most working-class people in the 50s and 60s.

The first professional production of mine that my parents saw was Wally Shawn's *Marie and Bruce* at the Royal Court Theatre. My parents didn't swear. And there's a lot of profanity in that play. So to them it was as if I had lured them to a high place and then pushed them off a cliff. They came to other productions. Not a lot. And they didn't say much about them. My Mum was very upset by Caryl Churchill's *Fen* because she thought I spilled the beans about her family. Lots of the women in my mother's family were agricultural workers. And there were things in the play that my grandmother and mother had said. Actual statements. She was upset and angry. It was a betrayal.

I think they were proud of me. I didn't talk to them about what I did. I kept it very separate. I feared my parents' disapproval quite strongly, and I

DOI: 10.4324/9781003170808-39

protected myself from that disapproval by not telling them about the work. Silence was a weapon in my parental home. Sometimes, I think all my work is an attempt to get my father's approval. My father was not harsh. Far from it. He was loving and kind and gentle. He was a good man. But I needed his approval. My father was particularly adept at making things. He built an extension to the house, he could mend a car engine, he painted surprisingly delicate flowers on wooden furniture. I am useless. I can't drive. I can't swim. I can't ride a bike.

Kafka writes in his "Letter to his Father,"

> Sometimes I imagine the map of the world spread out and you stretched diagonally across it. And I feel as if I could consider living in only those regions that either are not covered by you or not within your reach. And, in keeping with the conception I have of your magnitude, these are not many and not very comforting regions.

"Diary: *Top Girls* in Tokyo, 1992"

Les Waters

[Editor's note: *Top Girls* is one of Caryl Churchill's most important and most influential plays. The action centers on the character of Marlene, an ambitious businesswoman in the early days of Thatcherite Britain who receives a promotion at the London employment agency for women where she works. The play continued Churchill's innovations – radical 40 years ago – with dramatic form. The all-female cast plays multiple roles. The third act takes place a year before the first two. Lines of dialogue often include a '/' mid-line to indicate when the next line should begin, generating overlap in speaking. And the play combines scenes of family and workplace realism in the second and third acts with a first-act dinner party to celebrate Marlene's promotion attended by notable female figures drawn from history, art, and literature.

Top Girls premiered at the Royal Court Theatre on August 28, 1982, directed by Max Stafford-Clark. Ten years later, Les Waters had the opportunity to direct the play in Tokyo with a Japanese cast at a new performing arts complex called the Tokyo Metropolitan Theatre. The contract provided a fee of 12,000 pounds (the equivalent of roughly $40,000 today), a 10,000 yen per diem ($150 per day today), hotel accommodation, and business class airfare for two round trips London-Tokyo, an August 1992 trip for pre-production planning and then the rehearsal period in the fall.

What follows are excerpts from the diary that Waters kept to chronicle the process. As he explains:

> This is the only time I made any record of a day-to-day rehearsal process. In the past, I have made notes/fragments about the preparation/

DOI: 10.4324/9781003170808-40

rehearsing of various productions but nothing substantial. Direct-ing Caryl Churchill's *Top Girls* in Tokyo and in Japanese seemed an occasion of some note and worth recording. I wrote every night about the process with no thought of this ever being read. In 1992, I was 40 and a different person.

Anything in parentheses below has been written by Waters in retro-spect from the vantage point of 2021 and added to diary text solely for clarification.]

*   *   *   *   *

TOKYO DIARY 1992

AUGUST 20
Fly to Tokyo

AUGUST 21
Visit Tokyo Metropolitan Theatre. 1st meeting with Mr Kuramoto, set de-signer. A series of floating platforms + expanding walls. The rural scenes are too rural + woodsy. The theatre seats 800. The proscenium is v. high. Not particularly good acoustics. Usually houses musicals.

Meet Ms Shiraishi (Muse of Tadashi Suzuki. Genius.) – to play Dull Gret/ Angie.
Meet Ms Adaichi – translator (of the play).

AUGUST 22
Meet Ms Matsukane – Waitress/Kit/Shona.

1st meeting with Ms Ito, costume designer. The research is good but she wants all the costumes of the first scene, except Marlene, to be beige or variants of beige. Office workers blue and interviewees orange. It's hard to visualize it for the 1st scene. Will they (the dinner guests) appear to be dead or will it just seem remote + flat.

Work on translation (4 hours).

(The first scene of *Top Girls* is a dinner party hosted by Marlene, a success-ful businesswoman, to celebrate a recent promotion. The guests are Isabella Bird, a nineteenth-century writer and explorer; Lady Nijo, a thirteenth-century concubine who became a wandering nun after she fell out of favour at the Imperial Court; Dull Gret, the subject of a painting by Pieter Brue-ghel the Elder; Pope Joan, a woman who disguised herself as a man and was appointed Pope in the ninth century; and Patient Griselda, a character from Chaucer's *The Canterbury Tales*.)

AUGUST 23
In a park that runs by the side of the Imperial Palace, a man catching enormous crickets (?) with a net + his tiny son putting them in a small green plastic cage. Some beautiful ponds full of carp.

Work on translation (7 hours).

AUGUST 24
Meet Ms Tane – Pope Joan/Louise. Work on translation (7 hours).

AUGUST 25
Production meeting. Set design now v. spare and elegant. A diamond floating platform with moveable walls. To be decided colour of floor + walls. Both Mr Takahashi (sound) and Mr Sawada (lighting) have worked with (British theatre director) David Leveaux on *Elida*. Mr Yano (production manager) suggests I consult David re tech etc. Situation re Ms Ito – will consider use of colour in 1st scene – if she doesn't like it, won't do it.

Meet Ms Buncho – Lady Nijo/Win.
Meet Ms Han (Star) – Marlene.

AUGUST 26
Meet Ms Midori (Star) – Isabella Bird/Joyce/Mrs Kidd.
Meet Ms Shiota –Patient Griselda/Nell/Jeanine.

Work on translation (6 hours). Endless misunderstandings of tone and of terms. 'Pissed' in English/'Pissed' in the US. What is a 'flying picket?'

AUGUST 27
No Ms Ito. She's still thinking it over + will do it if she thinks she can do a good job in colour. If you ask me, she's overcommitted.

AUGUST 28
Fly home.

OCTOBER 9
Fly to Tokyo.

OCTOBER 10
I'm in a single-cell room but can move to a Twin on the 25th.

(Staying at Hotel Edmont. At 6'3", I am much longer than many Japanese mattresses so I sleep on the bedroom floor for the next 2 weeks.)

OCTOBER 11

Design meeting. Ms Ito – Some colour in 1st scene. Win and Nell costumes to be changed. Took some explaining of their status + they're not little girls. I don't think Ms Ito understands character. Mr Sasabe (one of the producers) looks relieved there isn't a bloodbath.

The set is to be a deep red, if they can produce that in Japan. Why not? Sadly, the rake has to go for reasons of economy.

(I never understood why this particular deep red was problematic in Japan.)

OCTOBER 12

1st readthrough. Everybody nervous. Photos first – company, company + me – those awful cheesy group photos with director seated centre + 2 kneeling actors gazing up at him. Who are these for? Then, me on my own I'm sure looking like a X between Nosferatu and a terrified rabbit. Ms Han's + somebody else's manager are there. I'd been warned the readthrough would take an age with many pauses for sensitive, 'wet' reactions but it's not too bad. Ms Midori obviously wants to suffer but is a rather sprightly Isabella Bird. And I can understand it even following in the Methuen edition. The readthrough takes a time to get going as the /'s aren't understood. I make a little speech about England since 1945 and Thatcherism. I feel quite pleased with it and it's met with polite indifference.

(Thatcherism amounted to a systematic rejection of significant post-war achievements – the welfare state, trade unionism, nationalized industry, and a closely regulated British economy. A brutal assault on working class identity.)

(The script I used had the size and heft of the Gutenberg Bible. Each page split into three – Japanese, English, and phonetics. Like a musical score. Over time, I slowly began to identify some of the cultural differences, misunderstandings. I could hear it rather than understand it. As if someone was 'singing' the text off key, flat.)

OCTOBER 13

We start to read through the script stopping to ask questions.

Mr Yano takes me, Ms Takahashi (my interpreter and a truly wonderful person – on call 24 hours a day, 7 days a week) + the crew for dinner. A small restaurant tucked away in an alley + I'm sure is in no tourist guide. Yano is a fisherman + says this is the place to get the best fish so we have raw sliced mackerel, huge platters of oysters, grilled head of mackerel + a great tureen cooked at the table of meat broth into which go golden mushrooms, more mushrooms, tofu, chives, cress, lettuce. And *lots* of saki. Y drinks in the fish market at 8 in the morning. Who paid for this?

OCTOBER 14

We continue reading through asking questions about references, tone, and text. What style is this play? What do I want it to say? What is its message? How will a Japanese audience perceive it compared to a British one? Are we to make it Japanese? Is it set now? The last question seems outrageous to me. How would the last scene work? Thatcher isn't there now. There's an economic depression. But it is rightly pointed out that there were scarcely any 'Top Girl' agencies in Tokyo in 1982 so an audience would assume it is now + if you don't read programme notes? So perhaps an extra line in the 1st scene?

No sign of Mr Yano all day.

OCTOBER 15

An enjoyable day working on Scene 1. When it's going fast + they are hitting all the overlaps it's rather exhilarating. Of course, it's like the bullet train going through a station but it's good to have it that way rather than the line/pause/watch my reaction/pause/line syndrome. Much talk of how much do they know each other – it doesn't help if they do. Pope Joan's death isn't a surprise.

Endless revisions of the translation – it's obviously still too long-winded + formal – Ms Adaichi did the translation for the original production 9–10 years ago. What was it like? Everyone says the first scene was a disaster – a series of overlapping monologues. A lovely moment found between Nijo and Pope Joan about unwanted pregnancies.

Mr Yano and Ms Takahashi take me to dinner. I am going to see Noh next week. They both think it's dead – can't develop or generate itself any longer. They claim only a few old people know what it means. Shakespeare is performed here in simplified versions with the poetic verse removed. They are convinced that everyone in England understands all of it.

We all think the poster is dreadful + sexist.

(Indeed, the poster was dreadful and sexist depicting a woman both corseted and headless.)

OCTOBER 16

And the jet lag hits today. The cast endlessly revises the text with Ms A (translator). We read to the end + I try to give some idea of life in a Suffolk village. What would Angie + Joyce do? Joyce's cleaning jobs? Ms Midori (Isabella Bird/Joyce/Mrs Kidd) thought she was cleaning office buildings at night – that's what the Japanese word for 'cleaning' is. I'm particularly perplexed by Ms Han (Marlene) forcefully asking about the 'if' in 'If I don't come for another 6 years, she'll be 21, will that be ok?' What does it mean by "if"? What does she mean by "if"? Doesn't 'if' mean 'if?' This goes on for a long whilst until Ms H and Mr Y say there are many words for 'if' in Japanese and this obviously isn't the right one. Ms H has many questions about the end + we go through these in private. Asking to do this in private is v. indicative of the group – they are such top girls. They don't want to show their weaknesses. Objective for next week is to get them to relax.

(Most days after rehearsals, the actors would stand in line according to status – Ms Midori and/or Ms Han always at the head – to ask questions in private about the text and their character. Often important questions. So, what was rehearsal? What were we doing during the day if basic questions were not being attended to? What was actually happening? Why could important things not be asked in public?)

OCTOBER 19

Some additional thoughts from the last week. On Friday as I direct, in my bare feet, the rehearsal room keeper rushes forward with a cloth to wipe them + then I am rapidly shod in a pair of tabi. Again on Friday – lunchtime – a meeting between Ms Midori and Ms Ito. Ms M shows a delicate Victorian lace blouse, obviously an attempt at a pretty Isabella Bird. After 45 minutes, it's over. Ms Ito walks by me, smiles + says, 'No need to worry.' This woman could get them wearing large plastic bags on their heads.

Happy Birthday, Annie. I love you.

OCTOBER 20

To start a scene, you clap your hands. To stop a scene, you clap your hands.

An enjoyable morning working on the office scenes. Ms Han is now relaxed + concentrated + beginning to enjoy herself. After lunch back to the restaurant scene + things go out the window as we have a crew in from WowWow, a cable tv program + the actors shrink their performances either from tension or to suit tv. Why is it of any interest to watch rehearsals or a director talking to actors? Once they've gone, the problem seems to be the energy goes after Patient Griselda arrives. Too much generalized drunk acting? They view her as an alien? But *she's* the princess with the marriage that worked – a lot of talk – we begin to get it going again.

(The question of why the other women tolerate Patient Griselda was debated every day and never satisfactorily resolved. Why would successful women embrace a woman who is rejected and abused by her husband but never criticizes him? Why does Marlene invite Patient Griselda to her celebratory dinner in the first place? The problem of Patient Griselda stalked the rehearsal room.)

OCTOBER 21
Yesterday, a typical design meeting: within the space of a few minutes, the designer's precious silver chairs have become plain wood + the textured blue + red 'Callum Innes' walls and floor are now one solid sheet of blue. Hours of work and thought are erased in minutes.

To the National Noh Theatre. The Kanemaki play *Dojoji* is rarely performed + is apparently radical + and when the dancer/serpent performs stop-motion dance you can hear a pin drop. What I love is the alternation of extremely slow ritualized gesture + real time. They take an eternity to raise a heavy bell to the ceiling. It takes the time it takes. The transformation from woman into demon beneath the bell is pure magic. Masakuni Asami, playing the female role, is at the height of his powers and is wonderful. We wait for Asami at the stage door + the actors are transformed into grey-suited businessmen as if that's what they really are.

(Lesson learned. Perform in real time. Actions take as long as they take. Actions should be performed with real objects. Actions and objects should be authentic. Theatre happens in compressed time – a whole life passes by in two to three hours. When actions happen on stage in real time, both stage and auditorium are united.)

OCTOBER 22
A good day's work on the final scene. It takes a long time to get going as they're frightened of it but it does play like a dream at the end. And finally, they are more open about asking questions in front of each other + building a picture of the traditional English unhappy family. Things are going well + it's enjoyable + rewarding.

OCTOBER 23

Today's rehearsal is a long slog working through the office scenes. Ms Buncho and Ms Shiota (playing Win and Nell) don't really know how tough these women are. A *lot* of explaining. By the end of the day, they are beginning to understand they don't have to sympathize about Howard's heart attack. And the translator has softened the tone – Mrs. Kidd's 'You're not natural' comes out as 'You're cold' – not really it, is it? And how do you translate 'Could you please piss off?' into Japanese? Finally, the cast work out that a simple 'Sayonara' cutting across Mrs. Kidd is about as rude as you can get.

OCTOBER 24

What a day! Morning working back through the office scene. The toughness required starts to appear + and that is gratifying. After lunch on to the restaurant scene + it's a mess as we haven't touched it for days. The concentration is appalling. It's frustrating for all. After a pee break, Ms Midori is saying to all next time we should rehearse it in blocks + get it perfect but for the moment we can keep going this way. And all this said very condescendingly. And I go into an inner blind rage. Then, we hit the rocks on Patient Griselda and Midori says why would anyone find this interesting? + I see red, fling my script at the wall, storm off to put on my shoes + Ms Takahashi and Mr Sasebe run around. I return to try + sort this out.

(Looking back now, I have no idea what was sorted out or how it was sorted out. Was anything discussed? I doubt it. Did I apologize for my bad behaviour? I doubt it. I had been 'advised' by several European and American directors who had worked in Japan that it could be useful to have a tantrum in rehearsal. That it was expected of one. That it showed authority. The best one can say is that this is dubious advice. I don't believe that this particular meltdown was staged in any way. The anger rolled for hours afterwards and was followed by the usual feeling of humiliation. Once after another tantrum – I had thrown a coffee cup across the room and the producers had 'rewarded' my passionate behaviour with expensive leather gloves and two beautiful pears – Ms Shiraishi said 'Don't worry. Suzuki once broke my arm with a chair.')

OCTOBER 25

Move into my new room + although it's a normal twin size, it feels enormous after the cell of the past 2 weeks. By late afternoon, yesterday's mood has passed + I work on editing + work on the Patient Griselda scene.

OCTOBER 26

A good day working through Act 1 in detail. 6 hours on one scene.

We all go out to eat. We sit on tatami mats and eat and drink for 3 hours. Ms Tane launches into tales – in a surreal English – of travels in England, the USA, Germany, France, Portugal, Italy, China, Thailand, Malaysia, clubs in Kyoto with live sex acts, men fucking chickens, near sexual encounters in the jungle – she is a great entertainer. Everybody is delighted when they realize that we are in a version of the 1st scene + and they can speak at speed, eat, listen + the focus passes back and forth. Much talk + drink + gasps of horror at my tales of being robbed in London. For 2 weeks, I have walked around Tokyo with over 300,000 Yen ($4500 in 2021) in my bag and felt safe. And when I say that I wouldn't allow Jacob on his own on the street in London, you can hear jaws drop. Mine drops even further when I find out that the actors are not paid to rehearse. They are there dutifully for hour after hour. Ninagawa, the great director, can utilize a chorus of 100s + all they are paid is a transportation fee.

Tonight, on TV, the Emperor's formal apology for War Crimes against the Chinese.

OCTOBER 27

We run through the restaurant scene with food + it collapses. Nobody, save Ms Han, listens, talks to anybody else. Ms Shiraishi despairingly says 'I hate this' of Gret's speech. Bad afternoon – we all know it!

(Whoever believes that progress, particularly in the theatre, moves inexorably forward is delusional.)

OCTOBER 28

Slow detailed work on the restaurant scene – who's talking to who, how to listen and still maintain one's own train of thought, when to pick up bread, when to eat, when to drink, when to lean forward, when to lean back. Choreographing a dance. But much progress is made.

At the end of rehearsals, Ms Midori, possibly the one with the highest status, says 'Goodnight, Les.' The 1st time in nearly 3 weeks anybody has called me by the name I asked to be called by.

Talk to Mum on the phone tonight: she sounds so little + frail. I got a letter from her this week + her high, loopy writing is showing a spidery tremor.

OCTOBER 30
Ms Takahashi says that today's Japan is so concerned with class, status + politeness that it's nearly impossible to debate anything.

This evening receive a picture of a whale + little fishes from Jacob. And one of him with curly hair and Mummy and me behind a curtain + my 1st ever letter from him.

OCTOBER 31
The chairs for the set arrived yesterday. These are rather simple, beautiful, unvarnished, pale wood + cost about 100,000 yen each – 500 pounds each (roughly $1500 per chair today).

The number of US actors doing TV ads for cars and whiskey here. Keanu Reeves + Peter Falk for Suntory Whisky, Kyle MacLachlan + Jodie Foster for cars. How much were they paid? And Alfred Hitchcock for Toyota!

This morning's rehearsal fucked up by yet another TV crew. Tension creeps in + the energy drops so it doesn't look so big on camera. Ms Midori is so nervous that Joyce develops a nervous twitching of the hands. Ms M wants a bucket and a mop – the kids want to play with knives. Lack of trust that the text will hold.

(This happened numerous times throughout the rehearsal period. Not unique to Japan. The UK, the US, Japan. Let's add props/have something to do with the hands when faith in the text is low. Louder, faster, funnier, busier.)

(I was fascinated by Japanese TV. Strongly believing that if I stared at the screen with sufficient force, I would come to understand all that was said. The world of Bill Murray in Lost in Translation.)

NOVEMBER 1
I'm very homesick today.

NOVEMBER 2
Another long session working through Scene 1. It founders again on Patient Griselda. Why should these phenomenal women find her interesting? Of course, it can be kept running by Nijo's interest in romance/marriage/beautiful clothes but it does seem forced by Caryl. Is it an author's conceit? And there's an actors revolt building against Ms Shiraishi + her lack of concentration and decision as Gret. I've been excusing her on the grounds that it is difficult to sit + not speak + eat for hours + maintain concentration as we go back over dialogue but she is all over the place. She may be the company genius (producers' term) but she does need focusing.

Naff day.

(Naff. Untranslatable English word. Lame in the US? Maybe. Origins? Unknown. 'No apparent function.' 'Not absolutely first rate.' 'Nasty as fuck.' 'Not available for fucking.' Naff. We all have had a naff day.)

(I realize later that a possible explanation for Marlene liking Patient Griselda is that in the end they are both rural working class women who make good, Marlene through business and Patient Griselda through marriage.)

NOVEMBER 4

A good day's rehearsal on the final scene. Ms Midori gets rid of her props + is perkier. Still whines at times but at least she's fighting it.

Ms Takahashi showed me yesterday a flyer for a production of *Romeo and Juliet* next year in which the main players are cats. The Montagues are all black + the Capulets are all white. John Hurt to be the narrator.

At the Foreign Correspondents Club, Gareth Alexander of *The Sunday Times*, tells me that Schwarzenegger was paid $1,000,000 for his 15-second ad, Eddie Murphy $3,000,000, Kyle MacLachlan says 6 words in his – 'Good Morning. Come to my party.' Words are kept to a minimum to minimize the damage if it's leaked to the US media. Farrah Fawcett Major sued for $20,000,000 when CBS got a copy of hers. Also Sean Connery, and Charlie Sheen for shoes. The Club is one of those wonderful, cozy, enclosed worlds floating 20 floors above the neon of Hibiya. Someone practicing golf shots atop a building opposite. Playing golf atop a Tokyo club can cost 600 pounds a session. 'I can fly to the Philippines for 4 days, stay with friends, play golf + get laid every night for that.' Who said that?

Clinton wins the US election.

NOVEMBER 5

1st run-through – Act 1. The restaurant scene comes + goes + doesn't reach its highs and lows + the end is a mess but the other scenes hold steady. What shocks me is the lack of concentration in the room – people murmur, walk about, stage management wash up cups. The note session is interminable. Much much talk. We are talking through a cultural wall of opaque glass. Through its smoky thickness we can just about perceive each other. Ms Tane is so confused that she's surprised to hear that we all think the 1st scene is naturalistic or a heightened form of realism, she thought they were playing dead. I had thought the concept of the living dead would be embraced in Japan but it's obviously confusing. After notes + lunch, we look at the final scene and the 3 divas crack into it + by stunning the others raise hopes + expectations + set a new level of achievement.

NOVEMBER 6

Stagger through Act 2. Generally, it's more secure than Act 1. I ask Ms Midori to be firmer on the line 'Don't come back' (Joyce's dismissal of Marlene, her sister) + she looks puzzled + asks 'When do I say that?' I point this out to Ms Takahashi who checks the translation and finds 'Don't talk to me about the past.' How much else is changed? Ms Midori hates her costume for Mrs Kidd + there is much discontent about Ms Ito. They're angry that she hasn't been in rehearsal to watch or discuss their character + I find out *now* this is the usual custom in Japan. We agree that what I and they don't like will be changed. Later, I find out they don't know they will be required to move the furniture – this is rare – so is scene-change light – better face that one tomorrow.

(When I ask the translator later how 'Don't come back' has transmogrified into 'Don't talk to me about the past,' she firmly states that no Japanese woman would ever talk like that to her sister. It couldn't be done. It could never be said. End of conversation. Challenging and as frequently confusing as it is to work in a language that is not one's own first language, it is disturbing to realize that the translator is rewriting the text for her own cultural and ethical reasons. And also a source of embarrassment for all concerned when discrepancies between the English and Japanese texts are discovered. My interpreter is caught in a storm of lies and evasions.)

NOVEMBER 7

Morning working through Angie and Kit scene. Ms Shiraishi (Angie) stops and says:

MS S:	You do it. You understand this more than I do.
ME:	What? Do what?
MS S:	You do it. You understand Angie. And this play. You do it.
ME:	No.

PAUSE WHILST WE RENEGOTIATE.

MS S:	You do it. You understand it. Only you understand this play.
ME:	No. I can't act.
MS S:	Say the words and walk through the scene and say the words and I'll hold your hand and feel the vibrations through your hand.

PAUSE.

ME: Ok.

And Ms Shiraishi takes my hand and we walk through the scene, and I say the lines in English and she holds my hand gently and everyone is watching.

PAUSE.

MS S: Thank you.

And she looks me directly in the eyes and doesn't smile.

NOVEMBER 8
2pm. Meeting with Mr Sasabe (producer), Ms Nagamine (producer), and Mr Yano (production manager). They say they want the production to be mine + English whatever a Japanese audience might think. I hadn't thought it wasn't mine. What becomes clear is that they feel Ms Midori is making trouble + causing disturbances in rehearsal by worrying about props and costumes when they all should be concentrating on the acting. Trouble = thinking the blanket in the final scene is wrong and her costume as Mrs Kidd isn't suitable. Because I've backed her on this, they feel I have breached professional etiquette. Is questioning the colour of a blanket making trouble? They don't want me to change her costume but it's wrong + I want it changing. Yano asks if the budget can stretch to it? Mr Sasabe says, if I want then I can have it. So, I have it.

4.30pm. Cross town to Ms Ito's and it's sorted out within 30 minutes. A brief spat about professionalism between Ms Midori and Ms Ito but a change will be made.

NOVEMBER 9
Spend time working through Act 1. Gret takes wing through her speech – an astonishing explosion of deep notes, sudden yelps and shrieks. All are astounded. We put in the scene changes + despite sulking in some quarters they seem to work efficiently + fairly quickly. At the end of the day, we look at the final scene + Ms Midori pulls faces, puts in unexpected moves + generally upstages. When I give notes, she blocks all of them – says as an actress this isn't right for her – e.g., looking upstage – it may look alright from the outside etc. etc. – so I go for her, I think fairly mildly, but the ripples shoot around the room and when I leave at 7pm she's quietly running the scene with Ms Han.

Check out of the Edmont and move to the Fairmont Hotel. The Fairmont is nice. It's older, more fustian. Reminds me of the (pre-Ian Schrager) Gramercy Park Hotel in New York.

(The question I will always ask is what vibrations did Ms Shiraishi feel through my hand, when we rehearsed the Angie scene, that caused this fiery new Gret in today's rehearsal? Could she understand both characters in those moments? What happened? What could she feel? What did she intuit? What passed between us? Whatever happened removed any hesitations from her performance. I have worked with 2 actor geniuses. Ms Shiraishi and Kathryn Hunter in Caryl's *The Skriker* at the National Theatre. Neither actor has any personal vanity. Both occupy very little personal space. Both appear to have no artistic limitations. As if everything was possible for them if they wanted to do it. Humbling.)

NOVEMBER 10
We are heading down a long dark tunnel towards Opening on the 21st. Spent most of the day rehearsing Act 2. Ms Midori was late + sulked nearly all morning. A barrage of 'We are not as good as English actors. This is very hard for us, Les-San.' They don't know the blasts of energy they need + seeing as Japanese is twice as long as English, it requires great attack. The constant complaint is 'Japanese is a horrible language to act in. It's so descriptive and literary.' The constant question is 'How do I listen to this?' whenever anyone has a long speech. The Japanese equivalent of 'What do I do in the pauses?' Over dinner, I vent my frustration to Mr Yano who explains that this is the most frequent question in rehearsals. For the Japanese, the high art is to listen. To speak is easy, to walk and to listen, that is the great achievement. One of those grey, hard work days.

7pm. Sound meeting. It's all John Adams: *The Chairman dances, Grand Pianola Music, Harmonielehre.* I love this stuff. Ms Takahashi and Mr Yano say, 'It's interesting.'

NOVEMBER 11
The actors rehearsed the 1st scene till 9pm last night, and this morning we run through that scene, I give notes + they run it again. It goes like an express train + is twice as fast as in England but there's twice as many words to say.

2pm. Run through the entire play. The room is packed – Mr Sasabe, Ms Nagamine, the LX designer, the LX assistant, the sound operator, the other translator I met at Caryl's in London, various managers and agents, and several husbands and boyfriends. First scene goes like a rocket (2 mins shorter), they blast through it all + it tires out towards the end. Voices are going. There's no formal training here + seeing as 80% of the company smoke 2 packs a day there's a lot of strain and choking and spluttering. But it goes well + they play as a company + people are impressed – the other translator in particular.

NOVEMBER 12

A morning of notes and encouragement to try out things and claim the play as their own. There's a feeling of having passed some sort of test yesterday. I ask Ms Nagamine if she thinks it went well. 'Yes, very good.' The other interpreters' presence and approval worked wonders.

4pm. Costume parade and photo session. Ms Ito has done a rather fine job. The wigs are awful. Shona's looks like some fun thing from the current club scene. But everything else is fine. Ms Midori appears in make-up that makes her look like Bette Davis in *What Ever Happened to Baby Jane* – huge false eyelashes with painted lines beneath her eyes. But let's tackle that later. Company meal + the costumiers buy us drinks + and on the way to the subway, minus Midori, much merriment + 'What are we to do about her make-up?' Apparently with her own company, she wears even more, big bows in her hair + little girl dresses with leg of mutton sleeves.

A traditional Japanese ghost wears a white kimono, a small triangle on its brow. The dead were buried in barrels like this + holds its hands limply in front. It has no energy. The actress who recently died when her car went into the ocean was performing in an unlucky ghost play + hadn't been before to bless herself at a shrine as is the custom.

(Does this explain in any way the frustration and confusion of playing a ghost/the uneasy dead here? In Caryl's world, the dead have the same needs and wants as the living. They are not limp in any way. They are full of energy.)

NOVEMBER 13

We run through Scene 1. Dreadful, gloomy, sloppy. Everybody apologizes. Ms Tane has injured her voice, Ms Midori's is raw, Ms Shiraishi is protecting hers.

Friday the 13th and also one of those days in Japan when there is 'no God.'

NOVEMBER 14 & 15

I can't really remember what happened early in the day as the end of rehearsal + evening were so emotional.

There's a run in the afternoon which is better + I give notes. There is a frayed quality around – a worry if they don't get enough notes, a resentment if they do. I ask Lady Nijo to trim the beat before 'When your lover dies – one of my lovers dies.' At the end of notes, she brings this up and suddenly it all comes out. Ms Midori has been asking them to change things for her convenience. She asked Ms Matsukane to change the timing of clearing the main course as she can't concentrate etc. I am filled with anger and resentment and, of course, can't express it + just seethe. Later, I force the producers into a meeting – they say they are too busy – and vent my anger/ hurt. How can I control things in the rehearsal room if I do not understand the language? Most of Ms Midori's notes go on behind my back or during the lunch break. I feel a lack of support from the producers. Mr Sasabe says the actors feel I am favouring Ms Midori. All this is emotional for me + I walk out of the restaurant + back to the hotel, phone home, burst into tears, and am a huge mess. I decide to punish the producers + leave a message with Ms Takahashi to tell Mr Sasabe that I am deciding whether to stay or not + will let them know in the morning + ask the front desk not to put through any calls till the morning.

An awful night feeling completely wretched + lonely + sad. First morning of going to work + not looking forward to it. Mr Sasabe is still awaiting my decision. On the subway, I meet Ms Buncho (Lady Nijo/Win) + Ms Han (Marlene), who are surprised + shocked that I am angry etc. Ms Han – thank god for Ms Han – attempts a conversation but it goes nowhere. Mr Yano calms me down outside the rehearsal room + word of how I feel electrifies the place. How will I react? What is going to happen? Ms Matsukane (Waitress/Kit/Shona) apologizes for my 'upsets' + 'offence' because they have been rehearsing on their own but Japanese actors do this after a director has given notes.

Because of codes of status + etiquette, how do you discuss/mediate/rehearse anything? There's blame + anger + then it's backed off. We start with the restaurant scene. I ask Ms Midori/Isabella not to stand on 'Such superstition.' She objects, gets heated, I say 'No,' there's tension, she is about to do it again, I bellow 'No! This is how I want it,' she says loudly in perfect English 'Yes. I can do that. Fine.' We rehearse, she doesn't, I'm pleased, they're pleased, she sulks, and that's that. A run in costume at 1.30pm – not bad – they're all tired. I ask Ms Midori to change an element of Mrs Kidd's entrance, she says 'Yes,' accepts all notes, and the air is cleared. They are all very happy + 48 dreadful hours are over.

NOVEMBER 16

2pm. Caryl arrives + I realize (and so do the producers) that it's the 1st time I've looked + felt happy in weeks. It's as if I've come out of prison or been in the dark more accurately + re-emerged into the light. Poor Caryl in that awful bleary jet-lagged way gets the full account.

A brief visit to the theatre to see the set. Well, it's all blue + some horrible creases where it had to be folded to get in through the scene door.

Back to the hotel + a meal + a walk + a talk with Caryl.

(Caryl claims that I talked non-stop for 7–8 hours. So much for my noted laconic nature. I spent more time on my own in Japan than any other country or during any period of my life. It was hard work. Demanding both as a director, but also as a non-Japanese speaker in a different culture. Certainly exciting. I enjoy being off balance, not knowing exactly where I'm going. Being a director is isolating, making a production feels isolating as if one is in a bubble and the rest of the world is passing by – the Emperor apologizes, Clinton wins 43% of the vote and becomes the 42nd President of the United States. My major experience of this period is isolation – the isolation of not knowing the country, the language, and the theatre.)

NOVEMBER 17

Out to the preview theatre – IMA Hall in Nerima – to start the tech. David Leveaux said the LX designer was very good and he is. We start with actors at 5pm on Act 1. They've been in since 1pm running lines. Some sea change has occurred: they're pleasant, positive + working as a group. I buy them all a plastic monster from the toy store near the theatre and they say how perceptive I am + compare them.

The scene changes are smoothish + well covered by the John Adams. The hall has bad acoustics. On stage the sound bounces back + in the house it's like listening to a transatlantic phone call.

Madonna's *Sex* is issued.

NOVEMBER 18

Tech Act 2 – 1–5pm. Smooth again. Office to last scene is a lengthy transition + needs tightening. I don't like the way it looks. It's been cut back so much it looks undernourished + if it's not perfect + seamless – those fucking creases – looks rather dog-eared. At the preview, the set designer, who won't be there on Saturday for Opening Night, thanks me + profusely apologizes + is genuinely mortified about the creases + swears they will get them out.

Ms Han asks if we will have a curtain call. I dread working this out because of the status of these women – who stands where? – + she suggests we don't have one. Caryl arrives. Ms Tane attempts a conversation in English about *Cloud Nine* – 'more entertainment than *Top Girls*' – and about how as Betty she had to masturbate.

The dress rehearsal is really rather good. Caryl, I think, is genuinely pleased. A sprinkling of boyfriends, managers + fellow company members. So, will 'boyfriend' notes appear tomorrow? . . . 'It suddenly came to me last night that I should . . . etc. etc.' But I'm pleased.

Off for dinner with Ms Nagamine + Mr Sasabe + Caryl. Her gluten-free diet becomes the centre of attention.

(November 18 was also Jacob's 5th birthday. Although I called at 1am and spoke to him then, it is not good to miss a child's birthday. Not good not to be there. Not good at all. I missed at least two of all three children's birthdays when they were young. It's just not good.)

NOVEMBER 19
Notes at 1pm. Caryl there to give them support. They're quite cheerful. Their peer group must've given them the OK last night. There are no boy-friend notes. A general note for the top girls section to be naughtier + to enjoy themselves. Caryl found it weak + they certainly don't have the buc-caneering spirit of the actors in the original London production.

Preview – 7pm – IMA Hall. Goes well – not as good as last night. They look like rabbits in a car's headlights in the 1st scene. It's tense + pushed. Midori being particularly overblown + irritating. She's good when she is simple but that's rare. The last scene is rather shouty. The audience is 80% women + that's usual. There's no applause at the intermission + that's usual. Somebody places flowers on the stage at curtain call + that's usual. Backstage a small line of friends + fans to present the actresses with bouquets. Ms Yoshikawa thinks tonight's audience was naive + not used to seeing many plays + the response will be more sophisticated particularly towards the 1st scene at the Tokyo Met.

Mr Yano drives us to dinner + back to the hotel + the rain starts. It's a ty-phoon. My 1st performance in Japan + a typhoon!

NOVEMBER 20
To Ueno in the typhoon. It's really coming down. Ueno has that squalid Kings Cross feel + it's very dirty by Japanese standards. There are people

sleeping in the subway + cardboard shelters in the park. A lot of Iranians looking for work – Japan's underclass. Too wet to visit the shrines so into the National Museum of Art + a special exhibition of Japanese treasures. Beautiful, perfect scrolls – *Words that give clues leading to the Enlightenment of Zen* + the Gaki Zoshi *The Scroll of Hungry* Ghosts – a really frightening 12th-century depiction of a famine. Caryl says 'like taking a sketch book to Somalia.' A Korean Crown 4th Century. Early pottery dancing figures and a coat of white + purple decorated with snowflakes + white flowers. It's the most beautiful piece of clothing I've ever seen.

In the evening to the Tokyo Foundation for a workshop on Kyogen for 'resident foreigners.' A lecture by Don Kenny + 2 kyogen – *The Snail* + *Two in One Hakama* performed by the Nomura family – 2 brothers + a son, Takeshi. Kyogen is increasing in popularity because of him. He's very funny – his demented elation on 'Dim, Dim, Moshie, Moshie' – + very handsome. His father and uncle both designated 'Intangible Cultural Treasures.'

NOVEMBER 21

To the theatre for noon and it doesn't look as bad as I thought it would. The set seems to fit well within the proscenium. The house seats nearly 900 + has poor acoustics in the best seats – 1/2 way back in the centre. Ms Han suddenly announces that she's unhappy with the ending. She feels she should stand + put her blanket around Angie who looks cold + pathetic. She's been nabbed by someone, probably by her manager who stares at me sourly at the Opening Night party. In 6 weeks of rehearsal, she's never gone for any softness in her playing of Marlene. I say, 'No, that isn't right' as I'm not prepared to argue this – it doesn't sound like her talking – Mr Yano talks however + presumably says what I would've said if I thought it worth the discussion + Ms Han seems quite happy.

The Dress Rehearsal is fine + so is the Press Night. A youngish, mixed audience + there's some response. It's easy to think it only works when they laugh as the silence is impenetrable. What do they make of it? Martyn Naylor (from Dramatists Play Service in Asia) seems ungraciously impressed – 'the overlaps aren't usually done here' – What does that mean? – 'or rather they are not committed to.' He finds the silence in the 1st scene after Pope Joan describes her death as 'telling.' Caryl + I are called onstage to take bows + I really enjoy that. A brief party after – we all make speeches + then home to bed.

NOVEMBER 22

Late night + I am packing + a sheet of paper is slipped under my door.

NOTES GIVING A CLUE - a hard play. For Les.

CHILD with clock playing 'Good Morning, let's go.'

20 PEOPLE IN WHITE sweep dry leaves into piles. This goes on for half an hour.

Enter a KING wearing coat with purple stripes + Korean crown.

He takes one of the people in white, undresses him, dresses him in a corset + chops off his head. The other people in white turn into HERONS + fly away. The king throws stones at them but misses.

The child takes a present to the king. He unwraps it. It's a large golden carp.

The king chops it into pieces and slowly eats them.

The child starts writing a sutra on a long scroll.

A HUNGRY GHOST watches the king eat, advancing slowly towards him.

This lasts for five hours.

Then, the child blots the paper + screams. The ghost reaches the king, who explodes.

The ghost sings 'Dim dim mosshy mosshy' and the child joins in. They sing it a hundred times.

Meanwhile, it starts to rain.

It's a typhoon.

There's a flood. The stage is twenty feet deep in water and black, white, and golden carp swim about in it. Everything has been washed away.

The child gets out of the water and flies away on the back of a heron.

The hungry ghost eats the clock.

Love from Caryl

NOVEMBER 23

Mr Sasabe and Ms Nagamine see us off on the 9.35 am bus to Narita. They pay our hotel expenses which is unexpected and generous. Sasabe: 'Tell me Caryl-San how do you write such inspirational plays?' Caryl: 'I think that's a nice statement rather than a question.' When the bus arrives, Nagamine links her arm through mine as we cross the little lobby at the Fairmont. I shall really miss them all.

On the flight Caryl + I look through the window at Siberia – is it Siberia? – in an endless twilight. Everything in shades of grey – tundra, mountain ranges, occasionally the silver of rivers + oxbow lakes + sometimes long straight roads but never any sign of habitation + then suddenly a light – it's very strong – not moving – looks like it's standing in a patch of cracked ice – is it a gigantic quarry? Is it a salt mine? Where are the salt mines? Who knows what it is? But it's the loneliest thing I've ever seen. Shortly after that, we travel into night.

David, Caryl's husband, at the airport: 'How was it then, Japan?' Caryl + I resist the easy generalisation and hardly say anything. From the backseat of the car, London looks old and raw and aggressive.

Home + baby Nancy is asleep + Jacob is up + it's lovely + just what I've longed for + it's great.

17. *The Skriker* at Royal National Theatre (1994).

18. *Apparition* at Connelly Theatre (2005).

"Just Nod and Say Thank You"

Keith Reddin

"What about Les Waters?"
It was 1985 and I was a playwright early in my career
Excited to have a production at the New York Shakespeare Festival
Joseph Papp legendary founder and producer at the Public suggested
Les to direct
I had been impressed by Les's recent production of
Caryl Churchill's *Fen*
The production was economical theatrical mysterious but
Les was British
How would he respond to a play about a period of American Cold War history
The Bay of Pigs invasion of Cuba orchestrated by the CIA

Even before *Fen* he ran the Royal Court Upstairs where he did the first productions of
Sam Shepard's *Seduced* and Wally Shawn's amazing *Marie and Bruce*
When I read he had done those plays by American writers I admired
I knew in some way he would respond to *Rum and Coke*
He knew American culture and theater well before he started working here in the US

We never met till the first day of casting in New York
I was immediately taken by his sharp humor, dark outlook, and brilliance
I learned early on in our collaborations to trust Les's choices
He seemed to have an instinct about people
He had a terrific connection to the actors and designers
I was struck with how little he seemed to "direct" in the traditional sense

DOI: 10.4324/9781003170808-41

He said very little to the actors in rehearsal preferring to induce
An atmosphere of organic creation
We were all collaborators
This often confused some actors who basically wanted to be told ("directed")
What to do, where to move, how to deliver a line
Only in the final days and in technical rehearsals did Les take a more vocal,
active approach

I remember one day Les invited David Hare
Who he knew (I would guess) from the Royal Court Theatre
To watch a preview and give us feedback
I was terrified and braced myself for the worst
But Les and David gave insightful notes and suggestions
(all of which I took)
Les did an amazing job
The production was a great success
Mr. Papp extended the run several times.

*   *   *   *   *

Three years later, I asked Les to direct my play *Nebraska*
Again the piece was on what I felt was
a very American theme and setting
The nuclear missile silos and the military men and women who worked on
them
Les responded to the play and we had
Another collaboration

Les and I often discussed the issue of class and
American versus British social structures
With *Nebraska*, it was important to show rank
Rank created status and power
On (I think) the first day of rehearsal at La Jolla Playhouse
Before the traditional first read-through of the play
Les had everyone pick a playing card from a deck
Then without looking at the card, each actor held it to their forehead
So that everyone else could see the card but the person holding it could not
Les asked us all to treat others depending on the value of their playing card
Thus, face cards (King Queen Jack) had higher status and were to be treated
Special with respect veneration
And low cards (deuce three four) were to be shunned or dismissed
The actors in the play were about to play characters with rank

And this was a way to take in a sub-textual lesson
In status as conferred by rank and use it in rehearsal later
(I think Les mentioned this exercise came from his time at Joint Stock?)
It was effective and actually quite fun

One scene in particular from the production of *Nebraska* stands out
Two characters who are on duty in the silo
On a 24-hour shift
Have been having tensions in their professional and personal relationships
To ramp up the sense of the uncomfortableness between them
Les suggested we have
Two minutes of silence
Now two minutes is an eternity in the theater
But Les instinctively sensed this could be
Powerful
We tried it
Two full minutes of not only no speaking but the actors did not move
Not even turn their heads
It was a true coup de théâtre which I remember to this day

In the years since I have seen how Les often uses
The power of silence to unsettle and at the same time
Burrow into the soul of the scene
From his productions of Charles Mee's plays to Sarah Ruhl's *For Peter Pan on her 70th Birthday*
As a director, Les is in my mind the master of silence
And stillness
Silence and stillness in his hands become quite active
And devastating.

*   *   *   *   *

The next year we collaborated on another play of mine
Life During Wartime
Both in San Diego at La Jolla Playhouse and in New York at Manhattan Theatre Club
It is perhaps the production I am most proud of
Les brought terrific humor and sensitivity to the piece
While not rooted in history, it had also I think a deeply American theme
Business, greed, capitalism (using the figure of John Calvin
Who some think of as the creator of the Protestant Work Ethic)

Les brought a sort of Caryl Churchill/British Labor/Socialist thinking to the play's look at
Salesmen and crime and violence

Les being a Brit directing what I thought of as
Inherently American subjects and history
His being in some sense an "outsider" or observer
Added a new dimension to our productions just as Wim Wenders
Working with Sam Shepard made *Paris Texas* so enthralling and moving
It is the nature of someone not raised in the culture to create a new understanding and bring surprising insights into
A work
His upbringing and sensibility were more often at service to very American themes
Interesting that since he moved here full time, he rarely did a British play
I know he did an adaptation of Virginia Woolf and Caryl Churchill's *Ice Cream*
I remember his other productions at the Public
Romeo and Juliet and Liz Egloff's *The Swan*
But look at what he worked on at Berkeley and Louisville
I think of his *Our Town, Long Day's Journey into Night*, Tennessee Williams
Classic American masterpieces that again benefit from his outsider objectivity and observations
The last decade I think has been primarily new work
By American playwrights
Sarah Ruhl in particular, Charles Mee, Jordan Harrison, Lucas Hnath, Will Eno
All really connect with him.

* * * * *

I feel I can take some small credit for Les teaching and working at UCSD
Back-to-back seasons (1989, 1990)
He directed *Nebraska* and *Life During Wartime* at La Jolla Playhouse
They required Les to use several just graduated UCSD actors
Among them Jefferson Mays in *Life During Wartime*
Jefferson had just graduated a few weeks before we went into rehearsal
Famous anecdote about Jefferson's professional debut in our production
He was cast in multiple roles (which later became a hallmark for him)
(*I Am My Own Wife*)
(*A Gentleman's Guide to Love and Murder*)
He was excited to be working on his

First professional show as well as being directed by Les
On the final night of tech, Jefferson got the flu or some food poisoning (not sure)
He showed up for first preview deathly ill
We were worried he couldn't go on but Jefferson was determined to prove
He was a total pro and said he could perform
Halfway through the first preview, he suddenly threw up all over a table
Then calmly cleaned it up with a napkin as he continued
It was scary and unnerving but the show went on
Afterwards an audience member came up to Les
And said he was a genius asking how he could make an actor throw up on cue like that night after night
I think Les just nodded and said thank you
But it was using the grad students so well and bringing their talents to light that impressed
the UCSD grad program
And it wasn't long after that he was hired to teach there
That and his work in California then brought him up to Berkeley and his term as associate artistic director there
And then Louisville
And then now . . .

*   *   *   *   *

What is often overlooked in Les's work and worldview is
A deep compassion for characters
He is, though he would never admit it, a person who is not afraid of emotion
He will try to hide it but he can express great love and sadness
We think of Brits in the cliché of being cold or distant
Les will allow work, performances, productions to express emotion but never sentimentality

He is also extremely loyal
One of the things we share is a desire to use the same actors from production to production
This not only saves time as one creates a vocabulary and working method
But is a product of
His faith and loyalty
He will work with some actors 10, 12 times
Together, we used a number of actors in all three plays
Rum and Coke, Nebraska, Life During Wartime
Then in the many readings and workshops, Les and I did together

It's not that Les doesn't want to go out of his comfort zone
It's that he knows (I think) that
Rehearsal periods are short and he tries to save time by working with
people he can trust and communicate with

Again and again
I am struck by Les's economy of direction
He is one of the only directors I know who can say
"I don't know."
More often it is
"Let's find out together."
Let's discover this scene, this character, this play
Together
It is direction by indirection, by posing questions, by observation, and then
A few incredibly incisive responses
Les is a writer's director, an actor's director, a designer's director
A man of sometimes Zen-like calm and knowledge.

* * * * *

Also on *Life During Wartime*
I remember Les flew over from London
And landed the night the US started bombing Iraq to start the first Gulf War
We met in a bar in New York for a drink and Les said
"Yes, well, life during wartime."

* * * * *

KEITH REDDIN is an actor and writer. His plays have been produced in New York and across the US, as well as in London, Berlin, and Tel Aviv. He has also written for film and television. In a 1991 interview in BOMB Magazine, he said, "The main theme of my plays, and I think of most plays in one way or another, is betrayal and coming to grips with that." He still feels the same way. Over 35 years, Les Waters has directed three of his plays and directed him as an actor in plays by Sarah Ruhl and Anton Chekhov.

National identity

My American career is totally dependent on Joint Stock's production of Caryl Churchill's *Fen* going to New York in 1983 and being acclaimed. That opened a door, and at the time, I thought, "Oh, this door is open. I'm going to walk through and see what happens." I worked at the Public, which was great sometimes, and sometimes . . . not. I was offered work at Arena Stage and at the Guthrie and at the Goodman. I didn't know how extraordinary that was. I didn't have to struggle as so many young American directors have to do. I was "that English guy who directed that Caryl Churchill play that the *New York Times* loved." Now it just seems like the most extraordinary luck.

If somebody asks me "What nationality are you?" I would probably say I was British and then have to correct myself. I am an American citizen now. In 2018, towards the end of my time at Actors Theatre, I became a US citizen. In Louisville. When the kids were young, there was a possibility of going back to England, so I thought, "Why bother?" And I always thought that America was overwhelming. America generates so much noise. Everything is dialed up all the time. In a couple of hours of watching news on MSNBC tonight, I heard the following – "the great city of Detroit," "the great state of Illinois," "this great democracy," "this great country," "this great melting pot," and "this great social experiment of ours." All this greatness. All of the time. What would the world be like without all this American noise? This country swallows you up and eats you alive, and I thought by preserving my English nationality I would have more distance from it. That being English could keep America at bay. That having an English passport meant I was an

DOI: 10.4324/9781003170808-42

observer of it all. Now I am living here and I am in it. In 2020, at the age of 68, I voted in a Presidential election for the first time.

A few years ago, my son Jacob was studying for a Masters in Political Theory at the London School of Economics and I flew back to take him out for dinner on his 30th birthday. It was the first time I had been home in 13 years. I got off the plane and had the same reaction I have always had since I started travelling: "This city is amazing. It is one of the truly great cities in the world. I don't know why I ever left." Jacob's birthday is in November, and London was beginning to put on all of its glitter for the holidays. I went to the National Theatre to buy a book in the bookstore, and the place was packed with people of all ages and the audience was diverse and I had a spiffy meal with Jacob, and two days later I thought, "Get me out of this place. It's hateful. It is vile." The moment you're born in England, you breathe this toxic air that is to do with class. I am a rural working-class man, who became a middle-class theatre artist, and I see it in operation all of the time.

I have no desire and no intention to return to England to live. When I read Colm Toibin's great novel *Brooklyn*, I thought this is my experience. I understand myself via this book. I don't feel English, I don't feel American. I don't know what I am. I could be American with an English accent?

I am aware that the accent gives me a certain status. It is palpable. People here think I'm posh, which is ironic given my origins. There are people who say, and always have said, "I love your accent. I love your dialect." It's fine. It's to my advantage. Early on, it was as if I was a young rock star from London. I have actually had people say, "I love it when you tell me to fuck off. It sounds so great with your accent." And I always reply, "Yeah, that's good. But you do know that I mean it? I am actually saying, 'Fuck off.'"

Something about lists

In 2000, I helped make and performed in a piece called *Phantom Limbs* at UCSD.

It was the brainchild of Jean Isaacs who taught choreography in the Dept of Theatre and Dance and made lovely dance pieces with her own company. She choreographed both *Big Love* and *Fêtes de la Nuit*.

Included 2 fellow faculty members, Charlie Oates (movement) and Jim Winker (acting/Shakespeare). Also Steve Schick, professor in the music department at UCSD. Who is one of the world's great percussionists.

Why it was called *Phantom Limb* I don't remember. Probably because Jean liked the term?

What we all did I don't remember. I do remember that Steve "drummed" cabbages at one moment.

I laid on a bed of ice in my pajamas whilst a recording of my voice listed everybody I have ever met. Both alive and deceased. From A to Z. Including death dates. The recording probably exists somewhere. Would be much longer now. Sadder. So many people I know have gone.

DOI: 10.4324/9781003170808-43

"Designing with Les: ' . . . back in the arms of a good friend.'"

David Zinn

My first instinct, in thinking about how to reflect *in words* the ineffable process of designing a show with Les Waters, is to honor what that process *feels* like . . .

And keep it brief.

In fact, I went back to look at the old notebooks I kept for *In the Next Room (or the vibrator play)* and *Girlfriend* – my first two shows with Les – to see if I was misremembering. Did I once take long copious notes that had now been forgotten, smoothed into that blur of a stretch called "process?" But no. Those notebooks are, essentially, empty. I mean, there are a couple notes for myself scribbled during what were probably the first rehearsals. A half-doodle. A mysterious phone number. A scribble. And then some tech and preview notes (those hard-to-read scrawlings made in the dark house of a public performance while you keep your eyes on the stage and move your hand in roughly the shape of the words you need to remember only for the next few hours). But . . . long notes from scholarly articles, or a million noodlings of complicated ground-plan solutions, or a record of long dramaturgical meetings and ponderings? Not a trace.

Which I think means that the design process was *easy* and as brief as I remember. With Les, it's usually an evening out at dinner and then a little bit of talk about the play but mostly life (and love invariably). And fashion. A lot of politics. And who we wished we owned a bookstore with. And then . . . somehow, it's the first preview and there's a room of costumed Victorians waiting to discover the pleasure of a vibrator for the first time. Or two boys

DOI: 10.4324/9781003170808-44

up against the vast empty expanse of Nebraska with a love they are just learning to express through music. People on the precipice – waiting to leap.

So, making work with Les is easy – it's just a matter of making hopeful, and forceful, collisions.

And Les likes collisions. Before I worked with Les, I think my primary notion of him was born from a photo I saw of his production of Chuck Mee's *Big Love* in which women in white wedding dresses seemed to be hurling themselves towards a bright pink floor – a picture of Delight, but also Violence. And, to me, indicative of a theater-maker who smashes things together: things like Risk and Simplicity and Joy (the kind of *adult* Joy that is mixed with Hurt and Love). And whomever made *that* event seemed like he'd be fun to work with.

It is a familiar trope to talk about "family" in theatre, but I think this is what Les, more than most directors I work with, builds. Family is how he makes work and it may explain the ease of the process, which is more like Gathering and less like Working. His affection for family is crucial, and it starts with his own. He loves and celebrates and talks about his own wonderful children and various family pets like any proud, beleaguered but doting father. He also has a long-running and fruitful collaboration with his wife and frequent designer (of said Pink Floor, above) Annie Smart. And also – and I suspect he would bridle at this entire comparison I'm making, like an uncomfortable father at a party given in his honor – "Family" is what he builds in the rehearsal room, a resilient and loving and frequently repeating (returning?) family of actors and designers whom he encourages to bring their own diverse energies to the material at hand. In my remembering, the start of a process with Les is like a parental pat on the back, a "just be back by supper" send-off to play for the day, trusting full well you'll come back home, messy and elated.

Les is a director who doesn't want to control the outcome at the start. He invites you to do your work – to build your world – and then lets *that* world collide with what everyone else brings, optimistic that the result will be, as they always are, worth watching.

And it's in using the architecture of home – of family – where I think we've made our best work together. Les (and I) like objects to be objects onstage – Real things and not scenic shorthands of those objects. So: A house. A room. A sofa. A dresser. Real and complete. Domestic things – which is where our memories are most deeply etched, in the architecture of "home." When those objects share space with the audience seated in what we in the theater call the "house," we've made a conversation, a provocation, a squaring-off of homeness – a place for memories to duke it out.

In *Girlfriend*, a musical with a book by Todd Almond and the music/lyrics of Matthew Sweet, the empty stage stood (stands?) in for the unfriendly expanse of Nebraska, and the orchestra pit (in this case, an intact teenager's bedroom from the early 1990s filled with a rowdy and loving dyke activist band) was smashed into in the middle of the expanse as an architectural artifact, colliding with the stage floor (or in later productions crashed into a giant disused drive-in movie screen). The tangible props our 2 boys needed were scattered around the space, loosely divided into their 2 rooms, and a couch did everything else, including becoming the very real bed where the boys spent their first night together, serenaded by bandleader Julie Wolf's beautiful voice and looked over by this room full of lesbian angels. Young love finding a place for quiet delight.

On another nearly empty stage, this one for Sarah Ruhl's *For Peter Pan on her 70th Birthday* at Playwrights Horizons, we placed the detritus of the hospital room on one side of the stage, for the play starts in a hospital room; and along the back wall was a house. An almost entire house, which was the emotional, and sometimes literal, container for this story of aging, remembering, and magic. And what I remember most is the transition from Scene 1 to Scene 2. The patriarch of the family has just perished in the hospital, and as the work light popped on, the father got up out of bed and slowly made his way to the house, as though not dead but simply returning at long last from a day's work. Meanwhile, one son picked up a trumpet to play "When the Saints Go Marching In," and the rest of the family simply put the hospital things away and moved to a table in the center of the stage. As the transition neared its end, the family dog came out of the front door to greet her now dead master – he joining her in heaven. Which in this case was just a familiar home, with the porch light on.

Les makes simple but muscular gestures that amplify the poetry of the playwright. He gives life to the process of transition – and *transition* is maybe what theater illustrates best. Onstage and offstage can stand in for the tension between life and death, of remembering and forgetting – holding colliding stories in space. Which is also what family does.

So maybe Les will indulge me my own family story. Sarah Ruhl's *The Vibrator Play* premiered in Berkeley, California, where my sister was then living. She came to visit me one day at the theater, along with my 3-year-old niece. We were in long, full-day 10-out-of-12 rehearsals – the subject of yet another play (by Anne Washburn) I was fortunate to explore with Les – and we took my niece Emma up to see the elaborate Victorian dresses I had designed. We thought she might get a kick out of all that *fabric* – something quite different than what she normally encounters in her rural Californian surroundings. The women of the cast were getting dressed and welcomed Emma into their dressing room, a place of transition I take for granted. I was amazed to see this child stand in awe at these incredible modern women clad in elaborate period ruffles and laces. Enraptured, and frankly kind of mind-boggled, her young brain wrestled with the Onstage-ness of it (the corsets! the petticoats! the wigs! watching hair be put on someone's head!) and the Offstage-ness of it (the modern dressing room, the stage management's announcements, cell phones, cough drops, laughter). She sensed (rightly) that she was in some magic liminal zone watching worlds collide, and that moment itself felt like the distillation of a play staged by Les. A beautiful collision, peopled by family: now and then, intimate and vast, beautiful and grave, heaven and home.

In fact, I made an *actual* family album for the New York opening night of *The Vibrator Play* to give out to the cast and creative team, something I've never done before or since – a book of photos taken during tech rehearsals of this warm and generous theater family that we had brought from Berkeley and expanded for our wonderful but improbable move to Broadway. We played at the beautiful Lyceum Theatre, and the edge of the stage, there was at sort of a convenient "counter" height, so it became a very easy spot to lean against while talking with the cast. And because the show was set in a very realistically depicted 19th century, the tension of the "fourth wall" (the invisible line between stage "house" and audience "house") became very heightened every time people from the "future" (us in the seats preparing the show for opening) leaned against the stage and broke the invisible plane to talk to people in the "past" (in their own 19th-century home, another set by Annie Smart). Like pushing into an old painting, the proscenium as its frame. In one of my favorite photographs of the album, Les is at the edge of the stage facing away from the camera and looking towards a slightly blurry and bustle-dressed Maria Dizzia. We see only the back of his head and his T-shirt that reads, in a way that clearly sows doubt but also feels true, "I have optimism."

Talking about Les really means talking about Love. Which he traffics in – although his reed-thin and vaguely 19th-century demeanor would seem to indicate someone altogether less warm. I believe he thinks we all are doomed, but quite beautifully so, and if the ship is going down, he clearly wants to be in marvelous company as it does. Les believes in love – young and old. He believes in Family. And he believes in simplicity – Les finds the poem of the play, if that makes sense. He trusts that if the poem is presented, simply and in the open, its contradictions and collisions intact, its heart will be available. Les creates the circumstances for, and moments of, deep affection and generosity. He believes in making big and bold choices and then just letting people get on with their work. There is never a threshold to cross with him, an "aha" moment or a target to work towards. There is just a continuation of a conversation which takes place . . . at dinner, in the rehearsal room, in front of an audience, on a walk after. Which feels like the essence of collaboration. And family.

*   *   *   *   *

DAVID ZINN *is a costume and set designer who works on Broadway and Off-Broadway. Sometimes far off. He grew up on an island on the West Coast but has lived on an island on the East Coast for most of his adult life. He has received some awards, which he's grateful for, but his passion is for tattoos (including designing the 2 that Les Waters sports on his forearms), queer performance, social justice, cats, and the collapse of the modern Republican party.*

Photographers

We photograph things in order to drive them out of our minds.

—Franz Kafka quoted in Roland Barthes,
Camera Lucida: Reflections on Photography

I was introduced to photography by the sister of a friend. Photography wasn't my first love. That was painting/sculpture. Rauschenberg's "Monogram." Francis Bacon. Bridget Riley.

I was at college in Manchester with the late Clare McIntyre. Originally an actor, then a playwright. *Low Level Panic, My Heart is a Suitcase.* She died of MS in 2009. Her sister Lel (Lesley) is a photographer and I liked her photographs and she educated me in photography. The looking, not the doing.

I collect photographs. It's an obsession. I have some interesting ones by Mark Klett, Becky Cohen, Markéta Luskačová, Jacques Henri Lartigue, Callum Angus McKay, Ryan Bourque.

Here's a list of photographers I like:

Ralph Eugene Meatyard
Francesca Woodman
Masahisa Fukase
Diane Arbus
Masao Yamamoto
Dawoud Bey

DOI: 10.4324/9781003170808-45

Lee Friedlander
Seydou Keita
Gary Winogrand
Markéta Luskačová
Peter Hujar
Adger Cowans
Robert Frank
Vivian Maier
Rinko Kawauchi
Sally Mann
Carrie Mae Weems

This list could go on and on.

A few more productions of mine

Nebraska by Keith Reddin, La Jolla Playhouse, 1989.
One of three collaborations with Keith. An underappreciated writer and a razor-sharp critic of American hypocrisies. One of many productions at La Jolla. Beginning of my life on the West Coast, also the beginning of my involvement with UCSD. Why my intense love of California? Why not may be the answer.

Action by Sam Shepard, UCSD Dept of Theatre, La Jolla, 2002.
The second time I've directed this play. Previously at the Belfast Arts Festival in 1975 in a deserted community center – during the Troubles. When will I do it again? I would love to do it again. A play that endlessly fascinates me. Simultaneously specific in its physical actions – reading a book, sweeping a floor, gutting a fish – and also awash in connections and allusions and poetry. One of several productions with the students at UCSD. Also *Icarus's Mother* by Shepard, also *India Song* by Marguerite Duras, also a workshop production of *Big Love*. I met Sam a couple of times and wish I had been free to direct his last show, *Heartless*, at Signature in NYC. That's a genuine regret. Not being able to spend time with Sam, to learn from Sam. I loved Sam because I thought he was America – the world of loners and oddballs and towns with crazy names such as Azusa and cowboys and Bob Dylan and farm houses in the middle of nowhere and Patti Smith and dying for love and Joni Mitchell and working-class America and driving forever down long long long empty roads. And he was charismatic and so very beautiful.

DOI: 10.4324/9781003170808-46

At the Vanishing Point by Naomi Iizuka, Humana Festival of New American plays, Louisville, 2004.
The lives of a white working-class community in Butchertown, Louisville. Meatpacking plants. How many plays are there about the working class that are not voyeuristic? No "ooh, let's look at the working people." Not patronising. No sense of the working class is just like us but grubbier and with a more limited vocabulary. I think productions are gifts, here's something beautiful, here's something useful, here's something you might not really like but you'll appreciate it sometime in the future. *Vanishing Point* is a gift for Phyl and Les, my parents. Revived in 2015 during the main season at ATL. A play about community and a play about a particular community. Music by Tara Jane O'Neil. A play about a photographer, Ralph Eugene Meatyard. A hero of mine. Performed by my frequent collaborator, Bruce McKenzie. A hero of mine. How do we see? What is there? What can we not see? And Time, that great fucker of all things, Time. What will we leave behind? How will we be remembered?

In the Next Room (or the vibrator play) by Sarah Ruhl, Berkeley Rep, 2009, later Lyceum Theatre, NYC.
On the opening night of *Eurydice*, before the show, Sarah and I had drinks. I don't watch Opening Nights. Too tense making. I offered Sarah a commission that night. If I remember correctly, she had two ideas – something to do with Demeter, something to do with something that I now totally forget, and a question. Had I read *The Technology of Orgasm* by Rachel Maines about the use of the vibrator to cure women of hysteria? Of course, I hadn't read the book, but who could resist that? A technically complex play to direct – two rooms on stage, action often in both. What can you see? What can you hear? Using the resources of a regional theatre to generate work for myself. My one and only show on Broadway. In the beautiful Lyceum Theatre. Production and theatre a perfect match. My friend Leigh Silverman said "People go to Broadway for the rides. Who has got the biggest ride? What is the newest ride? You didn't make a ride. You made an art installation."

Girlfriend by Todd Almond (book) and Matthew Sweet (music), Berkeley Rep, 2010, and then other theatres (Kirk Douglas, LA; Actors Theatre of Louisville).
About 2 young guys who have just left high school, who fall in love in a small town in Nebraska. The pleasure and terror of sex and love. The joy of discovering what the body needs. Great music mainly from Sweet's *Girlfriend* album, cast of two, all lesbian band, led by the great Julie Wolf. One of two musicals I have directed and one of my favorite productions.

I'm not an avid fan of my own work but this one is a good thing and makes me happy.

Our Town by Thornton Wilder, Actors Theatre, Louisville, 2014.
A famous play for the theatre's 50th anniversary season. A play I knew of, had read once at college in the 1970s, and had never seen in either the US or UK. A play everybody knows or claims to know or believes that they know. A play that knows exactly what it wants to do and does it with skill and precision. A learning experience. Emotional torture. Mimi Lien's 'empty' space plus blue chairs plus model town on rolling tables plus giant revolving moon. All of the acting apprentices. Wilder and Stein were great friends. Why is Stein a hip goddess and Wilder is cozy Uncle Thornton? A rose is a rose is a rose. Rehearsal is rehearsal is rehearsal. A day is a day is a day.

Macbeth, Shakespeare, Actors Theatre, Louisville, 2016.
Only my second Shakespeare. Can one actually 'see' the play *Macbeth*? Or is it smeared with such *Macbeth*-ness that it's obliterated? Everybody knows it. What happens in *Macbeth* if the audience are denied the usual hand holds? No Porter. No double double toil and trouble. In my white liberal world does anybody really believe in witches? What are you prepared to do to get what you want? The questions, the questions. Productions revolve around a vision and a question. What is the central question? Built around Andrew Garman as Macbeth. Built around Ryan Bourque's fight choreography. I love design and hope my productions have beauty and grace but this was off the charts. Set by Andrew Boyce, costumes by Kristopher Castle, lights by Mark Barton, sound and music by Christian Frederickson. Built around the music of JLin and particularly Black Origami. Every day at the beginning of rehearsal felt like standing at the base of Everest and looking up and thinking how does one get up there? I don't burn to direct more Shakespeare. Maybe *Richard 2*? Maybe *Midsummer Night's Dream*? Maybe *Lear*?

Little Bunny Foo Foo, book by Anne Washburn, music by Dave Malloy, Actors Theatre, Louisville, 2018.
I never made a kid's show when the kids were young. Our kids – Jacob, Nancy, and Madeleine – who spent so much of their childhoods in theatres. Homework in the Green Room. Sleeping in dressing rooms whilst their parents were in tech. Belatedly a gift to them. A personal conversation with their younger selves. Often a production is a conversation with another director. Can anyone direct *A Midsummer Night's Dream* without being in conversation with Peter Brook's production? Aren't all productions of *MND* haunted by that one? This is common currency in the art world but not in the theatre. *Little Bunny Foo Foo* is perfect for kids and stoners. Brilliant team

of collaborators – all hail choreographer Barney O'Hanlon – and acting company led by the truly great April Mathis and Sam Breslin Wright. Unhinged looniness. So much discipline, so much buoyant chaos. This show has my favorite lyric:

> If I could make a wish
> And if that wish could come true
> The wish that I would wish is to be brand new
> I'd want to be something other than myself
> Possibly a woodpecker, a ferret, or an elf.

A loopy perfection.

Also the first time I have ever directed in the round. Hopefully the last.

19. *Macbeth* at Actors Theatre of Louisville (2016).

20. *Little Bunny Foo Foo* at Actors Theatre of Louisville (2018).

21. *Little Bunny Foo Foo* at Actors Theatre of Louisville (2018).

193

22. *In the Next Room* at the Lyceum Theatre on Broadway (2009).

"About Memory. About Ghosts."

Naomi Iizuka

This is my first memory of meeting Les. It may or may not be the first time we actually met, memory being a slippery and unreliable thing. Les and I are at the Mag Bar in Louisville. We're both there working at the Humana Festival. Though we're working on different shows, we end up in the same booth where we started talking about photography. We talked about photographers we loved. I'm pretty sure we talked about Nan Goldin. I think we talked about a book we both had come across and were fascinated by called *Wisconsin Death Trip*. We may have talked about the great Japanese photographer Hiroshi Sugimoto, but I think that was later. Mostly, we talked about the mystery of photography, how we see, how we try to document our lives, how we process the world around us, what we take in and what we miss. We talked about memory. We talked about ghosts.

The conversation with Les that began that day in a dive bar in Old Louisville evolved into a bigger, sprawling conversation between us that took place over the next couple years. This is one of Les's many gifts as an artist and a collaborator. He engages in fascinating conversations that provoke and inspire. We'd cross paths in different cities where we were working and we'd pick up where we left off. Les was fascinated with the ways in which photography as a medium resonated with theatre. At first blush, these two forms would seem diametrically opposed. Photography is about single moments frozen in time. Theatre, by contrast, is about a series of ephemeral experiences. And yet, as Les intuited and as I gradually learned, photography and theatre had much to say to one another. Both forms are preoccupied with capturing lived experience in authentic and surprising ways. Both forms present compressed,

DOI: 10.4324/9781003170808-47

elliptical stories that invite the viewer to fill in the blanks. Both forms are preoccupied with the possibilities and limitations of perception.

Time passed. I was working on a commission from Actors Theatre of Louisville. The theatre had asked me to write a play about Butchertown, a Louisville community on the Ohio River that had once been home to a thriving industry of meatpacking plants and stockyards. I spent time interviewing people who had worked in the plants and their families. I immersed myself in archival research. I developed some characters. I had some images. I had some writing that I was moderately happy with, but I was lost. The larger architecture of what the piece should be eluded me. I had bits and pieces of something, but I didn't know what the thing should be. Around that time, I reconnected with Les. We went for a walk around Butchertown as I told him about the piece I was working on. We walked past the Edison House and Beargrass Creek. We had a drink at Johnsons Bait and Beer. Les asked me if I had heard of a photographer named Ralph Eugene Meatyard. I had not. He told me to go look him up and so I did.

Meatyard's photographs blew my mind. I became obsessed. I did a deep dive into his work. An idea began to take shape for how to approach the piece I was writing, what the structure might be. This is another one of Les's many gifts as an artist and a collaborator. He's able to listen, really listen, and then make huge intuitive leaps. His mind has an uncanny ability to see connections between unexpected elements and knit them together in extraordinary ways. In our walking and talking through Butchertown, Les had an intuition that Meatyard might offer a clue to the puzzle I was trying to figure out in the writing. He was right. He was able to see a path through the thicket of writing where I did not.

Meatyard was one of the great American photographers of the 20th century, though his work may not be as well-known as others. He lived in Lexington, Kentucky, and was an optician by training. He took haunting, gorgeously strange photographs of his wife and children in abandoned buildings. Standing in ruined rooms, they wore rubber Halloween masks that were simultaneously grotesque and beautiful, alien and also deeply human. Meatyard was eccentric and prolific. He took photographs of Red River Gorge for his friend Wendell Berry's book *The Unforeseen Wilderness*. He took a series of photographs of twigs he called *Zen Twigs*. He took photographs of his friend Thomas Merton playing bongos and standing in a field. Meatyard's last work was a series of photographs called *The Family Album of Lucybelle Crater*. They were photographs that he took of himself, his family, and friends. The photographs are taken in living rooms and backyards that seem familiar, quaint even, but everyone is wearing a Halloween mask. In a very literal sense, identities are obscured. We wonder who these people are. We wonder about their lives. Make no mistake. There is joy and mischief in the work, but there is also something else, something thrumming just beneath the surface: an awareness of all that we don't know, a fierce longing for connection in a universe that is mysterious and at times terrifying.

Les and I ended up making a theatre piece together called *At the Vanishing Point*. It's about Butchertown, but it's also about Ralph Eugene Meatyard. It's about family and home. It's about how we see, how we try to document our lives, how we process the world around us, and what we take in and what we miss. It's about memory. It's about ghosts.

Les and I worked on *At the Vanishing Point* in 2004 in a site-specific production in an abandoned Butchertown warehouse and again in 2015 in Actors Theatre's Pamela Brown Auditorium. Revisiting the work after more than a decade was a revelation and a gift. In the intervening years, I had become a mother and my life had changed in countless ways. Les had moved to Louisville and taken over as Artistic Director of Actors Theatre. Returning to the piece was an opportunity to see the work and one's own life in relationship to the work with new eyes. There are images that stick with me from both productions. I remember the Photographer's children running at full speed through the space and then being all of a sudden very still. I remember the great actor Bruce McKenzie who was cast as the Photographer in both productions playing jazz on an old record player and showing the audience slides on an old projector. I remember the part where he talked about his wife, and how she appeared like an apparition in the vast darkness. I remember the beautiful, haunting song that Tara Jane O'Neil sang and Ben Sollee playing cello. I also remember so many moments in between performances. I remember sitting in tech with dramaturg Tanya Palmer in the freezing cold warehouse where we did the piece in 2004. I remember my son walking through Annie Smart's set, thrilled by the scaffolding and the grass. I remember standing with Les and watching and listening, trying to figure out the thing.

I realize now in retrospect that the piece that Les and I ended up making grew out of 15 years of conversation. We had begun a conversation about photography that turned into a long conversation about how we understand our lives both as individuals and as part of a larger community. It was a conversation that ended up including many other artists and eventually audiences. It was a conversation that wrestled with these daunting existential questions about nothing less than how you live your life. This is maybe Les's greatest gift as an artist and a collaborator. He understands that what we do is a kind of ongoing conversation with those that are with us now and those that came before. Les understands this in a way that few others do. He understands how to ask the best questions, open-ended and surprising. He understands how to listen. He has the patience to work through the knots and tangles of the process. He has an almost sixth sense about connections that are otherwise impossible to see. He sees them before you do. And then, he has the grace and generosity to point the way.

*   *   *   *   *

NAOMI IIZUKA *is a playwright whose best-known plays include* Polaroid Stories, 36 Views, Anon(ymous), *and* Aloha, Say The Pretty Girls. *Les Waters has premiered two of her plays,* At the Vanishing Point *and* Concerning Strange Devices from the Distant West, *and they are collaborating on two ongoing projects,* Out of Time *and* Black Mountain Women. *Her plays have been produced at Berkeley Rep, Actors Theatre of Louisville, Children's Theatre Company, The Goodman, and Brooklyn Academy of Music, among others. The recipient of numerous playwriting awards and fellowships, she is the head of the graduate playwriting program at the University of California San Diego.*

Evacuation list

On Friday, October 23, 2020, David White of the Berkeley City Manager's Office sent out the following:

> With high fire danger starting Sunday at 11am, everyone, especially residents in the Berkeley hills, should stay on heightened alert, keep phones charged and nearby, consider leaving the hills before Sunday afternoon – especially if they have trouble getting out quickly in a fire . . . A Red Flag Warning has been issued for the Berkeley hills from 11am Sunday October 25 to 5am Tuesday October 27. Current forecasts project winds in the region to be as strong or stronger than those present during 2019's devastating Kincade Fire and the 2017 wine country fires. Combined with record-low moisture levels, these winds are expected to create the most dangerous fire weather Berkeley has seen so far this year.

Evacuation list, Saturday, October 24, 2020:

3 full changes of clothes
Something to sleep in
Pair of indoor shoes
The red emergency kit
iPhone and charger
Laptop and charger
Masks and hand sanitizer
Meds
Something to read

DOI: 10.4324/9781003170808-48

Bottles of water
Passports
Documents (house insurance, proof of house ownership, birth certificates)
Tikki's carrier, cat food, cat litter, and box
Gus's harness, dog food, bed?
Blankets and towels for the animals
Do laundry
Bring in garden furniture
Wash the dishes
Take out the trash
Water the plants and lawn

(Annie also took photographs of the kids out of their frames and packed them.)

Our good friend Suzanne Pettigrew had offered accommodation but the winds never reached the potentially devastating speed so, along with most of the neighborhood, we didn't evacuate. The house is still here, my books and photographs are still here, the garden is still growing. Fires and a pandemic. A possible catastrophe within a catastrophe.

The Humana Festival of New American Plays

New plays can be very fragile. The plays in the Humana Festival rehearse fast. They don't have weeks of previews like in New York. This is the first time they are put up on their feet. During the interview process for the artistic director position at Actors Theatre, I spoke with a panel of playwrights and asked what they wanted for the Humana Festival, what was their biggest need. It was Time. More time to rehearse. More tech time. More previews. One preview and then Opening are clearly not enough. Creating new work demands time. The beauty of working for a company such as Joint Stock in the 1970s and 1980s, when the Arts Council of Great Britain was generous with funding, was that resources were used to buy time. I cut a show from the Humana lineup and reallocated monies for more rehearsal and more tech and an extra preview.

Eight of us read scripts for the festival. Sometimes six but usually eight. Six women and two men. If one of us had an obsession with a play and talked passionately about it and the need to produce it, that was always a factor. If we read a play at the beginning of the summer and sufficient people said, "Oh, this play is really interesting," and three months later, after reading many, many more plays we were still interested in that play, that always spoke to something. That was a sign of something. And then, did we think a play was important? Was it saying something about how we're living now? Whose story was being told? Whose voice was being heard? We would search for a range of voices. For diversity in the writers and different ways of telling stories. Hopefully stories that we had not heard before. Five naturalistic plays

DOI: 10.4324/9781003170808-49

by straight white male playwrights would not make an interesting Humana. Certainly not responsible.

Amy Wegener and I shared an interest in "messy" plays. I have an aversion to the perfectly crafted play where everything is neatly tied up at the end. Amy and I would read a play and think, "Oh, this is sort of great. It's messy and it's unresolved." We never programmed thematically. People thought we did but we didn't. We never sat down with the idea that this is the year of plays about gun control, this is the Humana Festival exploring the idea of citizenship, what makes an American, American. Of course, once the plays are selected and produced and performed, then connections appear because the human mind is programmed to make connections, to detect structure, to demand logic and intention. I once (jokingly?) referred to the 2013 Humana as the "OMG! WTF!" Festival, but that label could be applied to any Festival (or Main Stage Season) because of the history and politics and culture of the country we live in.

On a practical level, there are three theatres to program: the 633-seat Pamela Brown Auditorium; the 318-seat Bingham Theatre, a steeply raked arena theatre; and the intimate 150-seat Victor Jory Theatre. A play had to "fit" one of those three spaces. If we discovered a play with a large cast, a dozen or more, and we chose to produce that play, then that choice would affect the size of everything else. If we could, it was always helpful to have a "shiny" play in there, something by a recognizable name. A Sarah Ruhl commission or Will Eno's *Gnit* would help to draw people to the festival. I was the one with the power of veto, which I occasionally exercised. There were plays that I didn't like and didn't want in the festival and other members of the team could be very enthusiastic, but I just didn't like it. Rare, rare. And there were plays that I was not as enthusiastic about as the others, but commitment and passion are important and those plays went ahead.

One of the myths surrounding the Festival is that we had the choice of any play out there. It's simply not true. We lost plays to other theatres. Sometimes, agents submitted plays that were not available. Sometimes, directors attached to a project were working elsewhere.

The feeling I remember, most of the time, was "I wish the Humana Festival was more enjoyable." For a director who directs new plays, it was one of the major reasons for applying for the position at Actors Theatre. It's a prestigious festival, and it's a starry event. But it was hard work, for everybody involved, for the entire staff of the theatre, to produce a Main Stage season that ran from the end of the summer through to January and then follow immediately with a season of new American plays in the winter and spring. It was draining. It was physically and emotionally exhausting. Every year it reduced me to tears at some point. Meredith and I would say that our objective was not to cry in public. Or not to be caught crying in public.

It's disappointing when a show is crushed by the critics. It's harsh and demoralizing, particularly from *The New York Times*. Charles Isherwood was supportive of the plays that I directed, but there was a pattern in his festival reviews: one show would be praised, one would be acceptable, and the majority lightly dismissed. And one play he would crucify. That a critic cannot recognize the qualities of a play, what the writer is trying to do or what the production is trying to do, the particular circumstances of the production, and will quash it in a few sentences, that is deeply irresponsible. That play might have no further life.

When I first interviewed for the job in Louisville, I spoke about the need for a broad and vigorous commissioning program. How is it possible to create a festival of new plays without commissions? How is it possible to plan a festival without knowing that new play X by playwright Y about subjects A-B-C-D will be available in two years' time? How do we maintain a writer's loyalty? A commissioning program was a deal breaker for me and was agreed to by the Board and monies were reallocated to support this necessary work. In my time at Actors, 15 plays were commissioned and 4 were produced: Sarah Ruhl's *For Peter Pan on her 70th Birthday*, Chuck Mee's *The Glory of the World*, and Lucas Hnath's *The Christians* and *The Thin Place*. In addition, all writers for the Apprentice shows were commissioned: Jeff Augustin, Jaclyn Backhaus, Charise Castro, Sarah Delappe, Jackie Sibblies Drury, Idris Goodwin, Diana Grisanti, Rinne Groff, Dipika Guha, Cory Hinkle, Lucas Hnath, Claire Keichel, Basil Kreimendahl, Justin Kuritzkes, Martyna Majok, Meg Miroshnik, Ramiz Monsef, Brian Otano, Jihae Park, Jason Gray Platt, Amelia Roper, Jen Silverman, Anne Washburn.

I left Actors Theatre in the summer of 2018 and I am happy with that decision. I am not a believer in artistic directors staying for extended periods of time. Theatres need new blood. They need to change, to respond to the times. Since emigrating to the States in 1995, I worked at UCSD Department of Theatre and Dance (eight years), Berkeley Repertory Theatre (eight years), and Actors Theatre of Louisville (six and half years). It was time to de-institutionalize myself. Time to embrace a different kind of insecurity. But if I were to run another theatre, or in some parallel universe, I am still the Artistic Director of Actors Theatre of Louisville, one of my goals, my passions, would be to expand the commissioning program to include all theatre artists. Foundations and Grant Givers, and unfortunately the majority of theatres, rigidly insist that only writers are primary artists. The rest of us are only there to support, at best, to interpret the work of writers. We are considered second-class citizens. I don't identify as an interpreter, I am a director. The rest of us – designers and dramaturgs and stage managers and directors – are both collaborators and artists. How exciting would it be to commission a director or a designer to create something? Who knows what that would be? How wonderful would it be to fund a dramaturg? How delicious to say to a stage manager we think you are vital and necessary to our building and we want to support you in your artistic obsessions? We are skilled and passionate people who need to create, and financial support is a necessity. Theatre isn't our hobby. It's our profession. Why not a Humana Festival of New Theatre Artists?

"Partnership Leadership"

Jennifer Bielstein

I met Les Waters for the first time in 1997 when I was the marketing manager at Steppenwolf Theatre and he was hired to direct *The Designated Mourner* by Wallace Shawn. I remember being impressed with his directing and the respect he commanded from actors and the playwright. He returned the next year to direct Shelagh Stephenson's *The Memory of Water*. I'm not sure that he really has any memory of me from that time, but he always at least pretends that I made an impression.

Fast forward to 2011 and Actors Theatre of Louisville, where I had been managing director for five years already, working in collaboration with Marc Masterson. When Marc left for South Coast Repertory, we launched a national search for a new artistic director. The role of artistic director at Actors Theatre, with the opportunity to support an array of artists and to influence the field on a national level through the Humana Festival of New American Plays, is a plum position. We had a robust and inclusive search with many strong candidates. During the search, Martha Lavey, artistic director at Steppenwolf Theatre at the time, made sure that Les and I connected and helped us to interpret each other throughout the process. She was ever the supporter of people she cared about and I think she knew that we'd be really well-matched.

I remember Les arriving for the first round of in-person interviews – clean shaven as I remembered him from Steppenwolf. He remained a front runner and returned to Louisville weeks later, and there he was with his now-signature beard. I've never understood how it could have grown so quickly!? I'll also never forget how upon his return we were at dinner with a few members of

DOI: 10.4324/9781003170808-50

the search committee and someone asked him a question that I could tell didn't sit well with him. He slowly shook down his chain bracelets to the end of his long arm and deliberately rolled up his long white shirtsleeve, displaying a brilliant full-arm tattoo designed by David Zinn. Then, he leaned back and answered the question. From there, I knew that working with Les would keep me on my toes!

Les won the role and started as Artistic Director in 2012. He and I had a very collaborative and successful working relationship with a classical division of key responsibilities – he curated the art, I ran the business, and we came together on institutional planning and strategic choices – all with an amazing team. We understood each other, and we developed a complete trust that was grounded in great respect and mutual admiration. We each knew how and when to let the other shine, and stayed side-by-side, literally and figuratively, through it all.

It wasn't easy. To run a theater, especially one with a strong commitment to new work, is expensive. There was always the hope that the money and support needed to maintain Actors Theatre's leadership role in new play development and to launch new initiatives would just fall from the sky. We wanted to serve the local community and to advance the Theatre's national legacy. We went to numerous meetings with supporters to seek and to steward funds for that dual purpose. We encountered so much generosity and then there remained so much need. I remember sitting in my car one day talking Les off the ledge after he and I made a significant ask of some donors. They didn't immediately say yes, and Les was really frustrated. Part of my role was to ensure he felt motivated and engaged, and I succeeded to a degree that day, but the level of support we needed was more than we could quickly raise. Inspired by his Joint Stock roots, Les imagined creating work with the community in a big, bold way; we were able to launch a couple of projects but never on the scale that he/we envisioned. It is easier to find support for facilities than for the fleeting art that goes in them. Such are the limitations of the non-profit world.

When you work closely with Les, you get to know the whole person – family, friends, health, opinions, styles, and needs. When Les came to Louisville, he and his talented wife, Annie Smart, kept their home in Berkeley. He spoke longingly and lovingly of both. With Annie solidly grounded in her own successful career, they went through the challenge of a long-distance marriage. Les's love for Annie was always apparent, as was his love for and pride in his three children: Jacob, Nancy, and Madeleine. Theater is hard on relationships and on family. They were able to make it work, and it is important for other theater workers to see that with some creativity and commitment and, I'm certain, a few ups and downs, it can be done.

As a working partner, Les was terrific. He can be quite serious about the work, and then incredibly fun, sometimes dark, but always generous and respectful. Each season, he would set out an artistic vision and we would work as a team to figure out how to make it happen. I appreciated the constant exchange of dialogue, information, and ideas. Our offices were no more than ten steps from each other, allowing for frequent quick exchanges. I'm rather serious and focused at work, and whenever I'd hear a screech of laughter from across the way, either from Les's office or the desk of our assistant Janelle Baker, I'd run out to find some hilarious cat video or weird internet meme that Les had discovered while "working." And we all just buckled over in laughter!

I remember the range of work Les directed, starting with an intense production of Eugene O'Neill's *Long Day's Journey Into Night*. Todd Almond's *Girlfriend*, with Matthew Sweet's music as a guide, was a staff and community favorite. Lucas Hnath's *The Christians* kept Louisville talking and thinking for weeks non-stop. Chuck Mee's abstract and provocative *Glory of the World* was filled with emerging artists from our Actors Theatre Professional Training Company. And thanks to the vision and passion of Roy Cockrum, we had the exciting opportunity to remount this Humana Festival premiere and bring it to BAM, a career highlight for both of us.

I am sure that we appeared to many to be a mismatched pair, but we were great complements to each other. Les was willing to go with the flow and do what was needed – for the most part – to fulfill the institutional leadership aspects of his role. Each year, at Actors Theatre's annual fundraiser, a themed and costumed affair, we would be outfitted as a pair by the costume department, one year as Gianni and Donatella Versace, another with Les as the Conch King and me as a version of Carmen Miranda. We had the honor of leading the theater through its 50th anniversary – creating a block party for 10,000 Louisvillians, a fancy gala honoring key leaders and supporters, and a coffee-table book chronicling the theater's history – grateful that we were a piece of the puzzle for this storied institution at a very special moment in time.

I am certain that having an artist of Les's caliber leading Actors Theatre and the Humana Festival was exactly what the theater needed during those years. Les was able to leverage his artistic relationships to ensure the Festival was held in high regard as theaters, producers, agents, and critics from across the country and the world attended each year to experience multiple new plays in their world-premiere productions. It was such a pleasure to produce new work under his leadership by so many talented artists: Colman Domingo, Will Eno, Lucas Hnath, Naomi Iizuka, Branden Jacobs-Jenkins, Hansol Jung, Kimber Lee, Charles Mee, Sarah Ruhl, Jen Silverman, and so many more. I know he gave a jolt of energy to Louisville – sparking excitement and maybe even a little outrage – during his tenure. His passion and clarity around the work was a galvanizing force for Actors Theatre as a company during those years and remain a source of inspiration for me to this day.

Les and I were both always nervous to speak in front of the audience. We'd stand beside each other just before running down the aisle on opening nights or backstage before Humana events – in silence, trying to calm each other's nerves, Les in his pink Chuck Taylors and me in a fitted suit or dress. We would give each other a quick hand-squeeze and then go out, say our parts, and be so relieved when it was over. These are among the many moments I will never forget.

* * * * *

JENNIFER BIELSTEIN has been the Executive Director of the American Conservatory Theater in San Francisco since 2018 where she works in partnership with Artistic Director Pam MacKinnon. Prior to that, she was managing director of the Guthrie Theater in Minneapolis, managing director at Actors Theatre of Louisville, executive director of Writers Theatre in Chicago, and marketing director at Steppenwolf Theatre. She has a Bachelor of Arts from the University of North Carolina at Chapel Hill and an MBA from Bellarmine University. She is the immediate past president of the League of Resident Theatres. From her view in San Francisco (with a powerful pair of binoculars!), she can almost see Les across the Bay in the hills above Berkeley.

Chair exercises

A rehearsal exercise. A chair. I place a single chair in the space and I say, "Scott, tell me why this chair is the most beautiful chair you've ever seen." And you might say, "This chair is the most beautiful thing I've ever seen because it has four legs and it is very steady on the floor. The legs are slim. The seat is secure. And it has been well-used because there are all these marks and scrapes on it blah blah blah." Then I ask you to sit in the chair, and I ask the other members of the cast as their characters in the play, one by one, to say what they think is positive about your character. And one of them might say, "You're always kind to me," and another, "When I cry in Scene Three, you put your arm around me." And I ask, "Is there one line that sums that all up?" "Well, I do say, 'I love you.'" And everybody takes a turn in the chair.

I do it again and this time have somebody say why the chair is the ugliest, most revolting thing they have ever seen and they might say, "Well, it's got four legs and the legs are spindly and they don't sit right on the floor and it is badly chipped and scuffed blah blah blah." Then I ask the actor to sit in the chair in character, and once again the other actors say what their character thinks is negative about that character and what's a line that sums that up. Before the first run-through, I say to the cast, "Look, we're going to stumble through this for the first time and I want you to play all the opposites you were expressing earlier as strongly as possible." It's a very simple, straightforward exercise that reveals a surprising amount of material about the characters and their relationships to each other.

Here's another exercise that is to do with the distance you must travel in order to understand the world of the play. Early in the rehearsal period, I

DOI: 10.4324/9781003170808-51

take ten chairs and line them up from 1 to 10 with 10 being the highest and one the lowest. I ask the actors to enter the space and I ask them a series of questions. They are to make the questions personal to themselves and to answer by standing behind one of the chairs. In silence. I don't want them to talk about the questions. I don't want them to discuss the question with each other. I don't want them to interrogate me about the question. Just do it together as a company and I will do it along with them on my side of the chairs because it reduces my power as the director. It's important for the director to be seen participating, not judging.

So I might ask, "How much do you like the theatre?" And you could have two people standing behind the 10 chair, lots of people around 7 and 8, and so on. Or I could ask, "How well travelled do you think you are?" or "How educated are you?" or "How political are you?" Which is interesting because most people in the theatre will usually stand between 8 and 10, and then I will ask "How politically active are you?" and they will mostly shift down between 4 and 6. (It will be interesting to see how much the answer to this particular question changes because of the Pandemic and Black Lives Matter and "We See You, White American Theater.")

Later in the rehearsal period, I will return to this exercise, put out the chairs, and ask the cast to answer the questions from their character's point of view and not their own. It often reveals the gulf between the actor themself and their character in the world of the play.

"The Search Is the Destination"

Amy Wegener

At the center of a vast, dark stage, a lone figure sits in a wooden chair, his back to the audience, completely still, hands carefully placed on the small table in front of him. In silence, a series of thoughts projected on the rear wall of the cavernous set communicate flickers of awareness and sensation – thoughts describing ambient sounds, some identifiable like rain, others less distinct. The man remains perfectly motionless, his level gaze focused straight upstage, enveloped in the quiet. As time passes, you can hear the audience breathing, wondering. The man listens. The spectators take in the silence.

And then, suddenly, the image transforms. The lights become brighter, warmer, and a low rumble begins: an industrial-looking garage door opens in the back wall. Meditative solitude is replaced with a rush of motion and conviviality as a large group of men pour in, singing happy birthday and offering toasts in honor of Thomas Merton – the Trappist monk, activist, pacifist, mystic, writer, and more – each with a different point of view on his legacy. The play has become a party. Before long, the guys are running and climbing around the space. In a delirious sequence choreographed to the heavy guitar of King Tuff's "Black Moon Spell," they hang a dartboard and taxidermy trophies on the tall plywood walls, scoot around the stage, and set up game tables, snack bowls, and a refrigerator. Color and boisterous activity fill the warehouse-like set, remaking it into a kind of turbo-charged recreation room, a super-sized man cave. This is Les Waters's production of Charles Mee's *The Glory of the World*, which premiered in the 2015 Humana Festival of New American Plays at Actors Theatre of Louisville.

DOI: 10.4324/9781003170808-52

The wildly playful, arresting juxtapositions in this production are quintessential Les Waters – and not only because Les himself portrayed the contemplative figure who sat alone onstage. This example illustrates artistry that is unafraid of exploring the extreme edges and the messiness and mystery of life, drawing energy from that rather than trying to tidy the chaos or pretending to solve the riddle. The stage can hold silence that turns into raucous cacophony and back to silence in an instant, stillness and dance breaks, great precision within apparent mayhem, profundity and hilarity, and everything in-between. Like *The Glory of the World* itself – which Les invited Mee to write not to explain Merton's life, but rather to ponder how all of us contain volumes of contradictions – Les has a knack for expressing the irreducibility of experience, for holding paradoxical impulses in tension.

That ethos extends to the pre-production and rehearsal process as well. When Les directs, it rarely feels like there's a foregone conclusion that he's angling toward; he's more like the curious guide on a path that starts with acknowledged unknowns and no fixed destination. As a dramaturg fortunate to have worked with Les on many of his productions at Actors Theatre, I've learned a great deal from the model of leadership that he embodies. Being in a rehearsal room with Les is a master class on directing. Not because he claims to already have all the answers or to predetermine the outcomes, but quite the contrary – because his vision holds space for the questions and uncertainties that must be admitted in order to make new discoveries and inspire collaborators to bring our A-game to the work. There's a kind of relaxed rigor as ideas are floated in design meetings, as we chat with the playwright on breaks from a workshop or rehearsal, and as the actors come to inhabit their roles, encouraged to experiment with subtle adjustments. Of course, Les is decisive, too, but his choices are all the better metabolized because they evolve out of a shared exploration.

I admire the way that Les partners with writers to navigate the puzzle of a new play together, implicitly trusting the material and knowing that deeper understanding will come as the collaboration unfolds. It's evident that playwrights adore working with Les (as do I). He instills confidence that we'll figure things out along the way, that rehearsal is a necessarily iterative and accumulative learning process. It's a joy to be part of a room like that, to know that coming up with the perfect note that will solve things right out of the gate – even if that were possible – really isn't the goal. It allows me to be a sounding board in an authentic way, to respond to the work with wonder rather than any kind of premature certitude. Every play has a world all its own, and Les is expert at charting a course to let the topography reveal itself.

Les is often drawn to plays that contain the sorts of conundrums, rips in the space-time continuum, and weird staging challenges that his imagination is so well suited to tackle. I think of Lucas Hnath's eerie *The Thin Place*, a sly investigation of mind control and manipulation wherein Hilda, a woman with an interest in communicating with the dead, befriends a professional psychic who unveils the deception behind her technique. But Hilda counters with a chilling ghost story, whose coda is a phantom message from beyond that makes everyone in the theatre jump in our seats. Then the lights snap out, and the play's last movement takes place almost entirely in the dark, the space hypnotically lit only by one red light bulb as the characters hold a séance. With consummate irony, this theatrical summoning elicits the very response Lucas has been deconstructing all along by tricking the audience, creeping us out.

The title was inspired by an old superstition about the "thin places" between this world and the next that Les's grandmother had warned him to avoid as a child in England. With relish, Les would describe the dread of slipping through such a membrane, never to be heard from again. In a sense, the play is Lucas' nimbly rational mind working out why the belief in such ideas can be so hard to resist, placing logic in tension with the powerful psychological traps that might lead to experiences with the uncanny – among other, more insidious things. Les's productions of *The Thin Place*, staged in the most intimate venues at Actors Theatre of Louisville and Playwrights Horizons, were calibrated with exacting subtlety and economy of movement. For instance, he trusted that Hilda, played by Emily Cass McDonnell, needn't stir from her armchair to mesmerize while divulging her sensitivity to the supernatural. Even during the play's most seemingly naturalistic middle scene, a gathering where friends of the elder seasoned psychic debate the methods and merits of her art, every move, interjection, and sip of wine was finely orchestrated to build the twisting conversation. In a show with some surprising magic tricks, Les's restrained precision was a kind of directorial sleight of hand in itself, as he staged the play's intense dialectical argument while also keeping the audience off-balance with a growing suspense that would ensnare us in the end.

When it comes to directing plays that establish a reality and then pull the rug out from under us, Les might have a sixth sense. I vividly recall his unsettling production of Jorge Ignacio Cortiñas' *Recent Alien Abductions*, which like *The Thin Place* begins with an intricate and enthralling monologue from a character who appears haunted. A young man named Álvaro tells us of a sweeping conspiracy involving a lost episode of *The X-Files*, furtively weaving an enigmatic, winding tale that bends toward humor at times. And yet, the character seems troubled. It won't become apparent until later, but the story he spins is an allegory for a devastating trauma in his past, a secret that the play will gradually unfurl. In Les's Humana Festival production, this storyteller (a quietly compelling Jon Norman Schneider) stood planted on a dark stage framed by a greenish, rectangular rim of light, eventually vanishing in the gloom as the audience became aware of a house emerging into view upstage. As the play jumped decades forward to a time after Álvaro's death, the stage picture morphed into a brightly-lit Puerto Rican living room with white walls and doors opening to more interior rooms behind. Here, the mystery surrounding the young man's past would become grounded in a hidden family history.

Speaking of family history, my memory also turns to Sarah Ruhl's *For Peter Pan on her 70th Birthday* and its beautifully observed conversation between five aging siblings during and after their father's death. With understated attention, Les's direction evoked the strange way that time moves during a hospital room vigil. His care for the rhythms of Sarah's delicately constructed banter illuminated family relationships and sculpted the drama of anxious waiting. With the father's passing, the play's energy shifts: a marching band bursts into the space, playing "When the Saints Go Marching In" as a transition out of the quiet hospital scene. (In Les's original production, the audience was amazed to see a real band stomp through Actors Theatre's Pamela Brown Auditorium.) Soon, the brothers and sisters gather around the family table for a lively wake, drinking, telling jokes, arguing about politics, and reminiscing. In performance, the overlaps and cadences of their speech were like music, precisely calibrated in both script and staging, as the ghosts of their dad and the old family dog ambled through the room, unseen. And then, when it dawned on the siblings that without parents, they were the grown-ups now, they magically became their counterparts in *Peter Pan*, taking flight and hovering over Annie Smart's wonderfully changed set – now a colorful, outsized children's bedroom at the threshold of Neverland. Les is a master at orchestrating these fantastical turns, leaning into moments of evolution with an adventurous visual sensibility and a deft skill for engineering shifts in style, mood, and tempo.

And I'll never forget Les's production of *Evocation to Visible Appearance*, by playwright and Episcopal priest Mark Schultz. This bleak yet darkly funny play gives shape to the idea of the Devil, as encountered through the odyssey of a teenage girl confronting a fallen world that's crumbling all around her. Or rather, I should say that the play is the Devil, in Mark's sense of staging an encounter with a void, a nothingness, a doomed future made visible in order to contend with it. Supertitles between the scenes – in Les's production, ominously projected high above the stage – suggest that the play itself has a consciousness, an internal voice of its own that's moving things along. ("Shhh." . . . "There's no need to be afraid" . . . "It's coming," it tells the audience at the top of the show, as the house lights fade.) The scenic design by Andrew Boyce turned Actors Theatre's Pamela Brown Auditorium into a burned-out shell edged with detritus, and at various points in the production, lighting instruments literally crashed from the ceiling and furry demonic figures emerged from the shadows. In the final moments, the characters took up musical instruments to become a black metal band and played – loudly and thrillingly. The show's finale felt like a concert at the end of the world, with lights piercing through the hazy air and lyrics projected in scrawled text above – the play's final howl.

Whether depicting apocalyptic dissonance, rollicking celebration, or hushed stillness, Les fully embraces what is most peculiar and idiosyncratic about the worlds he brings to the stage. His productions often feel like expeditions through previously uncharted theatrical terrain. Here I'm reminded of Les's many journeys on foot through various urban landscapes, sometimes traveling for miles in his Converse sneakers. Because he doesn't drive, he walked whenever and wherever he could, later recounting the strange adventures he'd had while moving through the rush of humanity, observing life unfolding from city sidewalks. I suspect that this innate curiosity, this impulse to wander and seek out experience outside the theatre's walls, is not unrelated to his imaginative capacity. In fact, it was a daily walk past an unusual historical marker on a corner in downtown Louisville – a plaque commemorating Thomas Merton and his spiritual epiphany while standing in that spot, suddenly overwhelmed – that impelled Les to commission a play that took Merton as its jumping-off point.

Amid the many scenes in *The Glory of the World* that no one (except Les Waters and Chuck Mee) would have imagined belonging in a play inspired by Thomas Merton, there's a stage picture that is one of my favorites of all time. In the foreground, a spotlight falls on two guys in tuxedos, playing a comically slow guitar version of a perky pop song, wistfully crooning. Suddenly, a rhinoceros – actually several actors in a giant rhino suit – appears behind them and starts lumbering across the stage. Meanwhile, even further upstage on designer Dane Laffrey's set, guys wearing swimsuits have set up a plastic tarp and sprinkler, and they begin to leap and slide on their bellies, in moves simultaneously balletic and flailing, from one side of the stage to the other. The particular combination of music and imagery, the pace of the rhino reveal, and its ponderous walk past the careening, Speedo-clad sliders was ridiculous and sublime all at once, a prime example of Les's wickedly funny sense of humor.

That sense of humor – by turns dark, goofy, and wry – manifests not only on-stage but in his interactions with collaborators as well. (I don't know anyone who can sustain a running joke longer.) It is crucial to Les's ability to build rapport in the creative process and to bring many imaginations onto similar wavelengths. During rehearsals for *The Glory of the World*, it was fascinating to witness how Les, movement director Barney O'Hanlon, and fight director Ryan Bourque (yes, the play's crescendo was an epic, outrageous fight) were able to combine their expertise in the room, also energized by Christian Frederickson's bold sound design. As the piece came into focus, it was remarkable how the individual sequences they built established a dynamic overall trajectory even as the show kept transforming. For all its unhinged wildness, the production had a narrative logic and flow all its own – and the vision was wholly legible to the team in a way that made it possible to keep inventing and refining. How exactly this came about still feels a bit inscrutable, but it's a testament to the way that Les's guiding instincts and trust toward fellow artists enable everyone's most productive impulses to come to the fore within a shared vocabulary, built by the group.

Actors Theatre of Louisville has an open rehearsal policy that allows anyone in the organization to observe the work and seldom did a member of the staff or the Professional Training Company slip into the room without being acknowledged at some point with a grin and a welcome from Les himself. This may seem like a small thing, but having worked with many different personalities, I can attest that it is significant, and arguably even central to his artistry. Cultivating a sense of community with informal ease, signaling to the room in subtle ways that everyone's presence matters, makes all the difference in holding a space for relaxed, focused creative energy. Les set the tone for the cast and crew to bring their best selves to the process, to imagine and problem-solve together.

Perhaps I've moved between describing Les's theatrical imagination and what his rehearsal rooms felt like because both reside in my memory so vividly, and these moments come flooding back in an impressionistic, not always linear way. But I've also come to believe that the ethos shaping a collaborative process and what ends up onstage are symbiotic and inseparable. And now I'm thinking about Les's reappearance at the end of *The Glory of the World*. After a jaw-dropping, 14-minute fight sequence involving the entire cast and every conceivable mode of combat, from a swordfight to a chainsaw chase, the set is littered with stuff everywhere, trashed to the point of absurdity. Into this wreckage, the man from the beginning of the play, having quietly entered to watch from the sidelines, moves back to the center of the stage and stands there. Again, his thoughts are projected on the wall in the silence. This time, however, he meets the audience with a steady gaze, and we can observe his face and long, graying beard. A series of questions appear behind him and linger for a long moment, questions like:

"Does the silence scare you?"
"Is nothing sacred?"
"Is everything sacred?"
"What is the question? Salvation, damnation?"
"Who can explain those things?"
"What is to be taken seriously?"
"Is there anything serious?"
"Is there anything not serious?"

For me, this image epitomizes Les Waters and his work: a searching director standing on a gloriously transformed stage, looking directly at the audience, surrounded by questions about how to live.

*   *   *   *   *

AMY WEGENER is the Literary Director at Actors Theatre of Louisville, where she first joined the literary department in 1997. She has been part of the curatorial and dramaturgical team for nearly half of the 45 iterations of the Humana Festival of New American Plays, including a digital festival and online exhibition in 2021. In the process, she has mentored, worked alongside, and learned from a generation of dramaturgs and has co-edited more than twenty anthologies of new plays. During and after Les Waters's tenure as artistic director, she dramaturged ten of his productions at Actors Theatre, including Macbeth, The Glory of the World, and The Thin Place. She was also the literary manager at the Guthrie Theater for four years. An avid walker, she can often be found hiking around her neighborhood reading plays at the same time, mostly without tripping.

Some thoughts on somebody who is a stage manager

Somebody who is brilliant at pagination.
Somebody who is a stage manager and only a stage manager.
Somebody who will protect the show once the director has departed.
Somebody who can read the temperature of the room.
Somebody who is good with people.
Somebody who is fair.
Somebody who has great communication skills.
Somebody who is on time.
Somebody who realizes that the production is a living breathing thing.
Somebody with a sense of humor.
Somebody who doesn't roll their eyes.
Somebody who doesn't waggle their foot with impatience.
Somebody who is interested enough in this list and wants to contact me.
Somebody who has a plan for 1st day of rehearsal and 1st day of tech and 1st preview.
Somebody who is a speed thinker.
Somebody who is alive and present to the rhythms of a show in performance.
Somebody who wants to talk about the play.
Somebody who has a sense of adventure.

DOI: 10.4324/9781003170808-53

"The Trust Factor"

Paul Mills Holmes

To understand Les's work as a director, you have to look at how I do my job as a stage manager. I start each new project by mapping out a plan for the rehearsal process, the technical rehearsals, and finally the performance. The basics are always the same: read the play; make lists of props, scene changes, costume changes, and sound and lighting cues; tape out the set; get the rehearsal room ready; call a production meeting to talk through what is coming; and then get started. I don't spend a lot of time at the beginning analyzing the play. I wait for the director and the company to sit at the table, read the play, and then talk it through. That is when I can begin to figure out the why and how of the production.

Over the years, I have learned to keep an eye on the big picture. It is easy to get distracted by the little things – like how a piece of furniture gets on and off stage or whether a costume piece can be preset or how a prop tracks from one side of the stage to the other. I rely on my stage management team to keep an eye on these details so that I can concentrate on details more pertinent to the director's concerns, such as blocking and staging, the placement of sound and lighting cues, and whether the story is being told.

Working with Les always keeps me on my toes. The first show that he and I did together was *Long Day's Journey Into Night*. I had never done the play before, and it was his first production as Artistic Director at Actors Theatre of Louisville. I had seen Les's work as a guest director at the Humana Festival before: Chuck Mee's *Big Love* in 2000 and Naomi Iizuka's *At the Vanishing Point* in 2004. The acting companies made the material shine, and both were visually stunning, clear in their storytelling, and completely different. So, I

DOI: 10.4324/9781003170808-54

knew he would approach the O'Neill with an uncomplicated design and cast it with wonderful actors. But when I was able to sit in the room and watch him direct, it became clear that his approach to the work was on a different plane.

It was a somewhat foreign approach to me at first, but one that I was eager to learn. Working with dramaturg Amy Wegener, he edited the play down and eliminated the character of Cathleen, the Irish maid. Instead of the usual seaside cottage of the Tyrone family, with material walls and doors and period details in the decorations, he wanted the stage to be desolate and open to the surrounding sea. The furniture (including just the right wicker chair), the clothes, and the props were all carefully selected to set the scene and tell the story. What is usually a three-and-a-half-hour evening in the theatre was compressed into an intense two-and-a-half hours. As far as I was concerned, it was like a new play.

For Les, every play – whether it is *Macbeth* or an American classic like *Our Town* or *Long Day's Journey Into Night* or a Humana commission from Chuck Mee or Lucas Hnath – is a new play. He approaches every script with the same open mind. When the play is brand new and the ideas are radical and edgy and the playwright is madly rewriting between rehearsals and the director is thinking on his feet, that is when theatre is most exciting to me. Doing a new play with Les is always a challenge. Actors, designers, stage managers, and technicians have to be at the top of their game. My skills of diplomacy, kindness, and good humour are tested. There have been a few shows where I never actually understood why we were doing it or what the author was trying to say, but I always knew that I could ask. Sometimes, Les would give me an exasperated look that said how could you not know, and at other times, he would laugh and admit that he didn't understand the moment either and we would both laugh. At other times, he could say a few words and it would all become clear.

That's because Les communicates in a simple and direct fashion. He says what he means. You don't have to read between the lines. He can ask a question of a designer knowing that there might not be an immediate answer and that is okay. He does not feel the need to do the actors' work for them, but he can make a comment that will plant a seed that will help them to continue their work at home and come in the next day with movement forward. He knows what he likes and what he doesn't like. His notes are simple and to the point. This makes for such solid, grounded work that when it is time to leave the rehearsal room and move into the theatre the play is on such firm footing that time will not be lost during the long hours of tech solving problems or making adjustments that should have already been taken care of.

I remember a moment in rehearsal for *Gnit*, Will Eno's version of *Peer Gynt*. The production was loaded with big wagons of scenery, and I was getting nervous about a particular transition into and out of a scene in a vendor's shop. The more we did it, the more I realized we didn't need the large wagon that was going to come on for three minutes and then leave and never be seen again. When we were working on the transitions, I finally asked Les if he thought we really needed the wagon. I knew he liked to keep things moving onstage and this seemed to me to be a place where a simple prop would suffice. He looked at me and asked if the unit had been built. I knew it hadn't, and he said, "Let's cut it." End of discussion.

Being able to develop that kind of relationship with a director is what stage managers love. When you have the opportunity to work with a director many times, you develop a language and a kind of shorthand that keeps the paths clear for them to do the best work possible. Les and I did 13 plays together in seven years and because he came to trust me to look out for him and to be able to communicate his ideas and thoughts to actors and designers and technicians, we were able to make rehearsals easy and relaxed for all concerned. Technical rehearsals can be a nerve-wracking experience, and in the first few hours of tech, Les gets anxious. But once we get the opening three minutes staged, he settles in and lets the work unfold. He guides gently and lets folks do their work. He is generous with everyone in the theatre and does not lose his patience as can happen so often during these trying times. And as long as we have several bags of Cheetos on hand, the long technical rehearsals are pleasant and efficient.

On every opening night, Les likes to sit in the booth and watch the show. He watches from the audience during previews with the Assistant Director to take notes, and then on opening night, he is in the booth to watch. And whenever he comes back to watch a show, it is always from the booth. He will take notes as needed, and I will give his notes after the show or email them. Often, he will just listen to the play and not necessarily watch it. Since it is all about hearing it and not so much the visual, his notes are always succinct and clear. The only time he was in the booth where it became, how shall I say this, a distraction, was during a preview of *Girlfriend* at the Kirk Douglas Theatre in LA. He decided that it would be fun to do a running commentary on the show but even more on how I was calling the show that night. Clearly, he had taken his "Don Rickles Pills" because he was ruthless in one remark after another. I was barely able to keep from losing it. The trust factor was in full force that night, and at the end of the show, he just gave me that impish grin of his and thanked me for a good show.

In the end, the cleanliness and elegance of Les's work never ceases to amaze me. His directing feels invisible. Of course, you know it is there. Conceptually, what's onstage has to come from somewhere, but his collaboration with designers and actors is so trusting and so true that it feels all of a piece. Seeing a production of his is a satisfying experience. I may not always know why he picked a play. I only have to know he believes in the author and that his standards and his expectations are high. Mine are, too, and I think that is why we connected over the years. Our personalities are different. My somewhat relentlessly perky side balances out his darker, more English demeanor. But we share the same love of the process and the same boundless enthusiasm for theatre itself, and that's a big reason why we got along as a team.

*   *   *   *   *

PAUL MILLS HOLMES *is a production stage manager who was on the staff of Actors Theatre of Louisville for 28 seasons. He stage managed more than 130 regular-season productions at ATL, including every production directed there by Les Waters except for one. He spent 38 seasons at the fabled Totem Pole Playhouse in Fayetteville, Pennsylvania, and credits producer William Putch as an early mentor. Paul was a stage manager on* Oh! Calcutta! *during the New York City subway strike of 1979. And he was the original production stage manager on* Steel Magnolias *and on* Little Shop of Horrors, *which he later directed in Hebrew (in Tel Aviv) and in Japanese (in Tokyo) – neither of which he speaks! He is known to friends and colleagues as "Pablo."*

A cloud of direction

Art consists of its not being noticeable.

—Ovid

I don't like watching a play through a cloud of direction. Where the direction is drawing attention to itself: "Look at me directing this. I have directed every moment." I'm sure I have done that. Particularly as a younger director, when you have the opportunity, you want to show your stuff. You want to be seen doing it. You want people to notice you, to employ you. But sometimes, I watch a show and I think, "That's three productions worth of directing all at once." It feels as if I'm being told by the production how to respond to every moment. Of course, all productions are doing that in a way – teaching the audience how to relate to them – but if that is at the forefront of my engagement with the piece, then I am being forced into a passive role while the production does everything for me. While it answers all of its own questions. As an audience member, where do I exist in relation to this? Why am I watching?

The better hidden the author's views, the better for the work of art.

—Friedrich Engels

DOI: 10.4324/9781003170808-55

Opposites

I am addicted to opposites. To be precise, I am addicted to the space between opposites. It's important to look between the opposites at the space between two things. I have an acute sense of contradiction. I love contradiction in a production. If I am working on a play and somebody sticks a label on it that declares this is A GREAT TRAGEDY, I immediately think "If I direct this to be a great tragedy, that is reductive and that's all you'll see. Where is the opposite? What is the opposite? The opposite must exist there somewhere." If I see a show and an actor walks onstage and declares in some form or other I AM A BAD PERSON, and then they play a bad person (what does that even mean?) the entire time, I am defeated. And I think what can they do that reveals their character in an entirely different light.

I like queasy ground. I like things that are porous and travel back and forth between two poles. That intrigues me. I have always thought that everything was double-sided. That everything contains its reverse. And because I don't appreciate being told what to think, I need to keep the opposite spinning all of the time.

My maternal grandparents, Carey and Charles, were working-class socialists. I don't think they ever sat me down as a child and said, "You need to understand the principles of Hegelian dialectics." But when I did, I thought, "Thesis? Yes! Antithesis? Absolutely! Synthesis? Really? I'm not convinced." I don't believe that things resolve. Ever. I just don't believe it. I like change. I like the possibility of change. Cozy ideas of resolution and closure make me crazy. Change is the only constant. Productions should end with a big series of question marks. Shouldn't they?

DOI: 10.4324/9781003170808-56

Here's a favorite quote:

> I hate endings. Just detest them. Beginnings are definitely the most exciting, middles are perplexing and endings are a disaster. The temptation towards resolution, towards wrapping up the package, seems to me a terrible trap. Why not be more honest with the moment? The most authentic endings are the ones which are already revolving towards another beginning. That's genius.

—Sam Shepard, *The Paris Review*

"The Thing"

Sarah Lunnie

I met Les in the spring of 2012, when he became the Artistic Director of Actors Theatre of Louisville. I was the Literary Manager. I understood quickly, or thought I did, that he was a "cat" not a "dog." Don't fawn all over him, you'll only put him off; you have to let him come to you. He smoked but didn't carry his own cigarettes, so he always needed to bum one. That helped. He also couldn't drive because of his epilepsy, so sometimes he needed rides places. That first summer, I think, I drove him to a play development conference in New Harmony, Indiana. I'm not naturally a fill-the-silence conversationalist, and in the car, there were long stretches when we didn't talk at all. Les rolled his eyes during a lot of the formal conference events, including, I'm afraid to say, the readings, but he loved walking the grounds. There was a roofless church, and a pioneer cabin that the Scottish artist Jim Buchanan had converted into a camera obscura, which Les thought was great.

He had arrived at Actors just in time to see Ken Rus Schmoll's taut, troubling production of Lucas Hnath's *Death Tax* at the 2012 Humana Festival, and in response he decided to extend Lucas an offer of commission, his first as Artistic Director. I was thrilled. Lucas and I had developed a close collaboration working on *Death Tax*. Now, I would work with him as he wrote something new. This also meant embarking, for the first time, on an artistic collaboration with Les – and here I was nervous. Les's taste is so pure and unpretentious. His joy in what he loves is so real and so simple. But also he can be such a snob! And he wears his disdain, when he feels it, so openly! I remember once in an artistic staff meeting, he called someone (not present) a malevolent trout. It made me laugh and weirdly made me trust him, but

DOI: 10.4324/9781003170808-57

it also made me crave his approval. I really wanted him to think that I was smart. But I didn't know what it looked like to collaborate with a director on the development of a commissioned work. Or anything about how Les worked or, if I'm being honest, what (good) directing was.

It's funny to reflect on this, almost a decade later – how much I revered him, how unknowable he seemed – and how both of those feelings have and haven't changed. Right now, we're working together on another project, a series of short pieces commissioned by the National Asian American Theatre Company. "It's monologues and actors and a big empty space and one chair and one prop. Maybe a cigarette. Maybe an oxygen tank." (That's Les, in an email to the contributing playwrights, summing up the prompt, which is to write something for an actor over 60.) He took his inspiration from an Anna Teresa de Keersmaker dance piece called *Mitten Wir im Leben Sind*. In the midst of life, we are in death. As I write this in January 2021, the playwrights are sending us their first drafts. So, a few times a month, Les and NAATCO Co-Founder and Actor-Manager Mia Katigbak and I meet on Zoom to talk about whatever we've read lately. Yesterday, it was the first rough draft of Jaclyn Backhaus' "Black Market Caviar." Mia asked Les what he thought about it. "I like it," Les said. "I don't understand it, and that's always a good sign."

This strikes me as just about as succinct a distillation of his directorial credo as I can imagine.

Back in 2012, we had a bit of a false start, with Lucas taking up a project called *Kanye West Performs the Rise and Fall of George W. Bush* but quickly abandoning it for fear of a litigious muse. Then, in August that year, Lucas sent me an email with a Word doc attached. It contained an embarrassment of riches: seeds for plots, structural conceits, characters around whom a story might revolve. Each entry had an evocative dummy title ("Two Rooms," "Hot Shower/Cold Shower," "Mother [AKA, Guess Who This Play Is About]"), followed by a short description, 17 of them all told. "I'm in love with this man's brain," Les said when I showed him the file. Some of the ideas delighted Les, others flummoxed him; he thought all of it was fantastically interesting; I think he touched down lightly on a few entries that particularly intrigued him, but ultimately wasn't inclined to push Lucas in a particular direction. So, Lucas mulled a bit longer and fastened on the idea he'd nicknamed "Megachurch." The play would center on a pastor who sets out to liberate his congregation but ends up losing everything he built. This became *The Christians*.

Lucas grew up attending an evangelical megachurch with his mother, an ordained minister and hospital chaplain; Les's grandfather was a Methodist lay
preacher. Although the contexts could not have been more different, Christianity loomed large in both men's childhoods. I remember many of their
early conversations centered on those formative early experiences, where
they overlapped and how they differed. They were united by a shared desire
to investigate their subject seriously, without condescension. The trope of
the faith leader as a charismatic villain struck Lucas as facile and uninter-
esting. I remember him asking everyone he spoke with about the play what
rhetorical habits tended to make them mistrust a public speaker, so that he
(and eventually, Les) could avoid those gestures. He wanted to write a man
who was trying to do the right thing, who really *believed* he was doing the
right thing; someone genuinely likable, to whom a congregation or an audience might easily give their trust; a man with a long way to fall.

Other early conversations centered on the context of the performance itself.
Lucas was writing with ATL's Pamela Brown Auditorium, and Louisville, in
mind. He wanted to make a play for the festival's hometown audience, one
that would dramatize questions of deep personal and community concern.
A modified thrust in a two-level, 633-seat house, the Pamela Brown was a
perfect container for a play set in a megachurch. The play takes the form of
a church service, and Lucas felt he could use the architecture of the room
to collapse the boundary between the performance and audience, engaging
theatergoers as congregants.

The play premiered in the 2014 Humana Festival. Les's production was beautiful, full of mystery and pathos, evoking the tragic in a way that contemporary plays seldom do. He achieved Lucas' vision of closing up the distance
between the play and the room. The auditorium felt like a church: the stage
was an altar; the audience was the congregation; the actors processed from
the back of the house to enter the space with the house lights still on, disorienting audiences as to whether the "play" had really "started." Onstage, they
were flanked by a large Gospel choir. All of the actors were on microphone.
Les and Lucas' instinct to avoid anything that felt overly slick or polished
extended to exclude wireless mics, so the actors had to contend with long
cables as they walked, a constant negotiation between the desire to communicate and the immovable obstacle of the self. The choir sang hymns
and eventually left, en masse, in wordless protest. Their exit was quiet and
uncomfortable and took a long time. Ultimately, the pastor is left alone to
reckon with himself, his wife, and his God.

Every moment in the production felt – to borrow a phrase from Anne Washburn, another frequent Les collaborator – *attended to*. Rigorously attended to, I'd say. But that same quality that attracts him to work he doesn't understand, his attentiveness to mystery, his allergy to the easily reducible, made it difficult to grasp exactly *what* it was that he was up to at any given moment. He didn't say much. We had workshopped the play twice; by the time we gathered on the fifth floor of the Speer Building for our first rehearsal in February 2014, Les had been deeply immersed in the script, and in conversation with Lucas, for almost a year. Still, his instinct was to listen more than talk. We read the play. We took a break. "Shall we read it again?" Les said, and we did, again and again.

It's not that we didn't do "table work." Les encouraged the actors to stop as we read to ask questions or make observations. Lucas, a ruthless reviser of his own work, was also busy experimenting with new lines (or, more often, radical cuts) at the table. Nor was Les cagey when he had a strong opinion. He is perfectly comfortable giving a quick "no, that's not it" when he's confident that's not it. It's just that his engagement with this process was so restrained. Not so much quiet as spacious.

This has been my experience whenever I've worked with Les: he doesn't swallow up all of the oxygen in the room. He gives his collaborators – and the thing, itself, shimmering between us, this inchoate thing we're trying to make – his full attention. But he isn't trying to wrangle anyone or anything into submission, or pin something to a wall and name it and call it done. No one gets a prize for being clever in Les's rehearsal room. He's not afraid to admit when he doesn't know something, which makes room for everyone to be a little naive, to stay curious and attentive to what we're making. What is it, actually? Do we know? Are we sure? Are we, really? Shall we hear it again?

Starting with *The Christians*, many of the commissions Les extended during his tenure at Actors Theatre engaged in one way or another with the numinous edges of human experience, matters of faith and doubt and not-knowing, things elusive and half-in-shadow and difficult to grasp, ghosts and psychics and mystics and God. With Charles Mee's *The Glory of the World* (2015), he staged a 100th birthday party for the Trappist monk Thomas Merton, at once a raucous celebration of life and a serious investigation of the materiality of silence. With *Evocation to Visible Appearance* (2018), Les collaborated with playwright and ordained Episcopal priest Mark Schultz to stage "voidness," exploring damnation in suburbia with a black metal band. (Mark recently told me that he and Les sought not to make a play *about* voidness, but that, in its production, *was* voidness; an inquiry into the abyss that approached its subject and itself ruptured open.) And he and Lucas worked together again on *The Thin Place*, collaborating with the illusionist Steve Cuiffo to build a shapeshifting thriller for the stage that was also a serious epistemological test of the human psyche. Les may identify as an atheist; nonetheless, again and again, he tunes his ear to divine frequencies.

It strikes me, too, that Les's own language is often disarmingly imprecise, even as his meaning, in context, is – well, if not *clear*, then nonetheless present, undeniable, the space carved out around it for you to approach it, and see what it is he's trying to show you. He says things like, "I think it's this thing of" and "I'm not sure that's the thing" and "*That's* it, that's the thing." Or, he'll talk about what "the thing" *wants*, as though it has its own volition, often in relation to time – "I think it wants to move," "I think it wants to just *go*," "I think it wants to take a long time, and we just keep staring at it." It's as though something undeniable and irrepressible and *true* is operating at the center of our endeavor, with its own governing logic, and if we listen to it and attend to it and manage not to fuck it up, we can follow it somewhere we wouldn't have known how to point ourselves.

I love working with Les because he doesn't hurry us toward some fixed (and therefore limited) understanding of our shared work. He isn't troubled by what he doesn't understand. In fact, like he said on our call with Mia yesterday, he takes not understanding as a good sign. He finished the thought: "The ones I read and think 'I get that' – why would you want to rehearse it?"

* * * * *

SARAH LUNNIE is an independent dramaturg who works mainly on the creation and development of new plays. Her recent projects include Heidi Schreck's What the Constitution Means to Me, *Anne Washburn's* Shipwreck, *and Jeff Augustin's* Where the Mountain Meets the Sea, *created in collaboration with The Bengsons. She has been Associate Artistic Director of the Jungle Theater in Minneapolis, Literary Director of Playwrights Horizons, and Literary Manager at Actors Theatre of Louisville, where she curated and developed new work for the Humana Festival of New American Plays. She has a long-running collaboration with playwright Lucas Hnath and is a company member with The Mad Ones.*

"Responsion"

Lucas Hnath

While Les and I were workshopping *Dana H.*, we took a day to spend some time with a section about three-fourths into the play. I had the sense that at this point, the play needed to break form and do something we haven't yet seen, but I wasn't quite sure how I wanted to do it. As we were fumbling our way through this section of the play, Les thought for a moment and said, "Well, it's like the play has wandered into the thin place." I asked, "What's that?" Les said, "Oh you know, it's the place where the line between this world and another world is very thin."

He went on to explain that there were several thin places in the place where he grew up – locations where trees walked at night, where on occasion people were rumored to have disappeared. And then as if to explain "thin places," further he said, "It's like if you were to imagine an octopus in an aquarium pressed up against the glass . . . except that there's no glass . . . and no octopus."

And then, we took a "five."

The stories Les told me about thin places were both orientating to my work on *Dana H.*, and they also inspired an entirely new play, titled *The Thin Place*. Having worked with Les before, these kinds of anecdotes were already very familiar to me. It's one of the many pleasures of working with Les.

Strange stories of growing up in Lincolnshire. A foul-mouthed, possibly criminal neighbor named George. A past life regression gone scarily wrong. An uncle who would press push-pins into his bare feet so he could "tap dance" for the kiddies. Going to the pub with Sam Beckett.

DOI: 10.4324/9781003170808-58

Les is a natural raconteur, matter-of-factly stumbling into one remarkable story after another. But after spending many many hours in rehearsal rooms with Les, I no longer think of these stories as mere entertainment. I think these seeming digressions are, in fact, accomplishing serious dramaturgical work.

There is a model of new play development deeply rooted in the giving and taking of "notes." The writer submits a script; an artistic director or dramaturg or director reads the script and then gives the writer a list of comments or suggestions intended to make the script "better." Some writers embrace this process, some dread and merely endure it.

I do feel fortunate in that, by chance (and perhaps by choice of collaborators), I've very rarely been subjected to this process. But I do teach playwriting and I do see that my students get inundated with notes upon notes upon notes in their various classes. I'm not entirely convinced I've ever witnessed a script actually get better as a result of notes, or if it does, the note feels more like a band-aid has been slapped onto the play as opposed to a deeper recalibration of the thinking inside of the story. In the most troubling scenarios, I see playwrights lose their ability to hear their work with their own ears because they've over-relied on the ears of others.

Les however does not really give notes to the writer. In fact, he has claimed to know very little about dramaturgy or structure or storytelling craft.

There's something profoundly unfussy about Les's rehearsal room. We get together, we read the script. Maybe we read it a second time. And somewhere in there, Les will tell a story or two or three. Sometimes, it'll be a two-sentence anecdote. Sometimes, it's more involved. Sometimes, it'll happen at the top of rehearsal while folks are still settling in. He might talk about something peculiar that happened on the way to rehearsal. Or the digression finds its way into a lull – one of those "okay, so what next?" moments. Wherever it happens, I certainly don't think he plans it.

The storytelling has a couple of interesting effects, the most obvious of which is that it relaxes folks. The anecdotes are almost always dryly funny. They catch you off-guard. It's a way of signaling to everyone, "This isn't brain surgery, we're just making a play." It's the kind of thing that keeps people from getting too precious or, god forbid, pretentious.

But on another level – at the risk of being pretentious myself – the stories put the room into alignment with the primary task to tell a story. That's what a play ultimately does. It's helpful to be reminded of what a "story" sounds like, especially when the play you're working on is broken up into parts on the floor and it's hard to see what's what.

Which brings me back to thin places. Les's description of a thin place made concrete something that was, at that moment, nebulous in my mind. Those little anecdotes about eerie spaces in Lincolnshire gave me a corollary – a different but related image – that helped me to imagine – and subsequently write – a big theatrical gesture for *Dana H.* Les wasn't telling me about thin places as if to say, "You should make your play more like this." Rather, he was relating an experience that contained some really vivid and potent images in an attempt to both understand and parse the story he thought I was trying to tell.

From the playwright's perspective, this dialogue is immensely helpful. Much more so than someone instructing you to make that scene or that character more 'x.' The story lets you enter the process on your own terms and from the inside. When Les tells a story, he's essentially asking me a question. He's asking, "Is it like this?" And maybe it is. Or maybe it isn't. Either way, the anecdote helps make something that often feels like it's slipping out of my grasp a little more tangible, a little easier to grab hold of and study.

Even if the set of images that Les puts in front of me doesn't resonate, I might respond with a "no, actually, it's more like . . . ," and then I find myself painting a picture for Les or talking about a related experience that better captures the elusive thing I'm chasing, and the result of my spontaneous response is no less useful for all the same reasons I've been describing.

To be clear, I don't think the lesson for directors is to come up with a bunch of anecdotes to tell during rehearsal. Doing so would miss the point. Because even though Les might be talking, the stories come out of *listening*.

What Les is really doing when he talks about something that he experienced or when he describes an image is an act of creative responsion. He is providing an answer to an implicit question that you can only hear by listening very carefully. These stories are an attempt to parse an idea or a feeling. But instead of describing it baldly or prescriptively, the stories get at the notion by way of the primary language of theatre, that of storytelling.

* * * * *

LUCAS HNATH *is a playwright whose plays include* Dana H., The Thin Place, Hillary and Clinton, A Doll's House, Part 2, Red Speedo, The Christians, A Public Reading of an Unproduced Screenplay About the Death of Walt Disney, Isaac's Eye, *and* Death Tax. *He is a New York Theatre Workshop Usual*

Suspect, a member of Ensemble Studio Theatre, and an alumnus of New Drama-
tists. His awards include the Whiting Award, Guggenheim Fellowship, Kesselring
Prize, Outer Critics Circle Award, Obie Award, Steinberg Playwright Award,
Windham-Campbell Literary Prize, Lucille Lortel Award, and a Tony Nomina-
tion for Best Play.

Presence

Many years ago, Annie and I were living in Stoke Newington in North London and she was working on a show at the National Theatre. At the time, we only had one child, and one day, I took Jacob down to the National to see Annie in the break before the evening's tech rehearsal. I was standing on the stage with Annie talking to Bill Gaskill, the director of the production, and Jacob was sitting on the floor playing and we became very aware of Jacob just sitting there playing. And Bill said, "Oh, if only everything could be like that." Because Jacob was just being on the stage. He was not playing at being an unbearably cute little boy playing with blocks. He was just playing with blocks – stacking them up and knocking them over. He was fully present.

I am dumbfounded by actors who are truly present. No smoke, no mirrors. There, alive, in front of you. I think of Didi O'Connell in *Dana H.* She is acting under the tightest technical restrictions of anything I've ever done, and she is totally present. She is just there. How that happens, I don't know. When I watch a great actor and they are present like that onstage, it's thrilling, but I'm also deeply worried for them. I look and I think, "You're going to hurt yourself." There is Didi lip syncing every word of a story about emotional, sexual, and physical abuse, not getting up from her chair for almost an hour, and she is fully present. And I think, "That must hurt. That must be damaging." But of course, that risk is part of the thrill.

DOI: 10.4324/9781003170808-59

Humana on my watch

I was appointed as Artistic Director of Actors Theatre of Louisville in November 2011 and began in January 2012. I planned six seasons, 2012–2013 through 2017–2018, including ATL's annual Humana Festival of New American Plays.

Here are the line-ups for the Humana Festivals during my time. Full-length plays are listed first, followed by the multi-author anthology projects created for the apprentice Professional Training Company and then the annual program of ten-minute plays.

2013
Cry Old Kingdom by Jeff Augustin
O Guru Guru Guru or why I don't want to go to yoga class with you by Mallery
    Avidon
Gnit by Will Eno
Appropriate by Branden Jacobs-Jenkins
The Delling Shore by Sam Marks
Sleep Rock Thy Brain by Rinne Groff, Lucas Hnath, and Anne Washburn
The ten-minute plays:
    Halfway by Emily Schwend
    27 Ways I Didn't Say "Hi" to Laurence Fishburne by Jonathan Josephson
    Two Conversations Overheard on Airplanes by Sarah Ruhl

DOI: 10.4324/9781003170808-60

2014

Partners by Dorothy Fortenberry

The Grown-Up by Jordan Harrison

The Christians by Lucas Hnath

brownsville song (b-side for tray) by Kimber Lee

Steel Hammer. Music and lyrics by Julia Wolfe; original text by Kia Corthron, Will Power, Carl Hancock Rux, and Regina Taylor; directed by Anne Bogart; created and performed by SITI Company; music performed by Bang on a Can All-Stars and Trio Mediaeval.

Remix 38 by Jackie Sibblies Drury, Idris Goodwin, Basil Kreimendahl, Justin Kuritzkes, and Amelia Roper

The ten-minute plays:

Winter Games by Rachel Bonds

Some Prepared Remarks (A History in Speech) by Jason Gray Platt

Poor Shem by Gregory Hischak

2015

I Will Be Gone by Erin Courtney

Dot by Colman Domingo

The Glory of the World by Charles Mee

I Promised Myself to Live Faster by Gregory S. Moss and Pig Iron Theatre Company. Conceived and created by Pig Iron Theatre Company.

The Roommate by Jen Silverman

Wondrous Strange by Martyna Majok, Meg Miroshnik, Jiehae Park, and Jen Silverman

The ten-minute plays:

Coffee Break by Tasha Gordon-Solmon

This Quintessence of Dust by Cory Hinkle

Trudy, Carolyn, Martha, and Regina Travel to Outer Space and Have a Pretty Terrible Time There by James Kennedy

2016

This Random World by Steven Dietz

Residence by Laura Jacqmin

Cardboard Piano by Hansol Jung

Wellesley Girl by Brendan Pelsue

For Peter Pan on her 70th Birthday by Sarah Ruhl

That High Lonesome Sound by Jeff Augustin, Diana Grisanti, Cory Hinkle, and Charise Castro

The ten-minute plays:
  Rules of Comedy by Patricia Cotter
  So Unnatural a Level by Gary Winter
  Joshua Consumed an Unfortunate Pear by Steve Yockey

2017
Recent Alien Abductions by Jorge Ignacio Cortiñas
I Now Pronounce by Tasha Gordon-Solmon
We're Gonna Be Okay by Basil Kreimendahl
Airness by Chelsea Marcantel
Cry It Out by Molly Smith Metzler
The Many Deaths of Nathan Stubblefield by Jeff Augustin, Sarah DeLappe, Claire Kiechel, and Ramiz Monsef
The ten-minute plays:
  The New Line by Will Eno
  Home Invasion by Krista Knight
  Melto Man and Lady Mantis by Eric Pfeffinger

2018
Do You Feel Anger? by Mara Nelson-Greenberg
Evocation to Visible Appearance by Mark Schultz
we, the invisibles by Susan Soon He Stanton
Marginal Loss by Deborah Stein
God Said This by Leah Nanako Winkler
You Across From Me by Jaclyn Backhaus, Dipika Guha, Brian Otaño, and Jason Gray Platt

"The Art of Seeing"

Meredith McDonough

Cheetos. Glittery kittens with laser eyes. Laughter. Long walks. A collection of t-shirts. Esoteric records. Ventriloquist dummies. A melancholic figure by the sea. The smell of Listerine strips. Books and books and books. Silence.

I met Les in 1999 at Actors Theatre of Louisville when he was there directing Chuck Mee's _Big Love_. At the time, I was the Associate Director of the Apprentice/Intern program, and I would float in and out of rehearsals during the Humana Festival to observe an amazing variety of master directors. With some, I would leave with a concrete idea for staging or how to think about a script. With Les, it was immediately different. I couldn't put my finger on what he was doing. It was so subtle. What was that whispered aside to an actor? How did that seemingly unrelated story just open up an entire new understanding of the play for the cast? These moments were never big, so how was it that his work was _so big_? How did this place of sharing and laughter and personal history become the unbridled joy of watching actresses throw themselves on the floor or the manic hysteria of an actor screaming while hurling saw blades?

After observing that first process, I knew I had to study with Les. I wanted to know more, to get at that ephemeral something that he had. I assumed it would come to me in a class, or in some intense feedback, but of course I found that Les approaches teaching in a very similar way to his directing. It's not in grand statements, it's in quiet observation. Les "taught" by sitting in the back of your rehearsals every night – not occasionally, every night. He mentored by observing _you_ and where _you_ are in your process and then met you there. He was never looking to "change" you, simply to ask questions,

DOI: 10.4324/9781003170808-61

to feedback on what you were pursuing. He prods gently, asking you to clarify deeper, to be more specific. He wants the point of view to be yours, and he knows that can be found only through vigorous interrogation. He has a love of not only the process but also the tiny minutiae that make each of us unique. He observes that over time and then eventually reflects it back to you in profound ways. It's why so many artists want to work with him; you truly feel *seen*.

Les is a quiet and passionate observer. It's one thing to sit in your students' rehearsals, but he did it (albeit less frequently, to his chagrin) throughout our seven years at ATL. If Les wasn't in his office, you knew it was because he was up on the 5th floor watching rehearsal. He wasn't there to judge the work or because he had notes for the director; he genuinely loves watching the process, watching artists work. He asks questions, because he's curious; he wants to be there to watch the machine get built. He loves tech (not just because there are Cheetos there) but to see how another director crafts their production. He participates in your process in a way that makes the theatre a safer place to create your boldest and most vulnerable art.

Les is a great lover of photography. In 2004, I assisted him on the world premiere of *At the Vanishing Point* by Naomi Iizuka in the Humana Festival, a play made through interviews with residents of Butchertown in KY and inspired by the life and photographs of Ralph Eugene Meatyard. The play begins with a monologue in which Naomi imagines a photographer talking about what he sees. It's one of my favorite things in the play, and it always makes me think of Les. The Photographer says:

> i started using masks in my photographs not too long ago, the kind you get at the five and dime. i have this one photo i took of the kids in masks . . . there's something about seeing a person put on one of those masks, and you can't really see their faces, and there's a kinda mystery and strangeness that comes out of that that i think, well i think is there all the time, it's just the mask, it lets you see it in a way that you couldn't otherwise. all the everydayness, the realness of it is still there. the poison ivy and the tears and the ice cream afterwards, that's all still there. but it's as if inside of all of that, the masks, they let you see this other thing. for me, i guess, it's about how you see. it's about the act of seeing a thing, and how it connects to other things and is part of a whole. because on some level, how we form connections, how we see a thing and shape it in our minds, it's very personal, i think. it's about who you are and everything that makes you who you are, and how that comes together to form a certain way, a way of looking at the world.

It's about how you see. It's about the act of seeing a thing. In other words, how you see is who you are.

Once during my second year of grad school, Les pulled me aside and asked me how many art books I owned. I said I didn't know, maybe three? And he told me that was evident in all of my work. I was startled – how could looking at art or photography change my work? Was it just about design? It took me decades to learn that no, *it's about how you see.* We joked all the time in Louisville that his apartment was actually a museum bookstore – huge stacks of books covering his dining room table in a myriad of languages, opened to stunning landscapes or a mysterious portrait. I would also dig through to see which were new, excited for the surprises they contained. Packages arrived daily with some new edition or print or study of an artist's work that he'd found on the internet late at night. He is constantly looking for new inspiration, constantly looking to be surprised.

He's also a collector of postcards; he has 100s of them. The beautiful, the silly, the melancholic, the macabre. For each show he directed, he had the same process: he would fill this enormous 6′×10′ corkboard that took up his whole office wall with postcards. Each image was carefully chosen as if to tack down the ephemeral. Crazed children, glittery kittens, ventriloquist dummies, decrepit landscapes, students scribbling on a chalkboard, a lone bear with a tiny hat. An open book of sorts, a collage, a pastiche, they were a visual representation of his mind and the myriad of ways it was seeing the play, seeing the world at that time. There was seemingly no external logic to it, but it made complete sense to him. I can't tell you how much I respect that sprawling freedom. The images would be there for months, and there was always something new to discover in them. It was sad when one came down. I could feel the palpable loss of that momentary obsession. There is so much melancholy in what we do. Something needs to end for something else to begin.

But for Les, I don't think it's ever really over. It's an accumulation over decades of work. Of images, of experiences, of observations, of curiosities, of the people who make up his world. And because of that the work is so big, so full of the heart of humanity and the relentless pursuit of some huge unknown.

*   *   *   *   *

MEREDITH MCDONOUGH is a theatre director whose work focuses on the development of new plays and musicals. She was the Associate Artistic Director of the Actors Theatre of Louisville under Les Waters for six years, where she directed six world premieres for the Humana Festival of New American Plays and numerous other productions, including Angels in America and Peter and the Starcatcher. Prior to Louisville, she was Director of New Works at TheatreWorks in Palo Alto, California, as well as the New Works Director for the National Alliance for Musical Theatre. A proud native of New Jersey, she studied at Northwestern University and received her MFA in directing from UC San Diego. During the pandemic, she became a resident of Minneapolis where she makes a killer sourdough pretzel.

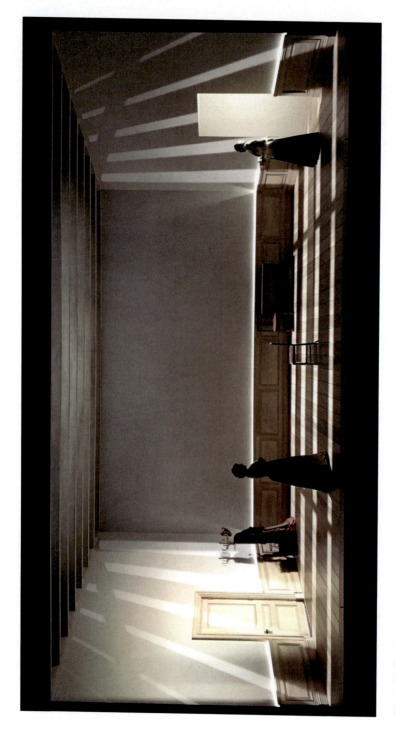

23. *A Doll's House, Part 2* at Berkeley Repertory Theatre (2018).

24. Insignificance at Royal Court Theatre (1982).

25. *Dana H.* at Kirk Douglas Theatre (2019).

26. *Dana H.* at Kirk Douglas Theatre (2019).

27. *Long Day's Journey Into Night* at Actors Theatre of Louisville (2012).

247

28. *For Peter Pan on her 70th Birthday* at Playwrights Horizons (2017).

Four more productions of mine

Not Quite Jerusalem by Paul Kember, Royal Court Theatre, London, 1980.
My first production on the main stage of the Royal Court. Critical (and box office) success. My "arrival" in the world of London theatre. A State of the Nation play, albeit set on a kibbutz in Israel. A pro-working-class play. The working-class characters occupy the center of the play, not some irrelevant side show of proletarian characters #'s 1–10. Hard work. Huge learning curve. Joyous. Revived in 1982 with the intention of moving to the West End. I very much wanted the prestige and money of a commercial success. Some cast members replaced with more "well known" actors. Mistake. Unhappy experience. Didn't move to the West End. Listen to your own voice.

Ghost on Fire by Michael Weller, Goodman Theatre, 1987.
An epic play in Michael's chronicles of the lives of the baby boomers. My first production in American regional theatre. Over 4 hours long at the first run-through. The joys of editing. Magnificent cast including the much-missed J. T. Walsh. I regard the Goodman as a theatre home and Bob Falls as a colleague and a champion – *Ghost on Fire, Big Love, Spinning into Butter, Dana H.*

Inside and *Intruder* by Maurice Maeterlinck, adapted by Caryl Churchill. UCSD Dept of Theatre, La Jolla, 1998.
Every year at UCSD, I taught a class in site-specific theatre with the third-year directors and actors. One year, Chuck Mee scripted a version of Strindberg's *Dream Play* for a backstage corridor at La Jolla Playhouse. Another year I became interested in both the plays of Maeterlinck and a mansion in the hills of Rancho Santa Fe. I asked Caryl to translate the Maeterlincks and

DOI: 10.4324/9781003170808-62

I worked with the directors and actors to make a performance melded to the specifics of this particular site. Not really a performance. More a whisper of a performance. The house was dreaming Maeterlinck.

Recent Alien Abductions by Jorge Ignacio Cortiñas, Humana Festival, Actors Theatre of Louisville, 2017.
Sarah Ruhl had introduced me to the plays of Jorge several years before. The pleasure of working with a writer for the first time. My first time working with any of these actors. The pleasure and terrors of that. The beauty of the writing and the thrill of watching Jon Norman Schneider perform the almost 20-minute opening monologue about a particular episode of *The X-Files*. The pain of letting someone go. I have been let go from a production and there's no way around it, it is a miserable, wounding experience. A big play about sexual abuse and gaslighting and the trauma of Colonialism. Confrontational in all the best ways.

Do's and don'ts for directors

Only someone who is well prepared has the opportunity to improvise.

—Ingmar Bergman

Start with a deep understanding of the script. My own preparation is a concentrated period of reading before the start of rehearsal. If rehearsals were to start June 1st, I would read the script every other day January through April. Sometimes the reading is fruitful, sometimes perfunctory. Some days many notes, some days just one. The point is to read the material into your body, read the script so that it is inside your bones. Not so that you have all the answers, more that you are full of questions. It's a commitment. That's January-April. And in May, I don't look at the script at all. That's the month of "forgetting" everything you learned the previous months. This way of prepping assumes that the script is "frozen" which of course it isn't when working on a new play. With Lucas, I may see the latest draft a day or two ahead of rehearsal.

It's not necessary to have an answer for everything. Say what you know when you know it; otherwise, keep your mouth shut. That's not easy to do because we think of "I don't know" as a form of weakness, a lack of authority. But if you have the answer to everything, what is the point of the process? Where is the collaboration? What is important for others to know is why you want to direct this particular production. What does it mean to you? At the meet-and-greet, it's not necessary to read a thesis-length description of the play and the means of production, but it will help everybody if they know why

DOI: 10.4324/9781003170808-63

this play and *this* space are important to you. Within the importance lies the vision. I remember talking about thin places during early stage *Macbeth*. Not in the sense of the supernatural but as an exploration of a moral queasiness, a philosophical grayness. Is there an ethical thin place where the world view is porous and once the Macbeth's have stepped through there is no going back?

Don't burn up all the oxygen in the room. You provide the vision, but the process and the production are not about you. Create space. Hold space for others.

Trust the people you are working with. You direct. They act and they write and they design and they dramaturg and they stage manage and they are electricians and deck carpenters and scene painters and costume makers and all the many professions that make a theatre production. Respect their abilities. Trust them.

Have a notebook with you at all times. I usually have at least two. One in which I note painters/photographers/plays/movies/the many things that friends and colleagues constantly recommend. In the other are notes relating to a particular production: lines of text that are elusive, staging ideas, sometimes bits of overheard conversation. My favorite from the workshop of *Fen* – a young man to a young woman on the local bus "Will you go out with me? I'm nice." Take out the notebook and write it down – it will stick. Then, put it away and forget about it. Look at it again later in the rehearsal period. Do these initial impressions/notions/ideas still have worth? Has the production become something else? Maybe so. Is that what you want?

You don't have to have all the answers, but you need to generate many, many questions.

Somewhere inside every play is one major question. Identify it. It may change over the process, but there's always that one major question. Not what is this play about, rather what question is it asking? Andrei Belgrader and I believe that *Happy Days* and *The Importance of Being Earnest* are soulmates, that they are linked by one burning question. What connects Samuel Beckett and Oscar Wilde? Yes, they are both Irish, and . . .

Give notes to the whole room. I'm not just talking note sessions after a stumble-through or a designer run. I'm talking notes during daily rehearsal. It helps if all the room can hear the notes given in order to better understand the world of the production. It is of great help to stage management who will maintain the production after your departure. I have to admit that I fail to do this much of the time and often give notes one on one to actors.

My favorite note is "Ignore bad direction."

You have the right to fail. When I worked at the Royal Court, the motto was "We have the right to fail." As long as you work hard and honestly, it is acceptable to say "I got it wrong" or "I fucked up. My fault."

Just because you're the director doesn't give you the right to talk with authority on all subjects. In the rehearsal room, I have heard male directors explain feminism to feminists, straight directors explain "the dating rituals" of gays to LGBTQ folx, and white directors explain systemic racism to BIPOC collaborators. Just shut up, listen, and learn. Employ a cultural consultant if the play contains subject matter that you have no experience of. And if it's uncomfortable, lean into it, deal with it.

Directing is biography, not therapy. You are a director, not a therapist.

Lucas says that writing is rewriting. In the world of new play development – the readings, the cold readings, the 29-hour workshop – rewriting is key and often for the better. But sometimes, the writing turns to mush in order to satisfy various directors and dramaturgs and miscast actors. So, if I am offered a script and I see that it is Draft 8 and has been developed at Sundance and Cape Cod and Ojai and at least one other good place, I will ask to read the original draft, to see the original spark, the initial messiness. Sometimes, this is useful.

You must learn to read the temperature of the room. You must be aware of what's going on in the room. Are we having a good day? Who is having a good day? Who is making progress? Why was yesterday so good and today just won't get going? Is someone unhappy because of the work? Because of you? Because their partner just dumped them? Or simply because the world is a total shit heap, and millions of people will keep having shit days until white supremacy and the patriarchy and global capitalism are all dismantled? So, all of these questions are your responsibility and you are going to have the answers for very few of them, but they make up the temperature of the room and it's crucial that you are aware of it. And having a great stage manager who is also expert in reading the temperature of the room makes life so much easier.

When you are working on a scene and it isn't working, often it is to do with the fact that the scene *before* isn't working and isn't properly set up to make the following scene work. The context isn't right.

Your work is political. Get it out of your head that beauty is your only goal. You may just want to make things that are beautiful. Beauty might make you swoon. But our work and how it is made and with whom it is made and where it is made are political because it's now.

Be nice to your assistant. They are there to learn and be of support. They are not there to collect your dry cleaning or wrap opening night gifts for the cast or walk your dog. Buy them food, talk to them about the process and what you are trying to do, buy them drinks. They have no money, so be kind and considerate. They may employ you in the future.

Your greatest asset is yourself. Your self. All the myriad things that constitute you are the best thing going for you. If you are so busy trying to behave like a director, you will cut off the oxygen to your creativity. I have watched actors in rehearsals so many times working hard and the only note that I have wanted to give and the note you can never give is "just be yourself." It's a note elusive to understand and impossible to live up to. But just be yourself in rehearsal. Talk about what books you are reading, what movies you have seen, what music you are listening to. Some of my directing is the telling of stories or references to other works of art. I find it useful to know what a writer was listening to when Draft 3 was being written. Letting your collaborators know what was inside your head as you prepped the production may be of use to them as they work on the project. If you are obsessing about how a real director behaves, then you are going to be unhappy and not alert to the shifts and eddies of the room. Be prepared and be present.

Get to the rehearsal room early. It gives you time to think in the space. And time to get to know your stage management team.

Don't be late. Ever. Being late is an offense.

Postscript for when you become an Artistic Director: Your duty is to protect the artists from the institution. Institutions run for themselves. Freelancers are paid poorly and usually regarded as a nuisance. They should be respected.

"Unfounded Belief"

Lila Neugebauer

It's raining inside an elevator. The elevator doors open and a barefoot woman in a pink skirt suit steps out, water cascading around her. She's holding an umbrella and a suitcase. She's entered what appears to be the bottom of a swimming pool, askew at a perilous angle, intricately tiled in aquamarine and dimly lit by crystal chandeliers. The woman's dead father welcomes her, but she mistakes him for a hotel porter. She wonders where she'll be staying. The dead father fashions his daughter a room out of string.

In September 2006, I had my first encounter with Les Waters's work: a production of Sarah Ruhl's *Eurydice* at Yale Repertory Theatre. I walked out onto Chapel Street afterward in a haze, unsure if I'd been in that tilted swimming pool for ten minutes or ten hours. The swimming pool was not in fact a swimming pool, but rather, a scenographic conception of Hades, the underworld. The rainy elevator was the river Lethe, whose waters, according to Greek mythology, stripped mortals of their memories en route to the underworld. Both that tiled interior and that elevator exemplified hallmarks – I would later recognize – of a Les Waters production: thrilling feats of design, perfect theatrical metaphors.

I had the remarkable sensation that day that I believe only certain live performances can engender: the feeling that the space-time continuum had been disrupted. I couldn't quite tell how that had happened, but I had an inkling it began when that man made that room out of string. There were no shortcuts to expedite the task, no cheats to prevent the audience's potential boredom. Instead, we watched the unwinding and tethering in real time. It took as long as it took. It was an act of fatherly love, staged poetically and

DOI: 10.4324/9781003170808-64

unsentimentally – a theatrical gesture more eloquent and immediate than any declaration of love might have been in that moment. I was mesmerized.

I got back to my off-campus apartment and googled: Les Waters. I was 21 and wanted to be a theater director. How did you become a professional director? I didn't know. I was preoccupied with the plays of Caryl Churchill and Sarah Kane. I fantasized about moving to London (where I'd never been) and stalking the halls of the Royal Court Theatre, where most of the plays I'd read and loved – or the productions I'd read about and imagined loving – began. Apparently, this Les guy was British. He had worked with Caryl Churchill. He had worked a lot at The Royal Court. And now, he was the Associate Artistic Director of Berkeley Repertory Theatre in California.

Eleven months later, I showed up for my first day of work in the literary department at Berkeley Rep. My boss Madeleine Oldham showed me my desk in our shared office and explained the "script database" that I would use to track play submissions, rejections, and the occasional "second read" recommendation. Toward the end of my first week, I arrived in the morning to discover a tall, grey-haired man sitting on the bean bag chair at the foot of my desk, reading *The New York Times*. We exchanged brief introductions, and he went back to his paper. He had a faintly wizard-like quality, with his grey mop of hair, and an effortlessly low-key fashion sense, complete with beat-up black converse sneakers. He was startlingly cool.

Les often read his morning paper in that bean bag chair. I gradually worked up the nerve to ask him bold questions, like, "How's your morning going?" or, later in the day, "Where'd you go for lunch?" Les would dignify my inquiries with courteous answers – yet he appeared disarmingly comfortable with silence. Weeks passed, and I summoned the courage to start inquiring about his directorial past, eager to hear about his collaborations with playwrights and, fundamentally, how he had become himself. One day, out to lunch with Les and Madeleine, I mentioned *Eurydice*, asking how he and his design team had come up with certain ideas; I expected a lengthy exegesis. Instead, he said something to the effect of: it just felt right.

Months later, Les asked me, "So, you're a director?" I confirmed that was my aspiration. He said, "You think like a director. You are a director." It was the kind of exchange that can bend the trajectory of a creative person's life: an artist you revere sees in you what you hope to be and, through the act of naming it, emboldens you to manifest it. Les was about to go into rehearsal for a Will Eno play called *Tragedy: a tragedy*; he had already hired an assistant director, but he invited me to observe some rehearsal if I could get away from my desk.

Les's comfort with silence – which I first encountered in that bean bag chair – was a striking aspect of his rehearsal room. When actors come to the end of reading or working through a scene, many directors hurry to offer reactions or instructions on next steps. Les tended to allow a silence. Following silences of varying lengths, Les would sometimes invite the actors to just – do it again. Or he would ask a question – often a seemingly simple question – which might lead to a seemingly simple new idea, say, sitting at a given moment rather than standing. And then that seemingly simple new idea would create the circumstances for something unexpected to happen. And usually that unexpected something . . . just felt right. Even I could tell.

At first, those silences felt long to me. But more and more, I recognized that time worked differently in Les's rehearsal room, just as it had in his production of *Eurydice*. There was never a fear of running out of time. The amount of time in a rehearsal was always the amount needed because Les's underlying faith in the trajectory of the work meant it could simply continue tomorrow. It took as long as it took.

I saw *Tragedy: a tragedy* eight times over the course of its run at Berkeley Rep. The play is an absurdist (yes) tragedy, which takes the form of a news broadcast, on a night in which the sun has set for good, never to rise again. It offers a Beckettian riff on certain inanities of American suburbia and the media – and an existential meditation on grief, death, and staring into the abyss. I kept going back, determined to figure out how the production was generating its impact on me: the feeling of something gradually breaking inside me – to hilarious, hypnotic, and ultimately devastating effect.

I never quite figured it out. Though I'm certain it had to do with Les's relationship to silence – and his heightened sensitivity to the workings of stage time. For many people who make theater, silence can be untenable, even frightening – hence, "Louder, faster, funnier!" In silence onstage, the audience might, for a moment, have to sit with themselves. They might not know how to feel or what to think. They might even think about what they had for lunch. Just as Les deploys silence in the rehearsal room, he understands how a particular silence on stage can beguile, unnerve, or entrance an audience. He's willing to allow unknowing and unease to linger. Not merely for the hell of it but in service of a carefully engineered consequence. The meticulously sculpted silences in *Tragedy: a tragedy* are what I remember best. The sense of suspension. Les made the central existential metaphor of

Will's play – eternal sunset – manifest in the visceral experience of watching it.

A few years after I worked at Berkeley Rep, I was Les's Assistant Director on Anne Washburn's *The Small*, produced by Clubbed Thumb at the Ohio Theatre on Wooster Street in Soho. *The Small* is an ingeniously bizarre and mystical play. To call it strange does not do it justice; it achieves a transcendent strangeness in its totality, an inexplicable coalescing of deep feeling. Entire sequences of the play – including a song – were written in an (invented) Elvin dialect, which actors Maria Dizzia and Susie Pourfar dutifully mastered, then intoned with ceremony, dressed as Elvin warriors/princesses. They were, in part, the psychic projections of a depressed character who finds respite in Live Action Role Play – played by Matt Maher – and they were also, just, well . . . Elvin warriors/princesses.

We all laughed a lot in that rehearsal room. Neither Les nor Anne are self-serious, they're both darkly hilarious. Their rejoicing in the quasi-absurdity of our investigations infused the process with joy. But they also took the crafting of that quasi-absurdity quite seriously, calibrating the tone and tempo of the play's strangeness with exactitude. While an invented Elvin language is a concrete instance, all new plays necessitate the discovery of their own felicitous stage language. Les's approach is a Rosetta Stone all his own – he listens attentively to the play in order to guide the invention of its three-dimensional expression. And when he doesn't understand what he hears, he listens some more. He welcomes this unknowing; he's interested in it, at home in it. Many directors feel a need to convey superior intelligence, power, and unequivocal certainty about any given matter, large or small, in rehearsal. Les has none of that. He is happy to say, "I don't know." And in saying, "I don't know," he achieves precisely what other directors are hoping for when they scramble to impose certainty: the trust of the room.

Observing Les in those rehearsals, I grasped more deeply his ability to shape an audience's engagement with unknowing. He values those spaces, locating in them an invitation to the imaginative collaboration between theatrical event and spectator. In his appreciation for the bewilderment, then wonder, the Elvin words induced, I was reminded of his faith in well-deployed silence. For a director who navigates texts and textuality fluently – across myriad styles, registers, scopes, and sensibilities – he also recognizes the limits of language. Just as in the construction of the string room in *Eurydice* and the deathly quiet before the final blackout in *Tragedy: a tragedy*, Les crafts space for something to happen between the play and the audience that text can't supply.

In the 15 years since I met Les, in the nearly 20 productions of his I've seen, I've continued to marvel at his relationship to silence onstage. And in a related (and often overlapping) arena, his ability to craft spaces of *unknowing* – of darkness, unease, even buoyancy – with singular imagination. Two recent examples come to mind, both involving blackouts.

The first was in his production of Lucas Hnath's *Dana H.* at the Vineyard Theatre in February 2020, the last play I saw before the global pandemic shuttered theaters. In that production, the actor Didi O'Connell recounts the testimony of the playwright's mother, Dana Higginbotham, a hospice chaplain who was held hostage for five months by a member of the Aryan Brotherhood. Her verbatim account is performed through Didi's spellbinding act of lip-syncing Higginbotham's words as recorded in a series of interviews. As her months in captivity take an increasingly hallucinogenic turn, the thus-far ascetic production spirals into a fever dream – with multi-colored moving lights kinetically accelerating, then sound continuing to roar through a prolonged darkness. And then, out of darkness, Didi's profile emerges, faintly backlit by a hotel window, an image we've heard her describe. The darkness is a portal through which we and she both journey, emerging at once more spectral and more embodied. I was chilled to the bone.

The second was in another Lucas-Les collaboration: *The Thin Place* – a thriller, a ghost story, and a kind of séance. The play investigates grief, the unknown, and how vulnerable we are to beliefs that may not reflect truths we know. The production featured the longest blackout I've experienced in the theater, long enough for the audience to move from discomfort, to boredom, into presence. Gradually, a tiny red light became visible. In seances, red lights are used to cajole the imagination. My brain began to fill things in – things I couldn't possibly have seen in the pitch black, but was, I'm sure, seeing. Or I believed I was seeing. That space provided an experience – and a real-time metaphor – that encapsulated the play's questions about where truth and feeling intersect. I left the theater with a disorienting sensation I recognized as the familiar aftermath of a Les Waters production: I had forgotten where I parked my car.

(I had taken the subway. I don't have a car.)

In 2012, Les left Berkeley Rep to become the Artistic Director of Actors Theatre of Louisville. During his tenure, we were reunited on several occasions when he hired me to direct at the Humana Festival of New American Plays. The last time I was in Louisville, on the Festival's closing weekend, I stopped by the administrative offices to say goodbye before leaving town.

The door to Les's office was ajar and I peered in. He wasn't there, but I noticed a recent addition to the wall, a framed quote from the Austrian–British philosopher Ludwig Wittgenstein:

> At the core of all well-founded belief lies belief that is unfounded.

I suddenly remembered that Les had once told me that as a young boy, he had sung in the church choir. He had a beautiful voice, but left the choir because he didn't like being looked at onstage. The image of Les in church at once seemed unlikely and made complete sense.

What does Les believe, I wondered?

A director's work is, you could argue, an enactment of their belief system. Our work – in process and production – reflects our taste, sensibility, values, and point of view; collectively, those elements comprise a philosophy of perceiving and being. If the practice of directing is an ongoing development and substantiation of those well-founded beliefs – what's the unfounded belief beneath it? Could *unfounded belief* be another name for . . . faith?

I left Les's office and scanned the hallways, but couldn't find him. I went to the airport and flew home to New York.

The next time I saw Les was at his production of Chuck Mee's *The Glory of the World* – a centennial birthday party of a play for renowned mystic and Catholic monk Thomas Merton. To my astonishment, Les told me he would be appearing in the play for several performances in its New York run at BAM. The show began and Les walked onstage – as Thomas Merton, but also as himself – and sat at a table, his back to the audience. A long silence passed. And then, 17 men in party hats charged the stage. Across seventy minutes, a high-velocity technicolor spectacle unfolded: raucous birthday toasts, sonorous reverie, metaphysical debate – all athletically staged – culminating in a knock-down brawl. And then:

SILENCE

Les returned, sat down, and again: a long silence. Into which a series of questions began to appear projected on the wall above him:

Does the silence scare you?

SILENCE

Is nothing sacred?

SILENCE
SILENCE

Is everything sacred?

SILENCE
SILENCE
SILENCE

Then more questions, more silence, and a swift black out.

Later that week, Les and I had breakfast in Brooklyn. I was struggling through a period of depression, which embarrassed me, but I knew Les knew about sadness, and so when he asked me how I was doing, I actually told him. We ate eggs and talked about everything and nothing. I had overscheduled myself that year; I was about to start a rehearsal process and worried I wouldn't find creative resilience. On our way out, I asked him to remind me how he found his way through the process when he had taken on too much. What kept him connected to the work? What kept him in it?

He told me that at the center of every play, he locates an unanswerable question. That question might change over the course of working on a play or over the years in his shifting relationship to that play. But if he could find an unanswerable question, it kept him from getting bored. It kept him interested.

Unanswerable? I confirmed. Yeah, he said.

Les greets a play, a rehearsal room, and a production with a relentless determination to ask the unanswerable questions. There's a kind of faith in that, I think. A faith in the intrinsic merit of a creative act that might itself produce more questions than 'messages' for an audience. A faith in the value of creative curiosity itself.

I'll try it, I said.

We stood on the street in silence for a moment. And then he smiled, waved, and turned and walked away.

*   *   *   *   *

LILA NEUGEBAUER *is a theater, film, and television director from New York City. Her work on new plays has included collaborations with writers Annie Baker, Sarah DeLappe, Lucas Hnath, Branden Jacobs-Jenkins, Zoe Kazan, Tracy Letts, and Simon Stephens, among others. She made her Broadway debut in 2018 with a revival of Kenneth Lonergan's* The Waverly Gallery, *starring Elaine May.*

As co-Artistic Director of *The Mad Ones*, Lila co-authors and directs ensemble-created work, including productions of Mrs. Murray's Menagerie *and* Miles for Mary, *which she is also developing for television. Her feature film debut starring Jennifer Lawrence is due for release in 2022. She has received an Obie award, a Drama Desk award, and a fellowship from the Princess Grace Foundation.*

The last list of films

Wings of Desire (1987) – Wim Wenders. Not my own favorite of Wenders' films but it makes Annie cry and therefore must be included.

Roma (2018) – Alfonso Cuaron

Diary of a Teenage Girl (2015) – Marielle Heller. Great cast including my daughter Madeleine.

Satyricon (1969) – Federico Fellini. A whole world.

I Know Where I'm Going! (1947) – Michael Powell and Emeric Pressburger

Pandora's Box (1929) – G. W. Pabst. Louise Brooks is Everything.

Silent Light (2007) – Carlos Reygadas

A Ghost Story (2017) – David Lowery

Safe (1995) – Todd Haymes

Lost in Translation (2003) – Sofia Coppola

The Conversation (1974) – Frances Ford Coppola

Last Year in Marienbad (1961) – Alain Resnais. Oh Delphine Seyrig!

Parasite (2019) – Bong Joon Ho

2001: A Space Odyssey (1968) – Stanley Kubrick. How many times have I watched this film? Twenty? Thirty? Always the same experience. In awe of its total control and precision and mystery. How is it done?

DOI: 10.4324/9781003170808-65

Double Suicide (1969) – Mashira Shinoda

Uncut Gems (2019) – Josh and Benny Safdie

Opening Night (1977) – John Cassavetes. The thrill of watching two great artists – Cassavetes and Gena Rowlands – take enormous risks.

Distant Voices, Still Lives (1988) – Terence Davies. Working-class life in Liverpool in the 1940s and 1950s. As if I'm in dialogue with lost members of my own family in England. All are gone.

The Turin Horse (2011) – Bela Tarr and Agnes Hranitzky. Brutal.

24 Frames (2017) – Abbas Kiarostami. The connection between photography and cinema. Mysterious.

Funny Games (1997) – Michael Haneke. Brutal.

King Lear (1971) – Peter Brook. Brutal.

Eraserhead (1977) – David Lynch. That feeling of sinking into something.

Breaking the Waves (1996) – Lars Von Trier. Brutal.

Ali: Fear Eats the Soul (1974) – Rainer Werner Fassbinder. Brutal.

Killing of a Sacred Deer (2017) – Yorgos Lanthimos. Brutal.

Pain and Glory (2019) – Pedro Almodovar. Great film by a great director about a director. Funny and generous. And brutal.

The need to do it

Sometimes when I am watching a production, I don't understand why the director needed to direct this particular play. Everybody can feel it when they go to the theatre and there's no urgency. If I see a production that is too neat, too tidy, if it has no passion, if I cannot feel an energy coming from the stage that declares, "I want to talk to you about something, I have something I must tell you," then I don't know where the *need* is. I am not saying it has to be manically wired, but if there's a lack of necessity, I don't have much interest in watching that.

I don't know how people function in the theatre unless they need to do it. It makes me loopy when people say, "Oh, I'd like to be a director." It's not going to work if you would *like* to be one. Maybe if you *want* to be one. But if you *need* to be one, that's something else. But if you don't *need* to be one, it's just an awful way to lead your life. I was going to say "make a living," but most freelance artists are paid so poorly they cannot make a living. They are exploited. According to a recent report from our union – On the Edge: The Lives and Livelihoods of Stage Directors and Choreographers – the average mid-career SDC member earns $17,000 from directing contracts per year. Yes, the theatre is my art. It certainly is a passion. Very importantly, it is my job. It is my profession. It is my craft. It is how I make money. There is an ugly contradiction where artists are put on a pedestal and at the same time treated like feckless idiots because they don't make real money.

DOI: 10.4324/9781003170808-66

"Dear Mr. Les Waters"

Raelle Myrick-Hodges

Dear Mr. Les Waters,

I am not a good writer. And I hate being precious. So this is hard. The fear that boils up inside is enormous. How do I express all the fuzzy feelings of what your work and your spirit contribute to me as an artist? I do not have fancy words and superhero sentences, but every syllable here is filled with genuine admiration and inner eloquence about how your work and your world propels me and the field of theatre performance forward.

My first panel interview for my first fellowship grant as a director was witnessed by you. It was in Cleveland. I had met the minimum requirements, but other candidates had lengthier resumes, more degrees, lots of schooling and such. You believed that the theatre establishment should invest in me. I remember the notes I received as part of the interview process and the sense of responsibility I felt knowing that you – that "cool" director who did *Big Love* – and others on the panel were saying "OK" to the little black girl who was foolish enough to start her own theatre company with only a hundred bucks and no college degree and no prior theatre training. If she could do that, perhaps it was the panel's duty to take a chance on her as a seedling director. That decision is one of the reasons I continue to do theatre today. I had done one prior internship and I was not really convinced at the time that theatre was a career for me. Perhaps it was my duty to take a chance on the landscape of theatre.

Since then, your work and your integrity has inspired me to "do what I want." To make work to share and not to lecture an audience. To develop a hybrid

DOI: 10.4324/9781003170808-67

process that uses devised theatre rehearsal techniques to support a narrative text-based play. Your Berkeley Rep production of Martin McDonagh's *The Pillowman* terrified me in the way that I "sympathized" with a terrifying character. That show influenced my work at the Arden on *The Bluest Eye*, Lydia R. Diamond's adaptation of Toni Morrison's novel. Katurian and Cholly could not be more different characters, but the fear and the ferociousness they embody is similar.

It may sound strange to say it out loud, but you love theatre. For an art form with little funding and little visibility, you believe in theatre as a place to commune.

You were an unassuming mentor for me. An advocate who championed my process and my prowess as an emerging stage director. I want to tell you Thank You.

Thank You for every single phone call about a stupid play that I did not "understand."
Thank You for every cup of coffee, every free meal, and every bit of advice for 20 years.
Thank You for the inspiration of *Big Love*, *The Pillowman*, *Peter Pan on her 70th Birthday*, *The Christians* and for giving me *Eurydice*.
Thank You for that beard. It. Is. Everything.
But, most important, Thank You for believing in me as a person who can be a creative artist and a citizen at the same time.

I think it is working out so far.

Talk soon,

RAELLE MYRICK-HODGES
"Theatre Artist"

* * * * *

RAELLE MYRICK-HODGES *is a theatre director whose work ranges from narrative text-based theatre to generative ensemble work. She has worked at California Shakespeare Theater, The Public Theater, National Black Theatre, and PlayMakers Repertory Company, among others. She acknowledges the mentorship of George C. Wolfe and Joseph Haj. As an arts administrator, she has been Artistic Director at Brava for Women in the Arts in San Francisco and Performing Arts Curator at Contemporary Arts Center in New Orleans. She is also the founder of Azuka Theatre in Philadelphia, a company dedicated to telling the stories of outcasts and underdogs. She teaches in the MFA theatre program at Brown University and the Actors Studio Drama School at Pace University. She will soon be directing her first opera.*

Things unfinished

In 1987, shortly before Jacob was born, I was in Minneapolis directing *The House of Bernarda Alba*, Lorca's great play about repression that should lay like a suffocating weight across one's ribcage. Garland Wright, the visionary Artistic Director of the Guthrie Theater, had asked me to direct. I was not an obvious choice. Despite a good translation by Timberlake Wertenbaker, handsome design by Annie Smart, Jim Ingalls and the late great Marty Pakledinaz, and a strong cast led by Miriam Colon, Christina Moore, Amy Aquino, and Brenda Wehle, the production was nothing more than worthy. It was solid. It was grey. No light, no shadows. Clear, well thought through but lacking excitement. On Opening Night, Joanne Akalaitis, who was also directing at the Guthrie – *Leon & Lena (and lenz)* from the works of Georg Büchner – remarked "Everything looked to be in the right place. Everybody knew what they were doing all the time."

In my arrogance, I mistook this as a compliment. What Joanne was politely pointing out was that the work was finished and therefore dead. I had rehearsed the play and polished it, and rehearsed the play and polished it, and rehearsed the play and polished it. We ran the play so many times. The production was a heavy expensive marble headstone on Lorca's grave. There was no space in it, no room for the production to grow. Nowhere for the performances and the production to expand. Nothing to be found out. It was finished and it needed to be unfinished. Somewhere something (or things) in the production needs to be left undone so that the journey can continue with the audience.

DOI: 10.4324/9781003170808-68

Advice from the photographer Robert Doisneau:

> I don't usually give out advice or recipes, but you must let the person looking at the photograph go some of the way to finishing it. You should offer them a seed that will grow and open up their minds.

29. *Suddenly Last Summer* at Berkeley Repertory Theatre (2003).

30. Image board assembled by Les Waters at the time of working on *Macbeth*.

31. *Red* at Berkeley Repertory Theatre (2012).

32. The Thin Place at Playwrights Horizons (2019).

33. *The Glory of the World* at Actors Theatre of Louisville (2015).

34. *Concerning Strange Devices from the Distant West* at Berkeley Repertory Theatre (2010).

35. Drawing of Les Waters by Ron Crawford.

36. *Eurydice* at Yale Repertory Theatre (2006).

Grief

I did not have a great relationship with my dad in my teens. It was the 1960s. I found him repressive and boring and dull and unimaginative. I was an only child. My parents were in a very unhappy marriage. My mother attempted suicide, more than once, and I identified with my mother and thought my dad was a terrible person. Simply not true. My father was an extraordinary person with a whole life that I didn't know about until after my mother had died. My mom had TB, my mom had TB twice, and my dad's focus was looking after my mother through her illness. My mother died of complications from TB in 2000, my dad died three years later. I was at UCSD. I still miss him. I miss his responsibility. I miss his gentleness. I miss his absolute love of his grandchildren. The loss was terrible. It was a physical thing. Like I was carrying a heavy rock inside my chest.

Grieving is discontinuous. There are days, or a day, or a part of a day, where you don't think at all about the person who has died. In the early stages, whenever that happened, I felt guilty. That there was something wrong with me because I wasn't thinking about my dad or my mom all of the time. What was wrong with me if I wasn't destroyed by pain? If there was no pain, how could I maintain contact with my parents? Now there are days and weeks and months that go by and then out of the blue, there's some memory that fells me to the floor. Some fragment that is living on its own some other place until without prompting it inhabits me. And I feel like I'm ten years old and I don't know where they are. I'm lost.

DOI: 10.4324/9781003170808-69

Pandemic reading list

On March 17, 2020, I wrote in my diary, "Day 1 of 2–3-week CoronaVirus lockdown." I thought it would be two to three weeks of staying at home and an opportunity to read. I love reading. Thought it would be the time for the "big reads" – all the greats that I haven't read – Dostoevsky, Cervantes – the time to revisit *Moby Dick* or Murasaki Shikibu's *The Tale of Genji* – the time to finally read Dorothy Richardson's *Pilgrimage*, whose four volumes have sat on my bookshelves for over three decades. But no, this hasn't happened. A 150-page book that pre-COVID would have taken an afternoon to read can sporadically occupy 10 days. COVID mush.

Normal People by Sally Rooney.

Elmet by Fiona Mozley.

Actress by Anne Enright. I usually don't like novels/literature about the theatre because I don't believe them and fault the research. This is very good. Rings true every step of the way. Funny. Painfully funny.

Funny Weather: Art in an Emergency by Olivia Laing. On why art matters. Not just inspiring, also focusing and offering support.

Training the Best Dog Ever by Dawn Sylvia-Stasiewicz and Larry Kay. In preparation.

People Who Led to My Plays by Adrienne Kennedy. Research for this project.

DOI: 10.4324/9781003170808-70

An Attempt at Exhausting a Place in Paris by Georges Perec. An attempt to describe all the things that usually pass unnoticed in Place Saint Sulpice. A birthday gift from Caryl Churchill.

Today is June 9, 2020. That's what I have read so far. Pandemic reading at the speed of tectonic plates. I don't have the attention – COVID paralysis – or I watch the news and there's a lot to watch and learn and support.

The Fox and Dr. Shimamura by Christine Wunnicke.

As if by Chance by David Lan.

Lot Six by David Adjmi.

July 11th. Gus arrives. He's a wirehaired pointing griffon. A birthday gift from my daughter Nancy. He has my father's eyes. Nancy says, "My Grandad had the softest eyes." And so does Gus. Often, I think I'm looking into my father's eyes.

Independent People by Halldór Laxness. Felt I was living inside the book. The book and me and my family on my mother's side of agricultural field workers.

Who Killed My Father by Édouard Louis. I wish this book existed when my father was alive. I wish my father, who scavenged for food as a child, who was too poor to receive a good education because his parents were not able to afford the school uniform, could've read this and felt seen. I wish I could see Ivo's stage version of this with the great Hans Kesting. Who identifies as working class in the US theatre? It is a problem that it is such a middle-class profession. Full of the children of the middle classes. I still wince when parentage is discussed. "Oh, my mother is a lawyer and my dad is an architect." "My moms are both therapists." Where are the children of the working class? The problem of not being seen, of not being acknowledged. Race. Class. Gender.

A Sorrow Beyond Dreams by Peter Handke. I first read this in 1976. I read it on Midsummer Common in Cambridge during a lunch break from Baldwin's bottling factory, where I was working. A book about Handke's mother's suicide. My father attempted suicide that year. I know so very little about it. I don't know how or exactly when. Somebody must have found him. Who? My mother? After I was told (by my mother) that he wanted to visit Cambridge, I said no. I deliberately turned my back on him. At that period of my life was I so ashamed of him? I had my own life to live. My mother attempted suicide the following year, a few weeks after I started work at the Royal Court. An overdose on prescription meds. My father found her. She was in a coma. We sat with her for days. She came out of the coma. Whenever I think about suicide (in general, not my own desires), I think of my mother. Rarely my father. I had two suicidal parents. Not one. Two. Since my mid-20s, I have been locked in a cycle of grieving for those who were not actually dead. I read the Handke again on Monday September 7, 2020. On first reading the book in 1976, I wondered if there was a production in this material. Yesterday, I read it searching for that impulse, the desire to make a production. When Lucas asked Caryl what it was like to work with me, she said that I was not afraid of difficult emotional material. I'm not. I enjoy it. I love the pain and the risk of it. With *A Sorrow Beyond Dreams*, something tells me not to do it. Not to risk myself. Not to inflict harm. And who to do it with? Philip Brannon? Thomas Jay Ryan? Bruce McKenzie? Conrad Schott? Why do it? Why stuff salt in that always open wound?

Today is September 8, 2020, and the Pandemic has killed 189,323 in the US. No end in sight.

September 9th. At 9 am, it's night. What light there is, is vivid orange. The air stings. Ash is falling. The wildfires across Northern California leave a massive layer of smoke across the Bay. With climate change and a lack of radical action will this be a yearly occurrence? I love Northern California, I love its beauty, I feel at home here, but is it liveable? Is this a new normal?

Another Country by James Baldwin. I have watched documentaries and interviews with and about Baldwin, including the 1965 debate with William F. Buckley, for many years. First time I have read one of his novels. Raw. Brutal.

Where We Go When All We Were Is Gone by Sequoia Nagamatsu. Short stories about Kappa and Godzilla and Yokai. Recommended by Naomi Iizuka. Thought it would be a useful portal into *Black Mountain Women*, our project with Martha Redbone and Aaron Whitby at the Public. These are too arch, too contained. *BMW* should be looser, more exposed, lacking in any armor.

October 23rd. I went to SF MOMA today. 1st time in a museum since mid-March. It was a relief and wondrous and I feel a tiny bit saner. I love this place. I love museums. Reassuring to see the Agnes Martin and Sigmar Polke and Julie Mehretu work again. A new face – Donna-Lee Phillips – her photographs exploring the relationship of photography and language in the 1970s: "This is a photograph." Art is not just illustration and decoration and entertainment. It's essential.

Hamnet by Maggie O'Farrell. I'm a nerd for historical fiction. I read all of Mary Renault and Jean Plaidy as a child. The present seemed endlessly confusing and unstable whilst the past was ordered and contained. A reimagining of Agnes (Anne) Hathaway's life. All the glamour of the Elizabethan world and the wrenching of absence – loss of a child, loss of a husband. My grandfather survived two of his children and always said it was the worst thing imaginable. Yes.

Confessions of a Bookseller by Shaun Bythell. In my multiverse, I own a bookstore in either Stinson Beach or Point Reyes, CA. Or to be particular, in my multiverse, I own Point Reyes Books and sit all day in a big leather armchair by the stove and read. Gus is by my feet. There are no customers to disturb me.

Caste: The Origins of Our Discontents by Isabel Wilkerson. Like most English schoolboys of my generation, my knowledge of the history of other countries abruptly stopped when a particular country departed the Mother Country, when that country liberated itself from the Empire and Imperial Rule. America, India, Africa. My History teacher, Mercy Grace Bradshaw, regularly acted out these "sad decisions" in class. (Culminating in a distraught re-enactment of the last night of the Romanov family on July 16, 1918. She wept. We teenage revolutionary schoolboys cheered. Not exactly British Imperial history, but Imperial History all the same.) As far as my formal education was concerned, there was an American Revolutionary War and a Declaration of Independence on July 4th, 1776, and then silence. No Civil War, No Abolition of Slavery, No Reconstruction, No Jim Crow laws. Silence. My knowledge of my adopted country has always been slim. Watching TV footage of the Civil Rights Movement in the 1960s provided some information. Whenever I complained about my sad teenage life (I was a committed complainer), my father, who had mysteriously lived in the States for several years in the 1940s – if you stand on the steps of New Dramatists on 44th Street in New York and look towards 9th Avenue, you can see the house where my father lived – my father always said, "So you think you are treated badly? Black people in America are treated badly. That's who is treated badly." And as our three children passed through the education system in California, I gathered information from them; they corrected me in my assumptions about systemic racism and white supremacy in the USA.

How to Be an Antiracist by Ibram X. Kendi.

White Rage by Carol Anderson.

Me and White Supremacy by Layla F. Saad.

December 3rd. Someone is dying of COVID every 30 seconds.

This Is Not My Memoir by André Gregory and Todd London. Annie and I had dinner with André and Wally Shawn when they were in London performing *My Dinner with André* at the Theatre Upstairs as a fundraiser for the movie. André talked and talked and talked.

Count Magnus and Other Ghost Stories by M.R. James. Since 1966 and the British TV Program *Mystery and Imagination*, I've been made quietly uncomfortable by the writing of M.R. James. Decades of reading Christmas ghost stories.

Today is December 20, 2020, and the Pandemic has killed 312,636. There is an end in sight. Two vaccines approved. How long?

January 15, 2021. First dose of Moderna vaccine. 2:45 pm. St. Rose Hospital, Hayward, California. Standing on line with Annie in a parking lot. Annie reading *The New Yorker*, me looking at all the health workers and people over 65. A sense of relief. The feeling that it is happening. That there is some possible end to this fear and anxiety and misery.

The Mirror and the Light by Hilary Mantel. Final volume in her trilogy about Thomas Cromwell. I roared through Volumes 1 and 2. This is over 700 pages but it took six weeks to read. My COVID brain? The narrative and character disappear under a mountain of detail and event. The last 50 pages are as good as anything in *Wolf Hall* and *Bring Up the Bodies*. That bereft feeling. No more Thomas Cromwell. No more of these novels.

I don't remember when I last hugged my youngest child.

Today is January 30, 2021, and the Pandemic has killed 450,381 in the US.

Adèle by Leila Slimani.

Beloved by Toni Morrison. Pain. Memory. The relentless cruelty of slavery.

Jazz by Toni Morrison.

Learning from the Germans by Susan Neiman.

Ghostways: Two Journeys in Unquiet Places by Robert MacFarlane, Stanley Donwood, and Dan Richards. Writing about two utterly unique places in England: Orford Ness and a "hollowed way" in Dorset. From the foreword, "The Irish phrase *Aiteanna Tanai* – usually translated as 'thin places,' or 'places of the shade' – refers to those landscapes in which the past is eerily restless, or the thresholds between realms are slender." And a few pages later,

"Drift loves lists. Drift is tide, gravity, storm, waves, wind, gyre, and coastal aspect, among other things." Thin places and lists. Thin places and lists.

February 12, 2021. Today, I received my second dose of the Moderna vaccine. The Pandemic has killed 492,119 in the United States.

Tell Me How Long the Train's Been Gone by James Baldwin.

Nature Cure by Richard Mabey. Depression and walking and Nature. Knowing that we are not central to the world but are part of its mystery. "Solvitur ambulando" – St. Augustine.

The Long-Distance Runner: A Memoir by Tony Richardson.

The Other Slavery by Andrés Reséndez.

Today is March 12, 2021, and the Pandemic has killed 545,377 in the United States. I am closing this list. One year of reading. 2020 was not the year of the big read. My expected big reads. Balzac's *La Comédie Humaine*. Thomas Mann's *Magic Mountain*. Jun'ichirō Tanizaki's *The Makioka Sisters*. George Eliot. Not to be.

Plus, I have watched so much television. I enjoy television, but I have watched an inordinate amount during this Pandemic:

343 episodes of *The Amazing Race*.
4 seasons of *The Crown*. I resisted this for so long. I detest the British monarchy. I have no interest in watching an interview with any of them. I don't thrill to the pomp and pageantry of their weddings and funerals. But then, I watched an episode and was overwhelmed by its sense of conviction. It knows what it is. It knows it's right.
3 seasons of *Dark*.
5 seasons of *Le Bureau*.
2 seasons of *Herrens Veje*.
And almost every Scandi-noir detective series made in the past 5 years.

And so much news. And then more news. The toll of the Pandemic. The murder of Breonna Taylor by the police in Louisville on March 13, 2020. The murder of George Floyd by the police in Minneapolis on May 25, 2020. The killing of 164 Black people by the police in the first eight months of 2020. The Black Lives Matter protests. The magnitude of the protests. The magnificence of the protests. The virus. The wildfires. The election. The vaccine. The insurrection. The virus. The vaccine. The virus. The vaccine.

"Don't Talk"

Bruce McKenzie

I.

The monologue ends. Then.

HIM: (*stands, folding arms, looking at a spot on the floor*) . . .

ME: (*looks, purses lips, pushing them to the side of his face, looks at the spot*) Enh.

HIM: (*looks at a different spot on the floor somewhere between the two of them*)

(*pause*)

HIM: Yeh.

(*pause*)

ME: It feels like if we're going to get that – if we like that thing, at the end, then I have to, y'know, on the table move . . . I can't

HIM: Yep.

ME: We don't want it twice.

HIM: Yep.

II.

The monologue ends. Then.

ME: (*sighs*)

DOI: 10.4324/9781003170808-71

HIM: (*blank look*)

ME: (*laughs*)

HIM: Do it again.

ME: Should I . . . um . . . with the . . . ?

HIM: (*grins. or not.*) Probably.

III.

The monologue ends. Then.

HIM: I'm having a little trouble . . .

ME: (*cocking his head*) On the . . . (*gestures vaguely behind him somewhere*)

HIM: Mm-hm.

ME: Yeah, okay.

IV.

I'm not sure how I can discuss a collaboration that operates "in the room" largely without (or past) words. I'm not sure I want to. Thinking back, I have the impression that beyond the table work – and even to a degree at the table – there's not a lot of talk in rehearsal about character junk, motivation, that junk. There's some, of course, yes, depending on who's in the room, etc. but it's usually just about understanding the sea-lanes rather than plotting a strict course.

Much more of our fundamental communication came/comes from the hours outside of rehearsal spent at restaurants, museums or galleries, at bars (when he was drinking), seeing films together. Or getting to rehearsal and talking about anything but the work at hand. For 15 minutes. Photography books, Trent Parke, or Luc Tuymans, Bela Tarr, Maggie Nelson, that farm-to-table place and why it sucked. We don't like exactly the same shit, it's not that, but we know intimately what the other likes, is moved by, and this guides our work together.

V.

The 2013 production of *Our Town* we did together is some of our best work and was very important to me personally. It interests me that when I made a list of the productions Les and I have worked on I left *Our Town* off the list. It completely slipped my mind. Perhaps I've fully absorbed whatever lessons it imparted or memories it left. They're unnecessary. Or don't really bear discussion.

VI. (a playlist)

Eric Chenaux – "Wild Moon"
The Fall – "Solicitor in Studio"
Clothilde – "A Ora So Cos'e"
Game Theory – "Girl Jesus"
Magnetic Fields – "When I'm Not Looking You're Not There"
Lower Plenty – "Girls They Stick Together"
Sandy Denny – "The Sea Captain"
Richard Youngs – "Mercury Lane"

VII.a. (simplicity)

I hate an unmotivated cross. There are exceptions, though this is not one of them. *Three Sisters*. The second leg of a co-production between Berkeley Rep and Yale Rep. Tuzenbach (Thomas Jay Ryan) and I (Vershinin) are sitting at opposite ends of this large room, of the stage, and I'm supposed to engage in a philosophical discussion of some kind about something or other and instead of crossing over to the dining table where Tuzenbach sat I just stayed put and started talking. We had been closer to each other on the thrust stage at Berkeley Rep. I had an inkling of a notion that I'd maybe wander over in that general direction at some point but why? We don't have to raise our voices. So, I sat there and Tom sat there, we played it like we were sitting next to each other, then the bit was done, and, yeah. Done and done. There was an intimacy to it and a fear of intimacy and an engagement, a necessity and a couldn't-give-a-fuck and entitlement and a narcissism that are all suggested. By sitting still. These are the kinds of layers Les enables and builds so beautifully in his work.

VII.b. (silliness)

Here's a cross we liked. Towards the end of *Three Sisters*, Vershinin has the line, "I have to go." I spoke that line, again didn't move, then walked to a single chair that was placed very far upstage and sat down. It was even better when we restaged it at Yale Rep and I had a *very* long way to walk. I'm not certain that that *is* silly exactly, but it partakes; I *am* certain that Les is silly, deeply silly. Amongst other things, sure, yeah, of course. In a serious way.

VIII. (donkeys)

I recently sent Les a limited-edition book of photo portraits of donkeys. I thought it might make him cry. It did. I also got one for myself. It made me cry too. I look at it often. *Au Hasard Balthazar* is one of our favourite films.

IX. (galleries)

There's a way in which we should also think of Les not as a director but as a curator.

X.

The monologue ends. Then.

HIM: (*raises his eyebrows, nodding. Blinks.*)

ME: Yeah, I think so.

Long pause. Reset.

HIM: (*turns to SM*) Pablo, who do we have tomorrow?

Apparently, rehearsal is over.

*   *   *   *   *

BRUCE MCKENZIE. *I have acted in American and international theatre for 35 years. I play(ed) music in three bands, Maquiladora (sweet, tweaked acid-folk), Buzz Or Howl (free-form psychedelic noise unit), Beggars (Vincent van Gogh possessed by Gram Parsons), and a solo incarnation, Peckinpah (blissed-out dronefolkambientamericana). With these, I've released albums in five countries and toured Europe and Japan. I am a Californian. I feel this is important somehow. I studied anthropology and philosophy at Johns Hopkins University before dropping out. Never studied theatre. Les and I have worked together on something like 16 productions of 10 plays. I wrote the Black Metal score for and acted in Ev-ocation to Visible Appearance. I write here about* Our Town, Three Sisters. *I was the Stage Manager, Vershinin. I was Nikos in* Big Love. *I played Stanley Kowalski for Ivo Van Hove. A long time ago.*

Kenneth Tynan

I bought a book of reviews by Kenneth Tynan the other day. *Curtains*. I wanted to look at them again because as a young man, as a teenager, I read his reviews in *The Observer*. I would get up early on a Sunday to walk several blocks to the corner store so I could get a copy of *The Observer*, which wasn't easy to find in a working-class steel town like Scunthorpe. That's how I found out about the work in London that I was not able to see. Tynan's reviews were so important to me. He was a magnificent champion of people's work. It was more than "Oh, I like the plays of so-and-so" or "There's a play by so-and-so." It was part of something bigger. It was really the beginning of the journey into all of this for me.

I would read *The Observer* religiously, the *Observer* art section and the *Observer* magazine. I don't even remember who the art critic was. In my early teens, I was very interested in the history of art. I even entertained the notion of going to the Courtauld Institute in London to study the history of art. I was especially interested in contemporary art. There was one particular cover to that magazine. I remember picking the *Observer* up at this store, starting the walk back to my parents' house, opening the newspaper, and finding the magazine with this cover photograph of the Rauschenberg combine "Monogram," the stuffed angora goat on a platform with an automobile tire around its middle, and it had a headline, something like, "This is the future of art." I remember looking at that cover and being incredibly excited and thinking, "Oh, this is it. This is it. I want to be in that world." Rauschenberg made these things that I'd never seen before and I thought they were beautiful, and ugly, and most importantly, very exciting.

DOI: 10.4324/9781003170808-72

And I wanted to be part of that world. I knew that somewhere, a hundred miles away, there were people living very different lives. That seemed to have more potent and imaginative pathways than the life that I was leading, and I just wanted to leave. Was there another option? I couldn't see it and I didn't know how to have Rauschenberg's *Monogram* and the life that I wanted in the town where I was brought up. Seeing that cover was as important to me as when I was a wee boy, a very small boy, seeing the pantomime of *Dick Whittington* and the cats dancing on the rooftops of London and thinking, "I want to do that, I want to make things like that."

Some of my favorite places

Like most they are connected to people and a particular time.

Weligama, Sri Lanka, the 1980s
North London, 1971
Caryl Churchill's old house, Islington, London
Drew and Sherman Fracher's farm, Abiding Grace, Kentucky, Thanksgiving, 2017
New York in the 1980s
Northern California
Paleochora, Crete, 1980
My Aunty Flo's house, Pleasley, Great Britain
Edinburgh
Chris Moore and Chuck Rosenau's house, Hudson Valley
Druidston, North Wales, 1991
Montelimar, South of France, 1971
Our house, Berkeley, now
Emily Bingham and Stephen Reilly's farm, Indian Bean, Kentucky
David McMahon's apartment, New York
Gumusluk, Turkey, the 1980s
Kathy and Henry Chalfant's house, Brooklyn Heights, the great blizzard of 2016
Sky Road, Clifden, Ireland 1995
22 Kynaston Road, London N16
Lincoln Cathedral, Great Britain, always

DOI: 10.4324/9781003170808-73

Ghosts

Of being a spectator, so to speak, of one's own absence.

—Marcel Proust

1959. I'm seven years old. My mother's brother Les is throwing a ball against the wall of my house. I lie in bed and hear the ball bounce. He died in 1951, the year before I was born. There was always confusion in my parent's house over who Les actually was. My father was Les, I am Les (but was always Leslie to my parents), and my mother's beloved brother was Les. For the purpose of clarification, I am not named Les after my father but after my uncle. To make things even clearer, my father called me Herbert for the first six years of my life. Herbert is not my middle name. There are no Herberts in my family.

1960. The beginning of a period of obsessive behavior. Food on my plate cannot touch other food. Everything must be separate, otherwise it is inedible. I invent elaborate punishments for myself to control unruly behavior. I band-aid cold french fries to the undersides of my arms. What did I do? My slippers must be perfectly aligned under the bed. I check them constantly through the night. The ghost of my uncle lies under the bed, waiting to catch my hands.

1961. I'm 9 years old. My maternal grandmother Carey, who I deeply love, has died and we are staying at her house before the funeral. On my way upstairs, she speaks to me in the voice of an owl. I cannot speak for several hours. For many months, I insist that my parents sit on the stairs outside my bedroom until I fall asleep.

DOI: 10.4324/9781003170808-74

1962. I'm 10 years old. Walking up the street where I live – 30 Lincoln Gardens, Ashby, Scunthorpe, North Lincolnshire – in the early hours of the morning. A man ahead of us crossing the roundabout bursts into flames. He's not worried. Suddenly, he's a column of light. Nobody else sees this.

1969. A man is walking. Late afternoon. Summer. Drowsy. Brumby Road. He has just died in the local hospital and is on his way home.

2003. Christmas Eve. We are staying at my father's house for the Holidays. Annie and the kids and I have taken over all the bedrooms. Against our protests, my father is sleeping on the couch in the living room. In the early hours of the morning, I creep downstairs to leave a stocking full of gifts for him. He is not sleeping on the couch. He's sitting in his armchair. Eyes closed. Is he asleep? I think so but am not totally sure. There is a low light. The curtains are closed. No lamps are on. A dull silver light is emanating from him. He's subtly glowing. My father is creating his own light. It's Christmas and my father dies 10 days later on January 3rd.

2012–2018. In Louisville, I live in several apartments in Victorian, or even earlier, buildings. One apartment in particular is very active. Footsteps. Strange dragging noises in the hallway behind the bedroom wall. A man stands at the foot of the staircase. Not tall. Wearing a long brown overcoat. Face turned away but what I can see of it is dissolving and reforming and dissolving again. I see him several times. Always the same. Same position, same coat, same morphing face. How did J.G. Ballard describe the portraits of Francis Bacon? As if the dead are trying to remember what they looked like.

2015. Get into Louisville very late at night. Flight delayed from the West Coast. Distressed to be back. I am missing my family. Why am I in Louisville? Why am I doing this job? Back in my apartment, I get into bed and turn off the lights. Something sits at the foot of the bed. I can feel the bed depress on the left-hand side.

2016. March. Long day's work at Actors Theatre. Humana Festival. I open the door to my apartment and there is a man sitting, facing a wall. I step outside. I walk back in. No man. No chair. What man is this? Is this a new man?

2019. January 17th. Berkeley. A diary entry: "At 1 in the morning as I am watching Project Runway All Stars, something comes up behind me on the left side and prods me in the shoulder. Very unnerving. As if something was in the wrong place."

2020. Late September. It's almost midnight and I'm the only one awake in the house. A chair at the dining room table scrapes on the floor. An exhalation of air. A small groan.

For many years, I was ill and finally on September 28, 1994, I was admitted into St. Barts Hospital in London with clinical depression. My life was saved by Annie and later by Dan Twomey, my analyst. In the time that I spent in Strauss Ward, I sometimes felt that the lenses in my eyes had been removed, not cleaned but removed, and that I could see with great clarity, and I often felt, when looking in the mirror above the sink in the room that I shared with Ian Wilson and "Yallery Brown," that I could put my hand, my right hand, through my face, that I had no solid face, that there was nothing there. As if a ghost is looking at a ghost to be.

Sometimes when I see a ghost, this feeling returns.

I see a ghost and everything falls apart.

"[aside]"

Maria Dizzia

"This is my father's shirt," Les said as he tugged at the open cuff around his wrist. We were on a break during rehearsals for Sarah Ruhl's *Eurydice* in Berkeley. I hadn't lost my father yet, so I don't think I knew what to say. Les smiled and moved past me to coffee or cookies or peanut butter M&M's. And from then on, Les's father was in the room with us or in the room in my mind – loving Les, imparting advice and then, one day, leaving. In some ways, it's obvious how Les built the connection between us – between director and actor, between a grown-up orphan and a young person with both her parents still alive – but in other ways, it was a mystery to me. Why exactly did I understand more now because he showed me his Dad's shirt? Because he still had it? Because he had decided to wear it? I think it was a little shorter in the arms than Les wore. It was plaid with green in it and soft. Maybe because it conjured a real person and not just the idea of losing what is dear and fundamental.

I think this is how Les directs. I can't know for sure because I'm the one being directed. Les never hints at what he's doing and, as a result, I never feel manipulated. I never feel like I'm being led in a certain direction or coaxed toward a result or like he wants to break a plate over my head.

Of course, he suggests that lines are better when you're not standing directly behind the furniture, when you're in your light, when you're audible and seem like you need something. But the depth of a character, the thing that drew him to the play in the first place, the thing in which he must inevitably see himself and then trust all these other people to enact – that he imparts

DOI: 10.4324/9781003170808-75

through stories and head tilts and by patiently letting actors work their way through a scene without saying anything.

Les has told me so many stories in the rehearsal room, but I don't think he's told me the same story twice. The stories he tells are about the play – what he sees and feels in it and then he trusts that you will understand. I directed once and I think I said "you know what I mean?" so many times. Les doesn't say that. He trusts that you do know what he means. And maybe that trust is how he directs. He trusts the actors to have an uncanny first read and then a desperate rehearsal process that gets more and more bungled until it all sorts itself out again. He trusts that he can communicate and that the people around him will deliver and that trust is in the air from the beginning. And maybe being trusted is all anyone needs to do their best, to reciprocate that trust in the text, and in one another.

I think the fact that I remember the stories speaks to what they meant to me as an actor. When Les was cold, his father would smack the back of his legs to warm him up. Your parents keep you warm, they make you laugh, they treat you like no one else, you kind of share a body. When we worked on Sarah's *In the Next Room*, he told me that when he was a kid, he used to run and vault himself onto his grandmother's couch. I imagined a little boy in pulled up socks (the socks are from another story) running toward this over-stuffed Victorian couch and flinging himself on it. I wondered if Mrs. Daldry should fling herself on things. If she should fling herself onto the examination table in her first scene or maybe she should start poised and gradually get more nimble and rowdy. Whatever the choice, now I knew there should be flinging.

During tech for *Eurydice* at Yale, we were working on the part where Eurydice says goodbye to her father to follow Orpheus out of the Underworld. We'd done it so many times already, in rehearsals and throughout a run at Berkeley. In the middle of a cue-to-cue without the cast – I was doing my favorite actor thing of snacking in costume while standing in the aisles – Les walked into the row of seats behind me and said, "I think stand on his feet when he hugs you." And I said "ok" and kept snacking in the dark. They finished focusing the lights and we were ready to run through the scene again. The actor playing my father and I started in that gentle, goofy way that happens toward the end of a long tech. And then, we got to the hug and I stood on his feet and it broke me into so many pieces. I sobbed and hugged him with everything I had, and then I ran away to find my husband. It resonated with me throughout the rest of the play, especially when I found my father again, lifeless on the ground, after we had shared something so enormous and intimate.

So, Les directs that way, too: he trusts the actors, he tells stories, he makes sure everyone can see you, and he gives you small wordless actions packed with history and meaning.

I always thought one of Les's most private stories was about singing when he was little. Les was a boy soprano and sang in a choir. The choir was professionally recorded once and Les had a solo. A few times, as an adult, he has heard the recording on the radio. I have tried to find it – I've googled "Les Waters boy soprano" and "Cleethorpes children's choir" – but I have never found it. I was always afraid to ask for more specifics . . .

I once called Les by what I assumed was his full first name, and the look he gave me made me think our friendship had come to an abrupt and bitter end. I wonder if that's the look his mother gave him when he finished his solo. Or maybe it was something cooler and more distracted. The boys finished their performance and Les returned to his mom after whatever hoopla must have surrounded a boys' choir's first professional recording in the early 1960s. He asked her how his solo went, and she said, "Your socks were uneven." Les loved his mom dearly and she loved him back. I had a teacher who told me argument scenes aren't interesting in the theatre unless the characters love each other. Les told me the choir story during *Eurydice*. We were staging the scene where she finally catches up to Orpheus, whispers his name, and he turns around. There's the feeling in Les's story of having first succeeded and then failing – most thoroughly and devastatingly – and the loss coming from a desire to be closer or to have a little more, to be reassured by your mom, and to bask in the joy of it. That's all a part of the scene as Sarah wrote it. The deeper meaning I've taken from Les's tale over the years is that the very thing that may have been mortifying to a seven-year-old is among the things we strive to achieve in the theatre as adults. To put yourself on display unselfconsciously. To experience the vulnerability of wanting to connect. To embody the dualism of being glorious with your socks uneven and understanding that maybe not everyone will get it, even when you love them.

These are all aspects of Les's work. His desire to connect with the audience, but on his own terms, to confront the way he sees the world, his aesthetic of leaving a few things undone – not burrowing into the actor, but guiding gently over time, making room for other people, for humanness, and for the story that, at its best, happens in the audience's imagination and not just on the stage in front of them.

*   *   *   *   *

MARIA DIZZIA is an actor who has appeared on Broadway, Off-Broadway, in regional theaters, and in film and television, including a recurring role on Orange Is the New Black. She has acted in four plays directed by Les Waters, two of them by Anne Washburn and two by Sarah Ruhl, including the Broadway production of In the Next Room, for which she was nominated for a Tony Award. She grew up in suburban New Jersey, attended Cornell University, and received her MFA in acting from UC San Diego. She was playing the role of Heidi Schreck in the national tour of What the Constitution Means to Me when the pandemic brought theatre to a halt in March 2020.

Comfort, solace

*LES, WHERE DO YOU TAKE COMFORT? WHERE DO YOU FIND
SOLACE?*

I read a lot.
Or rather I read a lot pre-Pandemic.
Novels/biographies/research material.

Surprisingly, I listen to very little music although I love it when I do.
I rarely go to concerts.
I love opera but see little. Maybe because I don't like the productions.
I think the last opera I saw was Mozart's *Don Giovanni*. At San
Francisco Opera. It was a birthday treat for Annie. Dreadful. Deadly. I
wanted to grate my face off.

I like dance. One of the highlights of 2020 would have been Pina
Bausch's *Palermo Palermo* at CalArts. Canceled due to the Pandemic.
Anne Teresa de Keersmaeker's *Mittel wir im leben sind* was a revelation
to me earlier this year in NYC. William Forsythe. Sidi Larbi
Cherkaoui. Crystal Pite. Bill T. Jones. All important. All very great
artists.

I'm not sure if any of this gives me comfort or solace. For too
long, I was very suspicious of comfort, solace. I thought it was soft.
Emotionally irresponsible to avoid the harshness of the world. I'm
not so sure now. I certainly want to find support. I deeply appreciate
illumination.

DOI: 10.4324/9781003170808-76

Work gives me pleasure.
Seeing work that I think is honest gives me pleasure.

I love the ecolect of theatre. All the idiosyncrasies and quirks of a
particular rehearsal room, all the tiny ways that theatre talks to itself,
defines itself. Why and how it's its own community. "Take a five,
everybody." "Thank you, Five."

Above all I like to walk.
I like to walk and think.
I like books about walking. W. G. Sebald's *The Rings of Saturn*. Teju
Cole's *Open City*. Woolf's *Mrs. Dalloway*. Joyce's *Ulysses*.
Sometimes, I practice walking meditation.

I have always wanted to undertake a big walk. Seattle to San Diego.
SF to NYC. A feat of endurance. I don't think that's going to
happen now that I'm 68. Maybe the 600 miles of El Camino Real in
California? Maybe the 147 miles of The Viking Way in the UK for my
70th birthday? My daughter Nancy walked part of the Pacific Coast
Trail. Over a thousand miles.

I love the slowness of walking. The endurance of it.
I love learning a city through walking, its cultures, its neighborhoods,
its history.
I love walking a landscape into my body.

"Still Connected"

Caryl Churchill

Blood in a bed and the opening of Keith Jarrett's Köln concert. A long dead boy scaring crows in the mist, a woman ironing in a field, opera soaring from the mouth of a woman who wouldn't sing. A man dancing with the pig he loves, someone changing gender as they speak, an angry woman rolling another up in a carpet. A contorted creature rattling damaged words.

I met Les in 1978 when he was about to be the assistant on *Cloud Nine*, I last worked with him in 1993 on *The Skriker*. Then, he moved to America.

Fen. Les came from the east of England, he'd read Mary Chamberlain's *Fenwomen*, and we shared a feeling that the piece would somehow be about people yearning for something different. It was a Joint Stock show, which meant researching something with a company before a play was thought of. We all stayed in a cottage for two weeks, listening to anyone who would talk to us. The book focused our attention on the women working on the land and we talked to workers and gangmasters, but some encounters were chance, we walked past a house and someone beckoned us in. When we finally opened the play in the cold Almeida Theatre, just reclaimed from use as a storage space, to an audience wrapped in blankets, it was in Annie Smart's amazing field in a room.

At the weekend in the middle of this, Les arranged for us to come back to London and see two Pina Bausch shows, one of the many things he showed me. The next play we did had dancers as well as actors, everyone spoke and everyone moved, and we worked with choreographer Ian Spink and another writer, David Lan, who was also an anthropologist. Joint Stock again, the

DOI: 10.4324/9781003170808-77

starting point was *The Bacchae* and we explored what it was like for people to be possessed, to be beside themselves.

A few years later, I finally managed to write a play I'd struggled with for years by realising it could have just three speaking characters and all the rest could be movement. And an opera in the middle. This time I'd already written the play, instead of approaching an idea with Les without having written anything, but there was no one else I could imagine directing it.

And then, he moved to America. He hasn't directed any of my plays since and I've seen only a couple of his productions, though heard about more. But I feel, perhaps irrationally, that our work is still connected. I miss working with him, I miss the ordinary and mysterious, the extremes of what can be felt or thought or can happen, the way it would look. I miss what makes us laugh.

There were other productions, there were and are years of friendship. It's hard to write anything at all about a network of memories and associations that mean a lot and which I wouldn't choose to tie down to words for myself let alone to be read. But that's some of it.

*   *   *   *   *

CARYL CHURCHILL *is a playwright. Her plays include* Owners; Light Shining in Buckinghamshire; Traps; Cloud Nine; Top Girls; Fen; Serious Money; Ice Cream; Mad Forest; The Skriker; Blue Heart; This Is a Chair; Far Away; A Number; A Dream Play; Drunk Enough to Say I Love You?; Seven Jewish Children; Love and Information; Here We Go; Pigs and Dogs; Escaped Alone; Glass.Kill.Bluebeard.Imp. *Music theatre includes* Lives of the Great Poisoners *and* Hotel, *both with Orlando Gough. She has also written for radio and television.*

What is Beauty?

My wife is beautiful.
My children are beautiful.
Sometimes, the sunset over the Bay is very beautiful. The light.
The reflection of Mt. Tamalpais in the water.

I don't have the descriptive ability to summon a sunset over the Bay. Either to a resident who has seen many or to someone who has never visited this luminous part of the country.

My father was beautiful. Handsome? No, beautiful.
My mother's hands.

DOI: 10.4324/9781003170808-78

A list catalogues experience

A list catalogues experience. It takes inventory. It gives insight into its writer.
It controls daily turbulence. It orders life.
Lists are both big and little.
We all make them.

Here's a little one.

> Grocery list – July 22, 2020:
> eggplants 2 medium
> parsley
> garlic
> apple cider vinegar
> granulated cane sugar
> tomatoes tinned 2
> sigis yoghurt
> fruit
> full fat greek yoghurt
> penne
> bread
> wine
> tomato paste
> margarine
> tea bags Taylors

DOI: 10.4324/9781003170808-79

And here's a big one.

My father died on January 3, 2003, of congestive heart failure. I was with him for the final week of his life, although he was in a coma. My parents had repeatedly told me as they aged that in the drawer of the dresser in the sitting room was a letter that would tell me exactly what to do when they were both gone. On January 4th I opened the drawer and there was a small blue envelope and inside the envelope a neatly folded single sheet of paper. On it in my father's beautiful copperplate handwriting was written:

> Return library books.
> Inform pensions.
> Go to Gas and Electricity companies.
> Go to Solicitors – Bell Watson, 15/17 Oswald Road. They have the Will. There should be no problem with the Will.
> Go to estate agents.
> I hope you know this but in case you don't, I want you to know that I have always loved you. I hope you knew that.
> I love you.
> I love you all.
> Dad

Appendix 1

Les Waters Biographical Timeline

(Rehearsal periods and significant productions are listed by the month of the first public performance.)

1952 – April 18. Born in Cleethorpes, a seaside town in Lincolnshire, northern England, the only child of Les, a steelworker, and Phyllis, a stay-at-home mother.

1954 – Waters family moves to nearby Lincolnshire industrial town of Scunthorpe.

1960 – Wins scholarship to attend St. Paul's Choir School, London. Father refuses permission to attend.

1968 – Summer. Participates in a production of John Whiting's *The Devils* directed by Mike Bradwell for the Scunthorpe Youth Theatre.

1968 – Hitchhikes from Scunthorpe down to London to see Peter Brook's staging of Ted Hughes' adaptation of Seneca's *Oedipus* at the Old Vic. The first of numerous solo theatregoing excursions as a teenager to London or Stratford-upon-Avon.

1971 – September 4. Marries high school sweetheart Gill Clark shortly before leaving home to study at Manchester University's Department of Theatre. By the time he graduates in 1974, the marriage is over.

1972 – Directs his first theatre production, Howard Brenton's *How Beautiful with Badges*, a play about "a tortured young working-class Maoist disguised as a boy scout." (Doolee.com). The first of several self-produced projects staged in Manchester's Stephen Joseph Studio.

1974 – Travels to Great Wilbraham to interview playwright Edward Bond as research for his undergraduate thesis and production of Bond's *The Sea*, a play that debuted at the Royal Court in May 1973.

1974 – Meets Annie Smart, a fellow student at Manchester. They become a couple in the next few years and over time long-term partners, spouses, and frequent collaborators.

1977 – October 31. Begins work at Royal Court Theatre as assistant director to director Charles Marowitz on his production of Peter Barnes' *Laughter!* (opened January 24, 1978).

1979 – January. Assists Max Stafford-Clark on world premiere of Caryl Churchill's *Cloud Nine* for Joint Stock Theatre Group.

1979 – May 20–26. Travels to the United States for the first time to conduct research in New York for his first professional production, the world premiere of Wallace Shawn's *Marie and Bruce*, which opens on July 13 at the Royal Court Theatre Upstairs.

1979 – June. Becomes Artistic Director of the Theatre Upstairs, responsible for artistic and commissioning programs in smaller, experimental theatre space at Royal Court Theatre.

1980 – June 5. David Bowie attends performance of Sam Shepard's *Seduced* at the Theatre Upstairs.

1981 – June. Becomes Associate Artistic Director of Royal Court.

1982 – July 14. Leaves Royal Court Theatre.

1982 – September 13–24. Travels to Upwell in Norfolk with Caryl Churchill, Annie Smart, and members of Joint Stock to conduct research for what will become Churchill's *Fen*. Directs the play's world premiere, first seen on tour at University of Essex Theatre in January 1983 and then in London at the Almeida Theatre.

1983 – May. Brings Joint Stock production of *Fen* to New York City for a run at The Public Theater as part of the "New York Salutes Britain" Festival.

1984 – February–March. Returns to US to direct an American cast in Caryl Churchill's *Fen* at The Public in New York.

1986 – January. Directs Keith Reddin's *Rum and Coke* at The Public in New York, beginning a period of directing off and on in the US while still based in the UK.

1987 – January. Directs Michael Weller's *Ghost on Fire* at Goodman Theatre in Chicago, his first resident regional theatre production in the US.

1987 – November. Birth of first child (and only son), Jacob.

1991 – May. Birth of second child (and first daughter), Nancy.

1991 – September 11. Marries Annie Smart.

1992 – November. Directs a Japanese cast in Caryl Churchill's *Top Girls* at Tokyo Metropolitan Art Space in Japan.

1994 – January. Directs world premiere of Caryl Churchill's *The Skriker* at National Theatre, his last London production before relocating to California.

1995 – September 18. Appointed full professor with tenure and head of the MFA directing program at University of California–San Diego in La Jolla, CA.

1995 – October. Birth of third child (and second daughter), Madeleine.

1996 – January 4. Annie Smart and three children (ages eight, four, and ten weeks) join Waters in La Jolla completing the professional and personal shift from the UK to the US.

2000 – March. Directs world premiere of Charles Mee's *Big Love* for Actors Theatre of Louisville's Humana Festival of New American Plays. Revives the production a year later, which plays at Berkeley Repertory Theatre, Long Wharf Theatre in New Haven, the Goodman, and Brooklyn Academy of Music. Both playwright and director win Obie Awards for *Big Love* in 2002.

2000 – September 3. Death of mother.

2003 – January 3. Death of father.

2003 – June 30. Leaves teaching position in UCSD Department of Theatre and Dance.

2003 – July 14. Becomes an Associate Artistic Director of Berkeley Repertory Theatre (under Artistic Director Tony Taccone). Goes on to direct roughly 20 productions there, including plays by Sarah Ruhl, Charles Mee, Will Eno, Martin McDonagh, Tennessee Williams, and George Bernard Shaw.

2004 – March. Directs world premiere of Naomi Iizuka's *At the Vanishing Point* for Actors Theatre of Louisville in a warehouse in Butchertown, an industrial neighborhood in Louisville

2006 – March 27. Experiences seizure in the courtyard of Berkeley Rep, which leads to a diagnosis of epilepsy.

2009 – October. Makes Broadway debut at the Lyceum Theatre with Lincoln Center Theater production of Sarah Ruhl's *In the Next Room (or the vibrator play)*, which he first staged at Berkeley Rep in February 2009. (During previews on Broadway, Waters gets the first of what eventually will be two tattoos designed by his frequent collaborator David Zinn.)

2012 – January 9. Becomes Artistic Director of Actors Theatre of Louisville. Directs more than a dozen productions there during his six-year tenure, including *Long Day's Journey into Night*, *Our Town*, *Macbeth*, and world premieres of new plays as part of the Humana Festival.

2015 – February. Directs Charles Mee's *The Glory of the World* for the Humana Festival, commissioned to celebrate the 100th anniversary of the birth of theologian Thomas Merton.

2017 – November. Travels to London for the first time since the death of his father 14 years earlier. Celebrates the 30th birthday of his son Jacob, studying at the time for a Masters in Political Theory at the London School of Economics.

2018 – June 13. Becomes a US citizen in Louisville.

2018 – June 29. Leaves his position as Artistic Director of ATL after six years to resume a freelance directing career.

2020 – March 13. Waters's production of Lucas Hnath's *Dana H.* at the Vineyard Theatre is shut down due to the COVID-19 outbreak. Takes refuge at home in Berkeley for the duration of the Pandemic shutdown of theatres. Numerous projects in development are postponed or cancelled; eventually, new projects – such as two with NAATCO – are conceived and planned.

2020 – July 14. Receives Obie Award for Sustained Excellence in Directing from Village Voice and American Theatre Wing.

2021 – January 15. Gets first dose of the Moderna vaccine against COVID-19 at a hospital in Hayward, CA. Second dose on February 12.

Appendix 2

Les Waters Directing History

This directing history lists all known professional theatre productions directed by Les Waters. It does not include staged readings, developmental workshops, plays directed in college, projects created with students while teaching at University of California San Diego, or occasional events such as ten-minute plays presented as part of the Humana Festival of New American Plays. The location of a theatre is included the first time that a venue is listed (and only then). Many productions are premieres, indicated as WP for world premiere, UKP for premiere in the United Kingdom, and USP for premiere in the United States. For plays and projects planned for when theatres reopened after the COVID-19 Pandemic, see the list in this book titled "Some things will be lost maybe."

1979-07	*Marie and Bruce* by Wallace Shawn (WP) Royal Court Theatre (Theatre Upstairs), London, England
1980-05	*Seduced* by Sam Shepard (UKP) Royal Court Theatre (Theatre Upstairs)
1980-06	*Three More Sleepless Nights* by Caryl Churchill (WP) Soho Poly, London; and Royal Court Theatre (Theatre Upstairs)
1980-08	*Cloud 9* by Caryl Churchill (co-directed with Max Stafford-Clark) Joint Stock Theatre Group at Royal Court Theatre
1980-11	*Not Quite Jerusalem* by Paul Kember (WP) Royal Court Theatre
1981-07	*To Come Home to This* by Carol Bunyan (WP) Royal Court Theatre (Theatre Upstairs)

1981-08   *Loose Ends* by Michael Weller (UKP)
           Hampstead Theatre, London, England

1982-04   *Not Quite Jerusalem* by Paul Kember
           Royal Court Theatre

1982-07   *Insignificance* by Terry Johnson (WP)
           Royal Court Theatre

1983-01   *Fen* by Caryl Churchill (WP)
           Joint Stock Theatre Group
           UK regional tour and Almeida Theatre, London, England

1983-04   *Fugue* by Rona Munro (WP)
           Traverse Theatre, Edinburgh, Scotland

1983-05   *Fen* by Caryl Churchill (USP)
           Joint Stock Theatre Group at The Public Theater, New York, NY

1984-03   *Fen* by Caryl Churchill (with American cast)
           The Public Theater

1984-06   *Minor Complications* by Elizabeth Bond (WP)
           Royal Court Theatre (Theatre Upstairs)

1984-08   *Abel's Sister* by Timberlake Wertenbaker (WP)
           Royal Court Theatre (Theatre Upstairs)

1984-11   *George Dandin* by Molière
           Leicester Haymarket (Studio), Leicester, England

1985-01   *Woyzeck* by Georg Büchner
           Leicester Haymarket (Studio)

1985-05   *Woyzeck* by Georg Büchner
           Almeida Theatre

1985-06   *The Overgrown Path* by Robert Holman (WP)
           Royal Court Theatre

1985-08   *Fire in the Lake* by Karim Alrawi (WP)
           Joint Stock Theatre Group at Edinburgh Festival Fringe and
           UK regional tour

1985-10   *Salonika* by Louise Page
           Liverpool Playhouse, Liverpool, England

1986-01   *Rum and Coke* by Keith Reddin (WP)
            Public Theater-Susan Stein Shiva Theater

1986-05   *The Seagull* by Anton Chekhov (adapt. Thomas Kilroy)
            Liverpool Playhouse

1986-09   *A Mouthful of Birds* by Caryl Churchill and David Lan (WP)
            (co-directed with choreographer Ian Spink)
            Joint Stock at Birmingham Repertory Theatre, Birmingham,
              England
            Regional tour and Royal Court Theatre

1987-01   *Ghost on Fire* by Michael Weller
            Goodman Theatre, Chicago, IL

1987-03   *Ourselves Alone* by Anne Devlin (USP)
            Arena Stage, Washington, DC

1987-09   *The House of Bernarda Alba* by Federico García Lorca
            (adapt. Timberlake Wertenbaker)
            Guthrie Theater, Minneapolis, MN

1988-03   *Fanshen* by David Hare
            UK regional tour and Royal National Theatre, London,
            England

1988-05   *Romeo and Juliet* by William Shakespeare
            The Public Theater

1988-11   *School for Scandal* by Richard Brinsley Sheridan
            Bristol Old Vic (Theatre Royal), Bristol, England

1989-06   *Nebraska* by Keith Reddin (WP)
            La Jolla Playhouse, La Jolla, CA

1989-09   *Our Country's Good* by Timberlake Wertenbaker (USP)
            (co-directed with Max Stafford-Clark)
            Center Theatre Group-Mark Taper Forum, Los Angeles, CA

1990-05   *Ice Cream with Hot Fudge* by Caryl Churchill (USP)
            The Public Theater

1990-06   *Life During Wartime* by Keith Reddin (WP)
            La Jolla Playhouse

1991-02   *Life During Wartime* by Keith Reddin
            Manhattan Theatre Club at New York City Center (Stage II),
            New York, NY

1992-03   *Media Amok* by Christopher Durang (WP)
            American Repertory Theater, Cambridge, MA

1992-11   *Top Girls* by Caryl Churchill
            Tokyo Metropolitan Art Space, Tokyo, Japan

1993-04   *The Swan* by Elizabeth Egloff (UKP)
            Traverse Theatre

1993-09   *Someone Who'll Watch Over Me* by Frank McGuinness
            Gateway Theatre, Chester, England

1993-11   *The Swan* by Elizabeth Egloff
            The Public Theater

1994-01   *The Skriker* by Caryl Churchill (WP)
            Royal National Theatre

1995-07   *Love* by Graham Reid (WP)
            West Yorkshire Playhouse, Leeds, England

1997-03   *The Designated Mourner* by Wallace Shawn (USP)
            Steppenwolf Theatre, Chicago, IL

1997-05   *The Importance of Being Earnest* by Oscar Wilde
            La Jolla Playhouse

1998-02   *The Memory of Water* by Shelagh Stephenson (USP)
            Steppenwolf Theatre

1998-05   *Nora* by Ingmar Bergman
            La Jolla Playhouse

1998-09   *The Summer Moon* by John Olive (WP)
            A Contemporary Theatre, Seattle, WA

1999-05   *Spinning into Butter* by Rebecca Gilman (WP)
            Goodman Theatre

2000-03   *Big Love* by Charles Mee (WP)
            Humana Festival of New American Plays
            Actors Theatre of Louisville, Louisville, KY

2001-01   *Glengarry Glen Ross* by David Mamet
            American Conservatory Theater, San Francisco, CA

2001-03   *Big Love* by Charles Mee
           Long Wharf Theatre, New Haven, CT
           (co-production with Berkeley Repertory Theatre)

2001-04   *Big Love* by Charles Mee
           Berkeley Repertory Theatre, Berkeley, CA
           (co-production with Long Wharf Theatre)

2001-10   *Big Love* by Charles Mee
           Goodman Theatre

2001-11   *Big Love* by Charles Mee
           Brooklyn Academy of Music (Next Wave Festival), Brooklyn, NY

2002-06   *Buried Child* by Sam Shepard
           American Conservatory Theater

2002-08   *Wintertime* by Charles Mee (WP)
           La Jolla Playhouse (co-production with Long Wharf Theatre)

2002-10   *Wintertime* by Charles Mee
           Long Wharf Theatre (co-production with La Jolla Playhouse)

2003-02   *Suddenly Last Summer* by Tennessee Williams
           Berkeley Repertory Theatre

2003-05   *Savannah Bay* by Marguerite Duras
           Classic Stage Company, New York, NY

2004-02   *Yellowman* by Dael Orlandersmith
           Berkeley Repertory Theatre

2004-03   *At the Vanishing Point* by Naomi Iizuka (WP)
           Humana Festival of New American Plays
           Actors Theatre of Louisville

2004-04   *The Mystery of Irma Vep* by Charles Ludlam
           Berkeley Repertory Theatre

2004-10   *Eurydice* by Sarah Ruhl
           Berkeley Repertory Theatre

2005-02   *Fêtes de la Nuit* by Charles Mee (WP)
           Berkeley Repertory Theatre

2005-03   *Hot 'n' Throbbing* by Paula Vogel
           Signature Theatre, New York, NY

2005-10   *Finn in the Underworld* by Jordan Harrison (WP)
            Berkeley Repertory Theatre

2005-12   *Apparition* by Anne Washburn
            Connelly Theater, New York, NY

2006-04   *The Glass Menagerie* by Tennessee Williams
            Berkeley Repertory Theatre

2006-09   *Eurydice* by Sarah Ruhl
            Yale Repertory Theatre, New Haven, CT

2007-02   *The Pillowman* by Martin McDonagh
            Berkeley Repertory Theatre

2007-02   *To the Lighthouse* by Virginia Woolf (WP)
            (adapt. Adele Edling Shank, music by Paul Dresher)
            Berkeley Repertory Theatre

2007-06   *Eurydice* by Sarah Ruhl
            Second Stage, New York, NY

2007-08   *Heartbreak House* by George Bernard Shaw
            Berkeley Repertory Theatre

2007-11   *Doris to Darlene: A Cautionary Valentine* by Jordan Harrison
            (WP)
            Playwrights Horizons, New York, NY

2008-03   *Tragedy: a tragedy* by Will Eno (USP)
            Berkeley Repertory Theatre

2008-05   *Cardenio* by Charles Mee and Stephen Greenblatt (WP)
            American Repertory Theater

2009-02   *In the Next Room (or the vibrator play)* by Sarah Ruhl (WP)
            Berkeley Repertory Theatre

2009-04   *The Lieutenant of Inishmore* by Martin McDonagh
            Berkeley Repertory Theatre

2009-10   *In the Next Room (or the Vibrator Play)* by Sarah Ruhl
            Lincoln Center Theater at Lyceum Theatre (Broadway)
            New York, NY

2010-02   *Concerning Strange Devices from the Distant West*
            by Naomi Iizuka (WP)
            Berkeley Repertory Theatre

2010-04   *Girlfriend* by Todd Almond, music by Matthew Sweet (WP)
Berkeley Repertory Theatre

2010-06   *The Small* by Anne Washburn (WP)
Clubbed Thumb (Summerworks Festival), New York, NY

2011-04   *Three Sisters* by Anton Chekhov (adapt. Sarah Ruhl)
Berkeley Repertory Theatre
(co-production with Yale Repertory Theatre)

2011-06   *Middletown* by Will Eno
Steppenwolf Theatre

2011-09   *Three Sisters* by Anton Chekhov (adapt. Sarah Ruhl)
Yale Repertory Theatre
(co-production with Berkeley Repertory Theatre)

2012-03   *Red* by John Logan
Berkeley Repertory Theatre

2012-10   *Long Day's Journey into Night* by Eugene O'Neill
Actors Theatre of Louisville

2012-11   *Dear Elizabeth* by Sarah Ruhl (WP)
Yale Repertory Theatre
(in association with Berkeley Repertory Theatre)

2013-01   *Girlfriend* by Todd Almond, music by Matthew Sweet
Actors Theatre of Louisville

2013-03   *Gnit* by Will Eno (WP)
Humana Festival of New American Plays
Actors Theatre of Louisville

2013-05   *Dear Elizabeth* by Sarah Ruhl
Berkeley Repertory Theatre
(in association with Yale Repertory Theatre)

2014-01   *Our Town* by Thornton Wilder
Actors Theatre of Louisville

2014-03   *The Christians* by Lucas Hnath (WP)
Humana Festival of New American Plays
Actors Theatre of Louisville

2014-09   *Marjorie Prime* by Jordan Harrison (WP)
Center Theatre Group-Mark Taper Forum

2015-01   *At the Vanishing Point* by Naomi Iizuka
Actors Theatre of Louisville

2015-03   *The Glory of the World* by Charles Mee (WP)
Humana Festival of New American Plays
Actors Theatre of Louisville

2015-05   *10 out of 12* by Anne Washburn (WP)
Soho Rep, New York, NY

2015-07   *Girlfriend* by Todd Almond, music by Matthew Sweet
Center Theatre Group-Kirk Douglas Theatre, Culver City, CA

2015-08   *The Christians* by Lucas Hnath
Playwrights Horizons

2015-10   *Luna Gale* by Rebecca Gilman
Actors Theatre of Louisville

2015-12   *The Christians*
Center Theatre Group-Mark Taper Forum

2016-01   *The Glory of the World* by Charles Mee
Brooklyn Academy of Music

2016-03   *For Peter Pan on her 70th Birthday* by Sarah Ruhl (WP)
Humana Festival of New American Plays
Actors Theatre of Louisville

2016-05   *For Peter Pan on her 70th Birthday* by Sarah Ruhl
Berkeley Repertory Theatre

2016-10   *Macbeth* by William Shakespeare
Actors Theatre of Louisville

2017-03   *Recent Alien Abductions* by Jorge Ignacio Cortiñas (WP)
Humana Festival of New American Plays
Actors Theatre of Louisville

2017-08   *For Peter Pan on her 70th Birthday* by Sarah Ruhl
Playwrights Horizons

2018-01   *Little Bunny Foo Foo* by Anne Washburn
music by Dave Malloy (WP)
Actors Theatre of Louisville

2018-03   *Evocation to Visible Appearance* by Mark Schultz (WP)
Humana Festival of New American Plays
Actors Theatre of Louisville

2018-09   *A Doll's House, Part 2* by Lucas Hnath
Berkeley Repertory Theatre
(co-production with Huntington Theatre Company)

2019-01   *A Doll's House, Part 2* by Lucas Hnath
Huntington Theatre Company, Boston, MA
(co-production with Berkeley Repertory Theatre)

2019-03   *The Thin Place* by Lucas Hnath (WP)
Humana Festival of New American Plays
Actors Theatre of Louisville

2019-06   *Dana H.* by Lucas Hnath (WP)
Center Theatre Group-Kirk Douglas Theatre
(co-production with Goodman Theatre)

2019-09   *Dana H.* by Lucas Hnath
Goodman Theatre
(co-production with Center Theatre Group)

2019-11   *The Thin Place* by Lucas Hnath
Playwrights Horizons

2020-02   *Dana H.* by Lucas Hnath
Vineyard Theatre, New York, NY
(co-production with Goodman Theatre and Center Theatre Group)

2021-07   *What If If Only* by Caryl Churchill (USP)
(virtual live-streamed production co-directed with Jared Mezzochi)
NAATCO (National Asian American Theatre Company)

2021-10   *Dana H.* by Lucas Hnath
Lyceum Theatre (Broadway)
(revival of Vineyard Theatre-Goodman Theatre-Center Theatre Group production)

2021-11   *Wintertime* by Charles Mee
Berkeley Repertory Theatre

2022-02   *Out of Time* by Jaclyn Backhaus, Sam Chanse, Mia Chung, Naomi Iizuka, and Anna Ouyang Moench (WP)
Commissioned and Produced by NAATCO
Presented by The Public Theater
Conceived and Directed by Les Waters

Index